PrincetonReview.com

WHAT TO DO WITH
YOUR PSYCHOLOGY OR
SOCIOLOGY DEGREE

By Jason Wall and Lisa Vollmer

Random House, Inc.
New York

The Princeton Review, Inc.

2315 Broadway

New York, NY 10024

E-mail: bookeditor@review.com

ISBN 978-0-375-76625-1

Publisher: Robert Franek

Senior Editor: Adrinda Kelly

Editor: Adam O. Davis

Director, Print Production: Scott Harris

Director, Production Editorial: Christine LaRubio

Printed in the United States of America.

9 8 7 6 5 4 3 2 1

2008 Edition

ABOUT THE AUTHORS

Jason Wall, a proud former psychology major, has worked in Student Affairs and Career Development for over a decade, including positions as a Career Counselor at UCLA and Director of Employer Relations at the Massachusetts Institute of Technology. He is currently a part-time Career Counselor at University of California—Berkeley and enjoys golf and wine in Napa Valley with his most trusted confidant, Winston-Hughes. Because networking really is the key to success, he is always available at jasonmwall@gmail.com

Lisa Vollmer is a freelance writer and editor, specializing in business, finance, and career-management topics. Drawing on her previous work experience in both investment banking and management consulting, she authored numerous career guides for San Francisco–based publisher WetFeet Press, including *Job Hunting in San Francisco* and *Beat the Street II: an Investment Banking Interview Practice Guide*. More recently, she has worked as a freelance journalist for the Stanford University Graduate School of Business and as a research editor at *Sunset* magazine in Menlo Park, California. She is a graduate of the University of Virginia.

ACKNOWLEDGMENTS

Foremost, I would like to thank Erica, for everything.
Additional thanks are necessary to Wall Brothers Consulting,
Albert E. Aubin of UCLA, and Christina Sedighi at Berkeley.

—Jay Wall

CONTENTS

INTRODUCTION

You've probably been on the receiving end of some puzzled stares from relatives and friends who wonder what in the world you're going to do with your psychology or sociology degree. The concerned parties most likely studied accounting or "pre-something" and knew exactly where their degrees would lead. Or you may have heard the more positive, but no more helpful, sentiment that you can do *anything* with your psychology or sociology degree. The trouble is: You don't want to do anything. You want to do something in particular, and the well-wisher's comment is more vague than instructive. In defense of the messenger, the skills and knowledge that psychology and sociology majors acquire during their studies of the brain and the behavior of groups readily apply to a range of industries, so the idea that you can do "anything" with your psychology or sociology degree is not that far off.

Psychology and sociology majors have achieved extraordinary heights in fields as diverse as politics, religion, and entertainment. Do Ronald Reagan, Martin Luther King Jr., and Jerry Bruckheimer ring a bell? These are just a few of the psychology and sociology majors who used their academic training to excel in work and beyond; there are countless others working in a wide spectrum of personally fulfilling occupations.

The trick is to connect the dots between your academic training and job openings, which is no easy task for many liberal arts students. You need help identifying the best jobs for you, finding available positions, and convincing the employer that you're the best candidate. Or, if pursuing an advanced degree is your aim, you need some insight into where to apply and what to expect when you get there. Well, congratulations—you've picked the right book to find answers to these and many other questions. Consider this your school-to-work translation guide.

Chapter 1 gives an overview of how your undergraduate studies add up to fabulous preparation for the working world. Chapter 2 breaks down the components of typical job listings to show you just how marketable your psychology and sociology expertise really is. Chapter 3 outlines a helpful framework for narrowing down career options based on your interests, skills, and values. Chapter 4 profiles a number of career paths popular among sociology and psychology majors, and Chapter 5 shows you how to land a job. Chapter 6 gives you the skinny on pursuing an advanced degree if your dream job requires more education or if you're not ready to leap into the world of work just yet. Chapter 7 profiles the top graduate programs to consider.

Profiles of notable psychology and sociology majors also are sprinkled throughout to keep you inspired. Remember: The sky's the limit. All you have to do is start reaching. Good luck!

CHAPTER 1

Discovering Your Strengths—Identifying your Marketable Skills and Knowledge

REACQUAINTING YOURSELF WITH THE MAJORS

Before we inundate you with all of the career options open to psychology and sociology majors, let's take stock of what you've gained from countless hours of exam preparation and thousands of dollars spent on tuition. Both majors probe the human psyche, examine interpersonal interactions, and give valuable insights into how to be successful in life and work. In order to successfully complete either curriculum, you must possess the analytical skills to master the intricacies of statistical analysis, the patience to carry out methodical research, the ability to craft compelling written arguments, and the know-how to explain individual and group behavior. Each of these skills is in great demand in today's marketplace.

The Swiss army knife of majors: The future of sociology

The Bureau of Labor Statistics predicts that the employment of sociologists will grow more slowly than average through 2014 because of fewer opportunities outside of government and academic positions.[1] On the other hand, there will be increased demand for people with the skills of the sociology major, when combined with other areas of expertise. Why are sociological skills gaining importance in the job market at the same time that growth in demand for sociologists slows? What does this mean for your future?

One possible answer can be found in the character of today's information-driven and data-oriented work environment. Course work in social research methods and statistics teaches sociology majors to gather information, collect data, and analyze findings—and qualifies them to meet employer's demands for people with these skills. Today's job market also requires people who can perform highly specialized tasks and still see the big picture. Sociology teaches you to view things in context, appreciate the complexity and interconnectedness of human life, and think abstractly and critically. In addition, the study of sociology provides valuable insights into ethnicity, national identity, and other social factors that affect how people and organizations operate into today's increasingly diverse business world.

As a sociology student you were taught to observe the interactions among groups and analyze the influence of group activities on individual members. You sought to understand the impact of gender, age, ethnicity, and socioeconomic status on a person's daily life; to analyze trends; and to forecast social and cultural change. Every industry is deeply interested in having this kind of sociological information about their clients, patients, students, employees, or other constituencies. Increasingly, organizations and companies rely on sociological data to give them an edge over their competitors.

---

1 Bureau of Labor Statistics. *Occupational Outlook Handbook: Social Scientists, Other.* U.S. Department of Labor. www.bls.gov/oco/ocos054.htm#outlook.

Final analysis: The future of psychology

According to the U.S. Department of Labor, the need for those trained in the field of psychology will increase over the next decade due to the great demand for services in social service agencies, mental health centers, substance abuse treatment clinics, research institutes, consulting firms, and private companies.[2] This demand for psychological services is linked to many problems facing today's society, from drug and alcohol abuse to domestic and gang-related violence to mental illness and learning disabilities. This has resulted in an increased demand for people with psychology training.

Changing demographics also play a role in the growing need for psychologists. As the country's population ages, more and more funding and research is focused on learning and memory, as well as stretching the subject of human development from childhood and adolescence well into the golden years. As people live longer, it has become clearer that physical and mental health care need to become more integrated, leading to the need for psychologists to work as part of health teams in hospitals and nursing homes. Additionally, we live in an increasingly diverse America, with people from every conceivable corner of the globe settling in cities, suburbs, and rural areas across the nation. As old and new members of existing communities figure out how to live together and how to accommodate the new mix of beliefs, languages and cultural traditions, they face a host of challenges in areas in which psychologists have expertise—the formation of identity, diverse learning styles, attitude change, and conflict, to name a few.

The remarkable advances in technology of the past few decades have also opened up new areas for psychological study and intervention. The study of the brain, artificial intelligence, Internet use, and computer gaming are just a few areas in which psychologists have much to contribute. And last, but not least, since 9/11 psychologists have been vigorously researching the psychology of terrorism and developing new intervention strategies and treatments for people suffering from trauma.

All this is good news for undergraduate psychology majors. While a career track as a psychological service practitioner often requires graduate training, quite a few entry-level jobs doing similar work are open to those with only a bachelor's degree. Keep in mind, you won't find them by looking for jobs for a "psychologist." That is a very specific title reserved for those with an advanced degree and license in a specific area of psychology. Fortunately, the knowledge of people that psychology majors acquire, along with the ability to collect, analyze and summarize data, are sought after in many other areas of work. Later in the book, you will learn about the duties, work environments, lifestyle considerations, and other factors related to common career paths chosen by psychology majors.

Making the connection: Putting your academic training to work

2 Bureau of Labor Statistics. *Occupational Outlook Handbook: Psychologists.* U.S. Department of Labor. www.bls.gov/oco/ocos056.htm#outlook.

Many prestigious (and not-so-prestigious) colleges and universities pride themselves on providing a broad-based liberal arts education in which specific job training—beyond periodic trips to your Career Services Office—is mostly absent. In their minds, if you want training for a specific career you should go to a vocational high school, community college, or one of those schools that advertises on TV. "Real" colleges and universities tenaciously carry out their calling to help advance knowledge by creating better students, not training individuals for careers.

With this in mind, it is no surprise academic departmental websites focus on what you will learn in class without explaining what value the lessons hold in the world of work. It's up to you to figure that out. Fortunately, we're here to help. Here's a secret: College *is* the real world except that its parameters are informed by hierarchies of knowledge rather than hierarchies of production. The distinction is most evident in the language used to describe what goes on in school and what is expected of employees in the world of work. Just remember that when academia hires, they use the curriculum vitae (CV), which is often up to eight pages long. Industry, which puts a higher premium on efficiency, uses resumes, which are one page. So while your statistics professors might have asked you to "perform a factor analysis on the causality of the variable," the industry professional would say, "Find out what the customer really wants." Again, it is all the same stuff, just a different delivery. Our goal here to strip away the academic lingo and help you put the skills you possess into straightforward terms that any employer will appreciate.

I USED TO BE YOU PROFILE

Jerry Bruckheimer[3,4]

Born in Detroit, Michigan on September 21, 1945

How You Know Him

An American film and television production juggernaut who has been the creative force behind (just to name a few) *Black Hawk Down, Pirates of the Caribbean, The Amazing Race,* and *CSI: Crime Scene Investigation* and its spin-offs.

Psychology or Sociology?

Bachelor's in Psychology

First "Real" Job

Mailroom assistant in a New York City advertising agency

---

3 Matt Smith. "Glory Road Interview with Jerry Bruckheimer." Lifeteen.com. www.lifeteen.com/
default.aspx?PageID=FEATUREDETAIL&__DocumentId=132232&__ArticleIndex=1.

4 Wikipedia contributors, "Jerry Bruckheimer," Wikipedia, The Free Encyclopedia.
http://en.wikipedia.org/wiki/Jerry_Bruckheimer.

His Educational Path

Jerry Bruckheimer grew up as a self-proclaimed photography fanatic and attended the University of Arizona where he graduated with a bachelor's degree in psychology. Also an avid film buff, he moved to New York City after college and started networking within the entertainment industry. After starting in the mailroom of an advertising firm, he wrangled his way into commercial production where he learned the ropes and gained increasing levels of experience. In time, he heard of an opportunity to produce a motion picture and risked his career and financial security to give it a shot.

How This Psychology Major Succeeded

During the 1980s and 1990s, co-producing with the late Don Simpson and hiring such high-profile actors as Tom Cruise and Eddie Murphy, Mr. Bruckheimer churned out a series of highly successful films for Paramount Pictures including the *Beverly Hills Cop* films, *Top Gun, Days of Thunder*, and *Armageddon*. Despite the death of his creative partner Don Simpson in 1996, Bruckheimer has continued to produce a large number of action movies including *Remember the Titans, Black Hawk Down*, and *Pirates of the Caribbean*. His clout and creativity extended to television success with hits such as *CSI: Crime Scene Investigation* and the reality game show *The Amazing Race*.

The Philosophy of This Psychology Major

"I was somebody who struggled with education. Whenever I had to read out loud, I was stumbling around, so I wasn't considered a bright kid. Don't let that hold you back; there's always something, and if you want it bad enough you'll get it. What you have to do is be honest about what you're good at, and I've always been good at organizing things . . . I organized a baseball team when I was like 10, a hockey team when I was 11 or 12. So I could always put things together, make them kind of work. I enjoyed getting the satisfaction of standing back and watching something work, which is what I do now. Kids today, when they're searching for something, get beat up by their parents and beat up by their teachers. You can't have all that negativity around you. You have to learn from it and try to improve."

"If you knew how much work it took, you wouldn't call it genius." [5]

—Michelangelo

5 Michelangelo. Quote. SOLO—Sense of Life Objectivists.
http://solohq.solopassion.com/Spirit/Quotes/index_6.shtml.

PRIMARY SKILLS AND KNOWLEDGE BASES

Before going out on job interviews, it is necessary to consider what you have to offer potential employers. Here's a quick rundown on the primary skills and knowledge bases that make psychology and sociology majors infinitely employable. Chapter 2 goes a step further and links the academic background overviewed here to specific qualifications sought in today's job market.

The Primary Skills

- **Writing (lots of it)**

    Psychology and sociology majors are required to generate a tremendous quantity of written material pertaining to a wide range of topics. Both majors easily write hundreds of pages of essays and other assignments during college. From weekly discussion papers for class sections to lengthy research papers, you honed your ability to present crisp, formal research findings and persuasive opinion pieces. Your typing skills and word processing knowledge are icing on the cake.

    Every job, without exception, requires the ability to communicate clearly and efficiently. Whether it is a simple follow-up e-mail or a major annual report destined for public consumption, the ability to write what you mean is critical. Be sure to save samples of your best work in case the jobs for which you apply (particularly ones related to writing, publicity, or promotions) request samples.

- **Critical and abstract thinking**

    You may not have spent as much time in the lab as chemistry or biology students, but your course work in experimental design or research statistics required you to develop hypotheses and construct and carry out experiments based on the scientific method. Indeed, this is arguably one of the best parts of both majors. Opportunities to conduct original research promote critical, independent thinking—exactly what employers are referring to when they say they want employees who can think outside the box.

- **Controlled research**

    By now, you're a pro at gathering and analyzing data and are intimately familiar with the scientific method (propose, test, evaluate, repeat) and, perhaps, even at developing your own experimental designs. Indeed, it is likely that your department required you to take at least one course in statistics and one in research methodology. On top of that, it is becoming more and more common for undergraduates to work as research assistants or interns, which only enhances your understanding of hypothesis development, the scientific method and quantitative analysis.

Lost in Translation: Your Research Skills in Plain English

Academic Jargon: Develop testable hypotheses based on theoretical constructs of the research.

Plain English: Guess what's wrong and come up with solutions.

Academic Jargon: Evaluate theories and research findings and apply the results to a given topic.

Plain English: Look at your options or how others have done it and pick a solution.

Academic Jargon: Interpret quantitative and qualitative data and extrapolate causality.

Plain English: Figure out what the numbers mean.

Academic Jargon: Use a statistical analysis tool to input and code the data.

Plain English: Use Microsoft Excel.

DATA COLLECTION AND MANAGEMENT

On the surface, it may seem that the ability to plot standard deviations or calculate a Pearson R has little to do with your future career choice, but make no mistake: Almost every position in today's job market includes at least some type of data management (managing budgets, tracking attendance, etc.). Consider the experience of Lana, who became a day care and afterschool program teacher at a YMCA after graduating from the University of Massachusetts—Boston with a degree in psychology. Believe it or not, Lana spends her days preparing arts and crafts activities and teaching the ABCs as well as using Excel and Access databases almost daily. Her job has a definite technical component, which may be surprising, and her undergraduate education more than prepared her for the responsibility. Lana says she got the job due to, in large part, the analytical and quantitative abilities she acquired in the course work for her major.

"I think I, a lot like everyone else in college, was certain the things I was learning in the classroom had no relevance to my future job. I wanted to be a teacher and work with children, and I had no interest in research and statistics. I remember my first group research project where we collected data by watching a public mailbox and tracking the number of deposits and the number of people who reopened the little door to confirm the letter had slid down after initially closing the door. It was completely boring and I was especially unhappy because I had to learn Excel to record the data. I laugh now because I was worried about typing two columns of numbers with nothing but ones and twos. I was hopeful that I would never even think about collecting data ever again. When I applied for my job here I specifically remember the job description saying that it required technical skills like database management, word processing, and spreadsheets. It was the database management that I was freaked out about. When I was in the interview, sure enough, I was asked to characterize my technical skills. Since I didn't consider all the papers I had typed to be anything special, all I had was the mailbox project so I told them I had collected and coded research data using Excel. There I was, trying to describe my two columns of ones and twos as if it were really impressive and I was sure she wasn't buying it. After maybe a minute explanation of my group research project, we moved on the next question. That was that, no follow-up. I was sure I had bombed that question. Obviously, I got hired, and I remember when I got the offer my soon-to-be boss said one of the things they were most impressed about was "research experience," and they were sure I could handle inputting the daily attendance list into Excel and updating the yearly Access database records."

GROUP PROJECTS AND INTERPERSONAL SKILLS

For many, this aspect of your education is so obvious that it is often taken for granted. Less formally, it's called teamwork or the ability to work with people. You've spent years learning about what makes people tick, and now it's time to put it to good use. Every employer looks for good people skills. (Seriously, try finding a job listing that advertises for weak interpersonal skills and an inability to work with others.) Your course work made you intimately familiar with the power of active listening, others' perception of you, and how to modify action to facilitate a positive outcome. With any career you pursue, you can expect to put the skills you practiced in the classroom and during group projects to the test.

The Primary Knowledge Bases

HOW LEARNING OCCURS

You remember the theories and research: constructivism, socialization, B. F. Skinner and his pigeons. All of the information you covered in either motivational psychology or socialization is directly related to understanding how humans process information and "get smarter." More importantly, it provides a window into different learning styles of other humans (your future colleagues and bosses). Employing the concepts of and information about how others learn can boost your success in the world of work. For example, it has been demonstrated that humans have a variety of learning preferences and that some are visual while others are verbal. When taken out of the textbook and applied to the "real world" of work, we see just how useful this ability to identify preferred learning styles can impact not only your productivity but how you are perceived (positively or negatively) at work. An interview with Jeff, a recent graduate from the University of Maine provides a great example of the pitfalls of *not* using what you've learned to your advantage.

"It was my first week on the job (a midsize marketing firm) and right away my boss gave me a bulleted list outlining everything he wanted me to accomplish during my first week of training. The last item on the list was to present a proposal outlining my contributions to one of our product campaigns. I should have known from the way he wrote everything down that he was a concrete guy. Well, I wanted to make a good impression so I worked, conservatively, 60 hours that week and was creating what I thought was a great PowerPoint show to pitch my elements to the project. Well, when I presented it, he was obviously distracted by all the imagery which wasn't directly related to the core concept I wanted to promote, and in the end, he essentially said my proposal lacked substance and that it was about the most unorganized set of ideas he had ever seen. I showed my presentation to a coworker who, after they stopped laughing and accusing me of kissing up to the boss with such an over-the-top presentation, asked if I'd noticed that everything I had received from the boss was a concise written list, no diagrams or visuals. . . . So, I distilled this hugo presentation that took me forever into a thorough bulleted list which took me about 30 minutes. I presented the list to the boss about a week later and said that I wanted to show him this basic outline before fully developing the bigger proposal. After reading it, he told me, 'It's great just the way it is,' and that he could finally 'visualize it' now that I had some focus."

Jeff's experience demonstrates that academic concepts can be successfully applied to work situations when you take some time to consider your audience and match them to the resources at your disposal.

HOW PEOPLE FORM ATTITUDES AND OPINIONS

Your undergraduate education gave you a tremendous foundation for understanding how individuals develop an appreciation for the dynamics of social interaction and organizational behavior. However, because much of what you learned was in the context of research, it may be very difficult to appreciate just how practical and applicable the knowledge you have acquired is to your future career. The real-world application of what you learned in socialization, research design, or social psychology courses might be to employ visual cues like smiling at everyone you meet and maintaining eye contact when you interview to ensure you are liked even before you have answered any interview questions.

CONCLUSION

Countless proverbs address the power of studying history and promote the idea that groups or individuals can only move forward if they understand their past. Hopefully, you now have a better understanding of your own academic history and the skills you have developed. Next you need to learn to verbalize what your degree represents in very practical terms that employers understand. In the next chapter, we will dissect the most common aspects of job listings and reveal how they relate to your newly defined skill set.

CHAPTER 2

Bargaining Power—What You Bring to the Table

THE POWER OF POSITIVE THINKING

Psychology and sociology majors typically take one of two extreme views of their career prospects: an extremely optimistic view or an overly pessimistic one. The optimists among you believe that your liberal arts background has prepared you for anything the world of work might throw your way and that the biggest challenge is to select just one job when your skills and interests are relevant to so many fields. On the other hand, some of you may lean toward a darker view of your career prospects and think that you are not prepared to do anything specific and that you have little to offer employers. Don't fret—this chapter will prove that the optimists are correct and that the pessimists are, well, pessimists. Your college experience has provided you with both the theoretical underpinnings and the practical experiences necessary to land a great job.

Unlike the electrical engineering major who aspires to be—you guessed it—an electrical engineer, you must educate potential employers about why your academic training is the perfect fit for their job opening. As a psychology or sociology major it is up to you use your resume, cover letters, and interviews as a platform for you to deliver a positive and informative sales pitch that touts your concrete qualifications for the job. In this chapter, all of the major skills, knowledge, and abilities you have developed in your major will be discussed in terms directly relevant to today's typical job listing. We are not just saying you're qualified to do anything; we are going to break down the core components of a typical job description and prove it. But hey, don't take our word for it. Read what Peter, a recruiter for a consulting firm, has to say.

"If you don't apply, I guarantee you won't get the job."

Peter Topkins, a partner at a large management consulting firm in the San Francisco Bay Area, takes time away from his primary work responsibilities to serve as a campus champion at his alma mater, Stanford University. He tags along with recruiters, whose sole function is hiring, participates in the first-round interview process, and weighs in on who should be called back for an on-site interview. Here Peter describes what he looks for and how he assesses individuals during first-round interviews.

"At our firm, and we're all fairly similar (which explains why it seems like the same 10 students get offers from all of us), the recruiters and I are looking for three primary competencies; the ability to research and gather information, the ability to analyze and solve problems, and the ability to communicate the findings in a clear and concise statement. That's it: research, analysis, and communication. If you can do those three things, you have 90 percent of what it takes to be a successful management consultant. The final 10 percent is the intrinsic motivation to work harder than everyone else. The specific major is definitely secondary to the more important characteristic of having been an academic standout in whatever field you chose to study."

Peter goes on to explain why he is always on the lookout for sociology and psychology majors.

"At our firm, and again we're not unusual, during on-campus recruiting, we have 'open sign-up,' which means we accept resumes from all majors; it is a fallacy that consulting firms only want business administration or econ majors. I am always excited to see psychology and sociology majors because I know, from my own experience, that liberal arts majors have all the skills we're looking for. Honestly, the biggest problem with applicants from these majors is that they don't apply, because they think they're not qualified. Think of it this way, if you don't apply, I guarantee you won't get the job. Or, once they've actually landed an interview, they spend the majority of their time apologizing for not having been a business major when they should be talking about their personal experiences. Lack of confidence will kill your chances every time."

I USED TO BE YOU PROFILE[1,2]

Martin Luther King Jr.

Born January 15, 1929, 501 Auburn Avenue, Northeast, Atlanta, Georgia

Why You Know Him

World-renowned civil rights activist

Psychology or Sociology?

Bachelor's in Sociology

His First "Real" Job

Nineteen years old and fresh from college, Martin Luther was ordained a Baptist minister. Immediately following he became Assistant Pastor of Ebenezer Baptist Church in Atlanta, Georgia.

His Educational Path

Dr. King skipped both the 9th and 12th grades and enrolled in Morehouse College without ever formally graduating from Booker T. Washington High School. In 1948 he graduated with a Bachelor of Arts degree in sociology and went on to be valedictorian of his class at Crozer Theological Seminary in

1 The King Center. "Biographical Outline of Dr. Martin Luther King Jr." www.thekingcenter.org/mlk/bio.html.

2 Wikipedia contributors. "Martin Luther King Jr." Wikipedia, The Free Encyclopedia. http://en.wikipedia.org/wiki/Martin_Luther_King,_Jr.

Chester, Pennsylvania, earning a Bachelor of Divinity degree in 1951. In 1955, he received a PhD in systematic theology from Boston University.

Dr. King also received close to 20 honorary doctoral degrees from some of the nation's most prestigious universities and colleges.

How This Sociology Major Succeeded

On December 1, 1955, while pastor of the Dexter Avenue Baptist Church, Dr. King launched a 382-day boycott of the bus lines in Montgomery, Alabama in response to the arrest of Rosa Parks, an African American woman who refused to comply with a Jim Crow law and give up her bus seat to a White man. The Montgomery bus boycott was just one of several feats that catapulted Dr. King into the national consciousness and established him as one of the nation's leading advocates for nonviolent change. The boycott led to King's arrest, the firebombing of his home, and ultimately a United States Supreme Court decision outlawing racial segregation on intrastate buses and all public transportation.

Following the campaign, King was instrumental in the founding of the Southern Christian Leadership Conference (SCLC) in 1957, a group created to harness the moral authority and organizing power of Black churches to conduct nonviolent protests in the service of civil rights reform. Dr. King smartly used his understanding of human perception, no doubt cultivated as a student of sociology, to promote nonviolent protests against the racist system of Southern segregation. He was confident that the extensive media coverage of the struggle for Black equality, with numerous newspaper stories and TV cameras recording the daily indignities, would produce a wave of sympathetic public opinion. He was exactly right and made the Civil Rights Movement the single most important issue in American politics in the early 1960s and, arguably, the century.

The Global Impact of This Sociology Major

The movements and marches that Dr. King led altered the entire fabric of American life and sent ripples throughout the world. His philosophy of nonviolent direct action and his strategies for rational and nondestructive social change galvanized the conscience of this nation and reordered its priorities. His wisdom, his words, his actions, and his dream for a new way of life are now intertwined with the American experience.

"I refuse to accept the cynical notion that nation after nation must spiral down a militaristic stairway into the hell of a thermonuclear destruction. I believe that unarmed truth and unconditional love will have the final word in reality. This is why right temporarily defeated is stronger that evil triumphant."

—Nobel Peace Prize acceptance speech, 1964[3]

3 The Nobel Foundation. "Acceptance Speech."
http://nobelprize.org/nobel_prizes/peace/laureates/1964/king-acceptance.html.

Locked and loaded: The skills employers demand (and you possess)

Here we will illustrate how the primary skills and knowledge bases described in Chapter 1 pair with the qualifications that employers seek. It is an interesting aside to consider just how similar job descriptions are across a wide variety of industries. Regardless of the reason for these commonalities, the fact that they exist can work in your favor, especially if you haven't chosen a particular career path and plan to apply for a wide range of positions. You might be surprised to see just how practical and versatile your skills are and how well you are prepared for the world of work.

WRITTEN AND ORAL COMMUNICATION SKILLS

Relevant primary skills or knowledge:

- Writing
- Group projects and interpersonal skills
- Controlled research

If you've browsed through job postings online or in the paper, you might have noticed that nine out of ten job descriptions have the phrase, "must have excellent written and oral communication skills" somewhere in the listing. Fortunately, you've probably written short-answer test questions in those flimsy blue books more times than you care to recall and had at least one class, if not several, that required group projects culminating in a class presentation. As you progressed thorough the curriculum, you undoubtedly began writing longer research papers, and by your senior year you likely were required to elucidate complex theories and arguments relevant to the human condition. All of these experiences are lethal ammunition to be unloaded during the job-search process. Save your best papers for applications that require writing samples, and remember those group projects for when you are interviewing and you are asked questions such as, "Tell me about a time when you've worked in a group" or "How would you describe your communication style?"

Your written and oral communication skills are some of the best coming out of *any* discipline. As a writer, you have not only developed the persuasive abilities possessed by English and communication majors arguing opinion, but you also can employ the direct style required of research and technical papers. This added understanding of when formality and precision are appropriate will serve you well in the world of work, as will those word-processing skills noted in the previous chapter.

In terms of oral communication and public speaking skills, you're also hitting on all cylinders. Even if it is not your preferred way to spend an afternoon, you should feel comfortable speaking in front of audiences both large and small given your group project and poster presentation experience. Your course work also should have made you comfortable making arguments in situations when there is no single correct answer. Not only will you need to employ this ability in your future job interviews, these debating skills will be valuable in future staff meetings and when selling your boss on new ideas and projects.

Relevant primary skills or knowledge:

- Group projects and interpersonal skills
- Knowledge of how learning occurs
- Knowledge of how people form attitudes and opinions

Right behind "excellent written and oral communication skills" the most oft-repeated job description text is, "must be a team player" or "ability to get along in a group environment is essential." Luckily, group dynamics is among your specialties (whether you knew it or not). Your time in college was saturated with studying precisely how humans function in group environments, the variables which positively or negatively influence group behavior (race, gender, and inequity issues), and even the keys to maximizing team performance. When questioned in an interview about your ability to function in a team atmosphere, you can easily dip into your academic training (you paid for it, you might as well use it) and explain your understanding of the key elements responsible for positive group environments and how you would bring this knowledge with you to the position.

The ability to approach, connect, and query others is critically important in today's workforce where collaboration within and between departments is increasingly widespread. From a theoretical standpoint, your course work has taught you volumes about human behavior, group dynamics, and productivity. The factors that help or hinder these interactions, variables such as active listening and leadership, are all part of your canon of knowledge. From a practical standpoint, you have been interacting with professors, fellow students, and college administrators for at least three to four years (maybe even five or six!). You undeniably have the double-edged ability to learn from colleagues *and* motivate others to achieve more. Vocalize these insights liberally in the cover letter or during the interview to prove that you can be an outstanding contributor and future leader within the organization.

RESEARCH SKILLS

Relevant primary skills or knowledge:

- Controlled research
- Critical and abstract thinking
- Data collection and management
- Knowledge of how learning occurs

Research is in your blood. You can ferret out anything about a problem—how it has been done before, where the relevant resources are, and who the experts are. Beyond that you can throw the data into a spreadsheet and have it spit out some charts, graphs, or reports to illustrate your findings. (Remember Lana's attendance database?) Your future boss can throw almost any problem at you, and whether it is collecting opinions about what is wrong, analyzing numbers to look for trends or fallacies, or observing current practice to look for improvements, you can dissect an issue, analyze its primary components, and hypothesize creative solutions.

SENSITIVITY TO OTHERS AND UNDERSTANDING DIVERSITY

Relevant primary skills or knowledge:

- Group projects and interpersonal skills
- Knowledge of how people form attitudes and opinions
- Knowledge of the effects of the environment on feelings and actions

Diversity is a hot topic in the world of recruiting and work. Federal Equal Opportunity Employment (EOE) standards have made the phrase "minority and disabled candidates highly encouraged to apply" quite common in your standard job description. Employers seek a more diverse workforce by engaging in minority-specific recruiting efforts and targeting people who can appreciate and thrive in that environment. As you begin your job search you will undoubtedly see job listings that have statements to the effect of "sensitivity to diverse populations" or "ability to succeed in a diverse environment." You will also see that more and more jobs are interested in bilingual applicants. Today, interviews are also peppered with questions meant to ascertain an applicant's appreciation for and experience with people of different cultures. In college you probably attended lectures, if not entire courses, dedicated to the study of words like racism, gender, identity, culture, norms, and values. Recognizing and understanding these hot topics should be second nature to you.

Speaking practically, you have interacted with students from diverse socio-economic and ethnic backgrounds during your time in college. You should have plenty of actual examples (getting away from classroom theory) of both personal exposure and classroom projects with a variety of people. The diversity topic, for both majors, is easily addressed in both the cover letter and the interview with statements such as, "As a <insert your major here> major, I studied the factors which positively and negatively affect human behavior and group interactions in <insert relevant course here>. I also lived, studied, and worked with students and faculty members from many different backgrounds."

PROJECT MANAGEMENT AND MULTITASKING

Relevant primary skills or knowledge:

- Writing (a lot of it)
- Data collection and management
- Group projects and interpersonal skills
- Knowledge of how learning occurs
- Knowledge of the effects of the environment on feelings and actions

Technological advancements such as e-mail, instant messaging, and smart phones, once heralded as harbingers of easier workdays and improved work-life balance, have only made work busier, more stressful, and more challenging. Back in the days before everyone had a phone on their belt or in their purse, when you left the office you were pretty much unreachable, and when you left for vacation you were *definitely* unreachable. No late-night frantic calls from "the boss with no life." Well, that has all certainly changed. Now, colleagues IM each other while simultaneously participating in a telephone conference call to make fun of someone in the phone meeting. Talk about multitasking. Checking e-mail from home is simply a given now, and most folks prefer a Wi-Fi hotel room so they can stay in touch.

Today's employees face heightened expectations and must cram more into one day than their predecessors (now one person can manage their own budget with Excel, create their own presentations using PowerPoint and draft their own annual reports in Word). To succeed, you must multitask and manage multiple responsibilities. Notice how many job listings have statements such as, "self-starter with the capacity to manage multiple, concurrent projects" or "ability to multitask and perform other functions as assigned." Every class you have taken has required you to use Word. In addition, you probably had to use PowerPoint for group presentations or handouts, and hopefully some type of database-management software like Excel or SPSS to track or manipulate data. The context (a course in college versus "a real job") has no bearing on the ability. Clicking "File" and "Save As" is no different at work than it is at school.

While in college, you had multiple bosses—also known as professors—and a limited time frame to discover their strengths, weaknesses, and idiosyncrasies. They each gave you several assignments ranging from large research endeavors to small quizzes (and, by the way, each one thought their project was the most important). You successfully provided them with the information they requested and got the job done. To do this, you kept track of a wide range of commitments using some sort of calendar system or you did it in your head, which is even more impressive. You prioritized your assignments either by due date or importance and allotted the appropriate amount of time for each.

Technical skills (MS Office required!)

- Relevant primary skills or knowledge
- Controlled research
- Data collection and management

If there is one skill that both sociology and psychology majors take completely for granted, it is their excellent technical abilities. You cannot type hundreds of pages of notes, mid-terms, take-home exams, and research papers and not gain better-than-average familiarity with the finer points of formatting and word processing documents. Laura, a recruiter for a management trainee program that hires dozens of sociology and psychology majors shares her thoughts.

"I am always surprised at how many of the students I interview from these majors who talk so negatively about their own technical skills. Even if they are not going to be overly positive, which they should at least try, they could at least say something neutral like, 'I did a lot of papers using Word' but they seem to actually go out of their way to sound unqualified. When I ask about their *basic* technical skills, I'm always hearing things like, 'Well, I didn't take any programming classes' or 'I've got some word processing but that's about all.' This lack of confidence is a real deterrent. If I like the applicant, I'll help them out and ask something like, 'Did you type any papers for school?' or if they have research experience on their resume, I'll ask if they used Excel or SPSS, and nine out of ten times they say 'yes,' so then I ask them to explain a little about either, and—lo and behold—we talk for five minutes about skills she said she never had."

Laura's observation about lack of confidence around technical skills speaks to an even bigger problem many sociology and psychology majors have when job searching. Because they often feel insecure going into the process, as they erroneously believe that their college experience has not adequately prepared them for a "real job," they often fail in the interview because they feel like they don't have great stories to tell or experiences to relay in the interview. The reality is that employers don't need earth-shattering expertise; they want basic proficiency.

Tanya, an Associate Dean at a school in Texas who is responsible for hiring Admissions Officers who can work together to share the heavy load of student applications, says psychology and sociology students must take a wider view of their abilities.

"I structure my behavioral questions so that *everyone* can answer them. For example, I might ask, tell me about a time when you were working in a group and the goal wasn't being achieved. I specifically do not specify 'at work' or 'at an internship' to give the applicant leeway to answer. Honestly, I'd accept a story about a time that person and a friend were driving and they got lost but then used some creative way like the position of the sun to get back on track. The point is I'm not looking for a miracle worker or someone that has supervised 12 employees and had a 1.2-million-dollar budget. I just want a well-thought-out, clearly expressed answer that answers the question. In fact, simple is often better."

Both Laura and Tanya's comment clearly show that your "basic" technical skills are adequate for any nontechnical jobs for which you might be applying. Remember, if everyone knew Word and Excel, they wouldn't ask for it in the job description. They don't ask for what everyone already possesses. When was the last time you saw a job posting that listed "ability to dress yourself daily and not drool while eating out with clients preferred" among its qualifications?

You are most likely excellent at word processing, Internet savvy, and possess a basic understanding of how spreadsheets work. Those of you who are slightly more advanced can create appealing PowerPoint slideshows for meetings and trainings and are comfortable using robust statistical analysis software such as Standard Analysis Software System (SASS) or Statistical Package for the Social Sciences (SPSS) predictive analytics. These skills are more than sufficient for most entry-level jobs.

Wrap it up; I'll take your skills

You should be feeling pretty confident now that you've explored the indisputable connection between your academic background and the qualifications needed for typical job postings. Now it's time to consider what jobs you should apply to in the first place given your skills, interests, and values. The next chapter guides you the through the process.

CHAPTER 3

Choosing a Path: Identifying the Jobs that are Right for You

WHERE HAVE I HEARD *THAT* BEFORE?

You've tried to be good-natured about it for a long time, but admit it—you're getting a little tired of having the same conversation over and over again. You know, the one in which a distant relative or a long-lost friend congratulates you on your recent graduation and asks what you studied. You tell them you majored in psychology or sociology and they immediately want to know what on earth you're going to do with your degree. You can detect a bit of cynicism in their tone—as though they don't quite believe you'll be able to be a fully functioning, self-supporting, tax-paying member of society just because you didn't major in accounting or "pre-something." Sure, the cynicism is wrapped in good intentions and genuine concern, but it's still there. And if you say you don't have a job lined up just yet, they try to buoy your spirits by saying something like, "Well, I guess you could always *teach* or something."

If teaching actually *is* among the options you're considering, then a comment such as this probably won't bother you. But if you have a different path in mind, or you haven't fully explored your choices yet, the implication—however subtle—that your career options are limited can be annoying. What's worse, it can be contagious—if you have this conversation frequently enough, anxiety can creep in no matter how passionately you believed in your academic choices.

You'll need to dismiss the notion that it will be harder to find a job with a degree in psychology or sociology than it would be with any other field of study under your belt. Sure, you may not pursue the same *types* of positions as your more vocationally minded classmates, but that doesn't mean you're any less marketable or qualified for the jobs that interest you—once you've determined what those are.

But maybe you already know that you have literally thousands of career options to choose from (Chapter 4 will introduce you to several). Perhaps your anxiety stems from not knowing which of these options you should pursue. Maybe all you know at this stage is that you'd like to secure a solid, respectable job—one that will make the best use of the skills and passions that you've cultivated in school, one that will convince Mom and Dad that paying your tuition was a worthwhile investment, one that doesn't require you to wear a hairnet or break the law. But of the jobs that fit those criteria, how on earth are you going to choose the one that's right for you? Don't worry—that's what the following chapter is all about.

First things first: Distinguishing jobs from careers

Before we go any further we should define both "career" and "job," because the two terms are not interchangeable. Most people who are just getting started tend to think of themselves as ensconced in a career only when they have a steady, full-time job with an ample paycheck and a respectable title—in an organization, or at least in an industry or field, in which they intend to stay for the foreseeable future. But that's not necessarily the case; you can still work toward your professional goals even if you know the position you're currently in, or the one you're about to take, won't last indefinitely.

What's more, you can still build a career even if the job that pays your bills isn't the one from which you derive the most professional satisfaction, or the one that provides the most opportunities for advancement. A career encompasses a lot more than any one full- or part-time job; rather, a career is *all* the things you're doing at any given point to advance your professional goals. You might work as a waiter while doing internships or volunteer work related to your long-term career aspirations. In other words, your career *includes* your current job, but that's not all it includes.

Taking that idea one step further, we should point out that you as a person are defined by much more than your job or your career. Your hobbies, personal interests, involvement in the community, relationships with friends and family—all of these things are just as important as your vocation when it comes to defining who you are. Obviously, satisfying and meaningful work that makes full use of your skills, abilities and interests is important (otherwise, we wouldn't be writing a book about it), but any specific job or career-related decision only makes sense if it's consistent with all of the other areas of your life that are important to you.

Granted, it's hard to avoid being identified by the job you do or the occupational field you're a part of. Whether you're applying for a credit card, renewing a passport, or making small talk at a cocktail party, everybody wants to know what you do. We obviously do a lot of things in life, but what most people care about is what we do for a living.

This cultural norm can be a real pain for people who get their intrinsic rewards from pursuits other than the activity that brings them their paycheck. We all know the type—wannabe actors schlepping trays of food, cab drivers writing the next Great American Novel between fares, and personal assistants who get their kicks from the hobbies they pursue on the weekends.

Add to this list those whose jobs are just stepping-stones to long-term career goals—e.g., recent grads in the mailroom on the slow road to CEO, aspiring attorneys copyediting while in law school. The jobs recent grads hold don't always hold their full interest or attention. Education usually pays off down the road, but initially, you may find yourself with a job title and job duties with which you'd rather not be identified.

Even if it doesn't exactly fulfill all of your professional goals, however, your first job shouldn't trigger a massive identity crisis—nor should your second or third job, for that matter. Most career experts agree that careers evolve over time, and they rarely progress in a linear way. Few people experience a professional epiphany at the age of 18 or 22 or 26, figuring out exactly what they want to do and sticking to it for the rest of their lives. Most people end up trying several different jobs—often in a number of different fields—before they decide what fits, and that's okay. At this stage, you are gathering information, investigating various options, and gradually refining your career goals as you find out more.

Over time, you'll start building on the themes and patterns you might already see emerging—a commitment to social service, a love of learning, an entrepreneurial streak. Your professional priorities and values might change, and your personal circumstances might change as well. When you move from one job to another to accommodate these changes, you carve out a career for yourself. You may decide to move after you've worked in a particular position for some time. Maybe you'll decide that you need to be closer to your family, or maybe you'll want to start one of your own. Perhaps you'll decide to return to school, and your graduate studies will spark an entirely new realm of intellectual and professional interests. Whatever the reason for the change in your personal circumstances, it's not uncommon for jobs to change along with them. No matter what's driving the change, your experience from your past job (or jobs) will probably influence what you do next. Let's say you loved the intellectual challenges your first job provided, but wished the work had been more team driven. Chances are, when you look for your second job, you'll be looking for positions that are decidedly more collaborative. Your second job will tell you even more about yourself and the specific things that float your professional boat, and you'll apply that knowledge and experience when looking for job number three. This process—the process of continually revising your goals, priorities, and values—is what allows your career to evolve over time.

So while you probably won't be able to map out the exact progression of your entire career right now, the good news is that you don't have to. Instead, you can focus on specific experiences that in one way or another weave together your interests, skills, and values.

Narrowing the field of options

Now that we've finished our pep talk, it's time to start thinking about what specific jobs make the most sense for you. As you may already know, there are countless personality tests and skills inventory tests out there intended to help you determine what type of work you're best suited for. But, at the end of the day, deciding what career you're going to pursue all boils down to something far less scientific and formulaic and far more instinctive: What do you like? What do you do well? What do you care about? The answers to these questions correspond to the categories "interests, skills, and values," which are often seen as the ABCs of career choice. By contemplating these questions, you're also addressing the question: "Who am I and in which environments will I thrive?" The key to finding a job you like is figuring out a way to balance your interests, skills, and values in a satisfactory way.

- Your **interests** are those things you enjoy doing, discussing, or daydreaming about. They include hobbies, sports, academic subjects, work activities, topics you read about, and anything else you like. They might be lifelong passions or just passing fancies. Your job is to decide which interests need to be part of your work life. You might major in art history but then work as a banker, reserving your art appreciation for museum visits on the weekends. Or you might have an interest so strong it must be a part of your daily work life.

- The category of **skills** encompasses three main areas: learned skills (tangible things we've learned how to do, such as creating spreadsheets in Excel or giving oral presentations); innate skills (aptitudes or talents); and personality skills (such as being hard-working, detail-oriented, or creative). Deciding which skills you enjoy using is important in defining a career focus and in finding a job you enjoy; as you'll read in Chapter 5, your resume, cover letter, and interviews are all opportunities to tell a prospective employer what specific skills and abilities make you a perfect fit for a job. If you trumpet skills you don't particularly enjoy using, it's entirely possible you'll land in a position you don't like very much.

- **Values** are things that are important to you. You probably already have a good idea of what personal values—e.g., honesty, integrity, loyalty, self-reliance—you hold most dear. For the purposes of this guide, however, we're referring to *professional* values specifically. Identifying your professional values helps you answer the question of what's really important to you in a particular position or work environment. The more closely your job—and your work environment—is aligned with your professional values, the greater the chances you'll be fully engaged and invested in your career at any given time. So what are examples of professional values? Here's a list—by no means exhaustive—to get you started:

  - Advancement opportunities
  - Autonomy
  - Availability of training/development programs
  - "Brand equity" (will people immediately recognize the name of the employer that I'm working for?)
  - Compensation package (base salary, benefits)
  - Contribution to society
  - Creativity
  - Direct contact with customers and clients
  - Diversity of daily tasks/responsibilities
  - Intellectual stimulation
  - Job security
  - Meritocracy (i.e., are the right people promoted? Does exceptional performance get rewarded?)
  - Quality of colleagues (e.g., colleagues that are friendly, supportive, and social)
  - Quality of direct manager
  - Quality of formal/informal mentoring
  - Prestige of the organization/occupation

- Predictability (in terms of hours, required travel, etc.)
- Relatively low stress level
- Work/life balance

What's your MVV (Most Valuable Value)?

The relative importance we place on each of the values above tends to change over time, reflecting not only changing professional priorities, but changes in our personal circumstances as well. There might be times in your career when making money is your top priority; as your career progresses, things like intellectual engagement or a sense of working toward the greater good might become more important to you. What's more, if you're still in college or have only recently graduated, you might not really know what relative value you place on the factors listed above; in most cases, it takes actually working in positions that represent different sets of pros and cons before you really have a sense of what's important to you. You may accept your first job out of college thinking that a better-than-average base salary and ample advancement opportunities are the most important things to you, only to discover that intellectual stimulation and colleagues that you can relate to are far more important, even if attaining these things means earning a lower salary.

Figuring out how you assign importance to these factors is a highly personal process—and you probably won't assess individual jobs or careers in the same way (or using the same criteria) that friends or peers would. For example, imagine what would happen if you printed out the list of values we provided above and distributed it to 20 of your closest friends and acquaintances. Let's say you asked each person to go through the list and assign a number between 1 and 10 to each value, where 1 meant that they assigned little importance to that factor, and 10 meant that it was a professional "deal-breaker." Chances are good that even among 20 people—a relatively small sample size—no two people would submit identical assessments. If you asked the same 20 people to complete the same exercise even two years later, their responses probably wouldn't be identical the second time around either.

Erin, who double-majored in psychology and German at a New England liberal arts college, accepted a job with a small corporate research firm after graduation. Three years later, she went back to school to earn her MBA. After her first year of business school, when her family and friends asked her what career she was likely to pursue after graduation, she admitted that she still wasn't sure. "All I know is that I have to work for a company whose name people will recognize," she said. "When people ask me where I worked before business school and I tell them, I always have to explain what kind of company it was. I'm tired of that. It's important to me that the next company I work for has instant name recognition." Though, not everyone assigns the same level of importance to brand equity, it's important to remember that there are no right or wrong answers when it comes to deciding what's important to you in a job. But you do need to give some thought to what's important to you in order to find a job in which you'll thrive.

At the end of the day, jobs (even the best, most desirable jobs) represent a set of trade-offs. Especially in the early days of your career, it may be difficult to get everything on your personal and professional wish list. Even so, the process of assessing (and continually reassessing) your priorities will enable you to figure out which tradeoffs you're willing to make and which things are too important to give up.

Major breakthrough

If you're getting stuck when it comes to figuring out your skills, interests, and values, spend some time thinking about what you've studied. Your major can tell you a great deal about the type of work you're likely to enjoy. Think of it this way: Many career experts say that the first step in determining your professional destiny is asking yourself what kind of work you'd do for free. In other words, if money weren't an issue, how would you spend your time? The rationale, of course, is that if you're truly passionate about the work you're doing, then you're far more likely to excel and advance in your career.

In a way, your major *does* represent the type of work you'd do for free. Not only were you not paid to study what you did, but chances are you actually paid (in one way or another) for the privilege of studying it. And if you're lucky, you had the freedom to decide what you wanted to study without spending too much energy on the myriad practical considerations that come with choosing a job. You didn't have to factor in compensation or benefits or promotion potential or the part of the country in which you wanted to live: You probably chose a major that you liked—or at least one that you thought you might like when you chose it.

Take some time to revisit the reasons you chose your major: what attracted you to your field of study, and what made it compelling enough to stick with? What made it rewarding for you? What made you glad you did it? What specific aspect of your major did you connect with the most? For example, did you enjoy the fact that it was research-intensive? Or that it involved a lot of writing? Did you appreciate that most of the work you did was independent versus collaborative (or was it the other way around)? Did your classes inspire intellectual debate and discussion that kept you engaged in the material? What specific classes did you find the most rewarding, and what about those classes floated your intellectual boat? How has your major—and the specific skills you developed while you studied it—contributed to success in other arenas? If you switched majors somewhere along the line (and many, many people do) think about what prompted you to switch gears.

Getting to the heart of what drew you to a specific major can tell you a lot about the type of work you'd find satisfying, and, conversely, the type of work that would be a round hole to your square peg. A case worker, psychologist, and a human resources manager might all have undergraduate psychology degrees in common, but it's very likely each one would have a different answer when asked what made their course of study so appealing and so valuable.

Balancing priorities

Once you've identified your interests, skills, and values, you need to weigh your priorities. It isn't always easy; sometimes two or more of these things seem to work against each other. Let's say you took an oil painting class as an elective while you were an undergraduate. The class was completely unrelated to your major, but it inspired a genuine interest in oil painting—and in the arts more generally. You've decided oil painting is something you want to pursue one way or another. However, when you look at the list of work-related values outlined above, you realize that job security and making a lot of money are important to you. If the starving-artist route is not for you, then you'll need to land a job that's more stable and more lucrative— maybe something on the business side of an arts-related organization. Or you may decide to keep your art interest "pure" by painting in your spare time and working a job unrelated to the arts in order to make money. (As we said at the outset of this chapter, the job that pays your rent doesn't have to satisfy all of your interests, skills, and values on its own). However you go about it, you'll need to decide what your priorities are before you can pursue a job that meets your needs. Here are some typical priorities of entry-level job-seekers:

- A foot in the door in an industry or sector in which I have a focused interest

- Any old job I have the ability to do and at least a basic interest in that will provide some professional experience and allow me to establish a work routine

- A job that will reasonably fit my interests, skills, and values but will more importantly allow me to live where I want and give me the amount of money I need to gain financial independence

- A job that bridges the gap to a new career field

These are all perfectly legitimate ways to frame your short-term career goals so that you can conduct a targeted, focused job search. In fact, they can be especially useful when looking for your first job, as many recent grads haven't figured out their long-term goals yet and need a framework to figure out which jobs to pursue. The key, however, is to continually ask yourself whether the jobs for which you're applying are consistent with your priorities—and to ask questions that will enable you to determine if your expectations about the job are realistic.

Foot-in-door disease

Many smart and talented folks with liberal arts degrees convince themselves to take jobs they don't really want because they want to get a foot in the door at an organization or in an industry in which they are particularly interested. There's nothing inherently wrong with this approach—as long as it's well informed and realistic.

Imagine, for example, your dream is to write for *Rolling Stone* magazine. Also imagine you are the most astute proofreader in the Western hemisphere—you can spot a wayward semicolon a mile away. Unfortunately, you enjoy proofreading about as much as you enjoy listening to chalk screech on a blackboard.

By stressing your exceptional proofreading skills on your resume, you could probably land a job at one magazine or another—as a proofreader. "That's okay," you say to yourself, "I'll have my foot in the door and eventually prove myself to be the great feature writer I know I am." Who could argue with the logic of this approach? By and large, organizations prefer to hire from within, so doesn't it stand to reason that you'll be able to work your way up fairly easily once people have gotten to know you and like you?

Well, maybe—but maybe not. First of all, you've got to ask yourself how long you can stare at columns of text looking for bad kerns and misplaced modifiers before you start thinking about the punctuation on your letter of resignation. What toll will all the dreaded proofreading take on your mind, body, and spirit? And do proofreaders at *Rolling Stone* have even the slimmest chance of being promoted? Only you can answer these questions, but in general, it's probably a bad idea to take a job you loathe because you suspect it might evolve into something else down the line. It might very well blossom into something better, but it also might not. Employees in virtually every industry can get typecast in the same way that actors and actresses do. You might very well be *Rolling Stone's* next great features writer—heck, you might already be able to write better stories than the person who currently inhabits that role—but if your boss sees you as a proofreader and nothing else, your chances for advancement could be slim. In fact, your proficiency in a role (even one you don't like) might paradoxically keep you from moving up. Your manager might decide that you are such a great proofreader he couldn't bear to hire someone else to replace you if you were promoted to features writer. That's why it's so important to talk to industry insiders in order to make informed choices about your career. During your informational interviews (which we'll cover in Chapter 5), be sure to ask about career advancement opportunities, promotion potential for specific roles, and the organization's philosophy and approach when it comes to developing its existing staff. After all of your conversations, you may very well decide that the foot-in-door approach makes the most sense, and that's okay. But you don't want to get your foot in the door only to find out that the rest of you will not be allowed in, nor do you want to get your foot in a door that you should have left closed to begin with.

GETTING FOCUSED

As we suggested at the beginning of this chapter, landing a job doesn't mean you've got your entire career mapped out. It also doesn't mean that you don't have to be focused during your job search; in fact, one of the easiest ways to sabotage your search is to come across as unfocused. These concepts aren't as contradictory as they may seem. You can be crystal clear that a job you're applying for is right on target for you at the present time, even if you're a little fuzzy on your long-range goals. Your cover letters, interviews, and follow-up correspondence—basically every moment of contact with prospective employers—must convey that you have a focus and have arrived at that area focus in a careful, thoughtful way. (We'll talk more about how to package your qualifications and career goals in a later chapter). But before you can convince anyone else that you should be hired, you have to figure out for *yourself* why any given job would be right for you and why you should be hired.

It helps to have a framework for thinking about the universe of job opportunities available to you. Every position you will consider can be defined on three distinct levels: the industry or field (e.g., social services, finance, education, government), the function or role you'd be fulfilling (e.g., counselor, account manager, analyst), and the particular company or organization you'd be working for. The function represents the core of what you do; the industry you're working in and the company you're working for provide context. For example, you could be an analyst in any number of organizations representing a range of industries. But the same function (analysis) would be an entirely different experience at a *Fortune* 500 company that makes semiconductors than it would be at a think tank. A role that's fascinating and rewarding in one industry might be utterly unbearable in another one.

While the same function can be very different depending on the industry you're working in, the reverse is also true: the same industry (e.g., advertising, government) can offer wildly different experiences depending on the function you have. Every field is highly complex and encompasses a variety of subfields and job titles. Each of these, in turn, requires different skills, credentials, and personality traits. In advertising, for example, there is a world of difference between the work an account executive does and the work a copywriter does. They are two different animals who happen to inhabit the same zoo. If you've identified the career field that interests you most, you've made a good start. And if you know the function you'd like to fulfill at your job (e.g., network administration), even if you don't yet know the industry or field you'd like to target in your search, you've also made some progress. But to make a compelling case to potential employers, you'll need to do legwork to fill in the missing piece. By "legwork," we mean research—checking out all available resources, online and otherwise—that will provide more information on specific fields and functions.

This book is a great place to start your research. And the Bureau of Labor Statistics—part of the U.S. Department of Labor—offers excellent career profiles of thousands of specific occupations. Whether you want more information on being a pathologist or a poultry farmer (seriously), the Occupational Outlook Handbook available on the Bureau's website (BLS.gov) will tell you about the training and education needed, average salaries, expected job prospects, job responsibilities, and other job-related details. You can also check out the websites of professional and industry associations (a simple internet search will turn up a lot of them). When it comes to research, there's really no substitute for good old-fashioned informational interviewing (a process that we'll describe in detail in the next chapter). If you need help, enlist the help of the career-planning office—their resources should be available to you whether you're a current student or an alum.

Practical matters

Balancing your interests, skills, and values is definitely an important part of the job-search process. It's an important part of life, for that matter—and it requires an enormous amount of introspection and emotional energy (if it didn't, networks like the CW wouldn't have any programming). There are also, however, significant practical implications you shouldn't disregard as you evaluate specific jobs. We've outlined a few of them below:

- **How much do I need to be paid?**

    A lot of people would like to think that, if given the choice, they'd rather make less money and do something they really care about than earn more money to do something they despise. Then many of these people go to law school, move to Manhattan, or take on a mortgage. The truth is, we'd all like to think that the most important factor determining our choice of profession is the ability to pursue our life's passion—to do work that's consistent with the very core of our being, that makes a difference in the world, or that makes the best possible use of our unique talents. However, unless you happen to be Oprah Winfrey, it can be difficult to balance these needs with the more immediate need to keep a roof over our heads, eat, pay off student debt, and eventually pay for Junior's college education.

    The truth can be a bitter pill to swallow. On average, graduates with undergraduate liberal arts degrees do indeed earn lower salaries right out of the gate than their counterparts in other disciplines. According to the National Association of Colleges and Employers (NACE), the average starting salary for class of 2006 graduates with liberal arts degrees is just under $31,000 a year. (By way of comparison, starting salaries for accounting undergraduates start at about $46,200, while finance/economics majors earn about $45,200 their first year out).[1] Gulp.

    We're not going to lie to you: living on $31,000 a year will mean living pretty modestly, especially if you have your heart set on living in a notoriously expensive metropolitan area (depending on the industry you choose, you may find you have to live in such an area in order to pursue the most attractive opportunities). Every year, Mercer Human Resource Consulting ranks cities across the globe according to their cost of living. In 2006, New York City, Los Angeles, San Francisco, Chicago, and Miami ranked as the most expensive cities in the United States.[2] If you're unsure how big-city living might affect your pocketbook, online tools such as Salary.com's Cost-of-Living Wizard enable you to figure out what you'd need to earn in one city to maintain the same standard of living you would in another.

---

1 National Association of Colleges and Employers. "High Starting Salaries Show Competition Heating Up for New Grads." April 6, 2006.
www.naceweb.org/press/display.asp?year=2006&prid=233.

2 Mercer Human Resource Consulting. "Worldwide Cost of Living Survey 2006—City Rankings." June 26, 2006.
www.mercerhr.com/pressrelease/details.jhtml/dynamic/idContent/1142150.

Salary.com, along with SalaryExpert.com and the U.S. Department of Labor website (BLS.gov), also provides salary information across various industries, functions, and geographic areas. Keep in mind that the salary ranges these sites provide are necessarily quite broad; you'll need to supplement this information with your own research. Occasionally, you'll be able to glean at least some salary information by browsing the postings on job websites, but, more often, you'll need to rely on insiders to give you a meaningful and realistic range. (You'll learn how to ask for salary information tactfully in Chapter 5, under "Informational Interviewing").

Of course, all of the salary information in the world won't do you any good unless you know how much money you really need to keep you going. Though financial planners use slightly different formulae to help people devise their monthly budgets, the following guidelines will give you a rough idea of how to allocate your net monthly income:

o   Thirty-five percent toward housing. This means your rent or mortgage, utilities, and the costs of any home repairs or improvements.

o   Fifteen percent toward repaying debt. This includes debt of both the student and credit-card variety.

o   Fifteen percent toward transportation. These costs include car payments, car insurance, parking, fuel, and cab, train, or subway fares.

o   Ten percent toward savings and investments. You are saving something, aren't you?

o   Twenty-five percent toward everything else. This means you've got one-quarter of your take-home pay to cover everything else: vacations, food, dry cleaning, clothing, recreation. Anything that you spend money on that doesn't fall into one of the aforementioned categories has to be accounted for here.

Once you've crunched the numbers, ask yourself if they paint a realistic picture: As we've said before, your salary won't go quite as far if you live in a famously expensive city such as New York or San Francisco, and you'll have even less wiggle room if you're staring down the barrel of substantial debt incurred during college or grad school. Keep in mind, though, that starting salaries are just that—starting salaries. Through job research, you'll (hopefully) find out how quickly and how often you can expect your salary to bump up, either through performance-based pay increases, annual bonus eligibility, or an annual inflation-based adjustment.

- **There's location, location, location ...**

  It's an age-old dilemma (or at least it's been a sub-plot of many sitcoms and motion pictures): Is it worth moving to a new city—perhaps one you've never wanted to visit, let alone live in—for the job opportunity of a lifetime? Though you're unlikely to face such a dramatic decision in the early stages of your career, giving some serious thought to where you'd like to live is important nonetheless. As you consider your options, be sure to ask yourself if the jobs/careers you're considering are available in that locale. Some industries have high concentrations of jobs in particular geographic areas. Finance jobs, for example, are predominantly in New York, Chicago, and San Francisco; technology jobs are clustered in Boston, Seattle, and Silicon Valley; publishing jobs are chiefly in New York; most entertainment jobs are in Los Angeles; and numerous government jobs are in Washington, DC.

  There are other factors to consider when deciding where you'll hang your hat: Are the job opportunities in your field of interest on the rise or at least stable for now? Are there interesting, varied places to hang out, like coffee houses, art galleries or museums, and movie theaters? Are there places you could take classes, such as colleges or universities, learning centers, or public libraries? Do there seem to be people you can relate to on an intellectual, artistic, recreational, spiritual, or other level that is important to me? What's the housing like? Is it plentiful, desirable, and affordable? How about the public transportation system? Do you need a car? Can you park a car if you need or want one? Do friends and family live there (or at least close by)? Is that important to you? How about your significant other? Speaking of significant others, if you don't have one but want one, does the city have a vibrant singles scene? Or is it a popular place for families to settle down and plant their roots? Consider these and any other questions that might be relevant to your situation: the extent to which you like where you're living plays a much bigger role in determining your overall happiness than you might think—it might be as important (if not more important) than the work you're doing.

- **... And there's relocation**

  So you've considered the list above and you've found a city that meets all your criteria. Congratulations! You've figured out exactly where you'd like to live—that's a huge weight lifted off your shoulders. Now, do you want to live there forever? Or just the next few years? It helps to have at least an idea of how you'd answer that question, because your response might help you determine how attractive a particular job opportunity is for you. Just as professional priorities often change over the course of a career, so do geographic priorities. Some careers can be pursued in just about any area of the country. If you're thinking about a career in social work, health care, elementary education, or family counseling (just to name a few), then you probably have more flexibility when it comes to geographic location than you would if you wanted to pursue a career in magazine publishing or the federal government—sectors in which job opportunities are highly concentrated in discrete geographic areas.

As an example, let's say that you've zeroed in on magazine publishing as a career field you might like to pursue. You know there are literally hundreds of magazines whose editorial offices reside in the New York metropolitan area, which is good news, as the city's energy and diversity—along with the sheer number of cultural and recreational opportunities it offers—have always seemed appealing to you. But while you'd love to live in the Big Apple for a few years, you sense it's not a place where you'd like to settle for the long term. Maybe you don't want to rent for the next 10 years. Maybe you can't stand the thought of choosing between a long commute and a tiny living space. Maybe the West Coast has always held a special place in your heart because that's where most of your family and friends reside. If you decide to move to another part of the country, can you parlay the skills you've developed in magazine publishing into another position in an unrelated field? While there are opportunities in magazine publishing on the West Coast, there are considerably fewer of them than there are in New York. If you do find a great editorial job with a West Coast magazine, what will happen if the company downsizes in three years, forcing you to look for other opportunities? Or what if you decide—for whatever reason—that the job or the company no longer satisfies your personal or professional goals? Are you comfortable knowing that there are considerably fewer places to approach for jobs if you decide to jump ship?

Keep in mind that even if your industry isn't highly concentrated in a specific geographic area, the organization that you're considering might offer more opportunities in a specific location (usually its headquarters city) than it does elsewhere. Let's say you've identified a great opportunity in the New York office of a Cincinnati-based consumer-products company. If staying in Manhattan for the foreseeable future is among your top priorities, be sure to ask whether career advancement is likely to require a tour-of-duty at company headquarters before you sign on the dotted line.

- **Leaving on a jet plane ... don't know when I'll be back again**

  If you ask people whether or not they like to travel, most would probably say yes. (We haven't done any scientific research to corroborate this point, mind you, but we think it's a pretty safe assumption to make). Most people think they like to travel, just as most people think they have a good sense of humor: It's rare to find somebody who admits to being either a homebody or a drip. If you like to travel and are looking for jobs that will enable you to hop around the globe (or at least the country), at least keep this in mind: Business travel and personal travel are two entirely different animals. Think about the last flight you took: Were there long security lines, interminable flight delays, hours spent in the middle seat directly in front of a screaming baby? Without a vacation on the other side of these annoyances, they can sap your strength—it takes a unique energy and stamina to excel at a job that requires frequent travel. If you think a jet-setting professional life means you'll get to see lots of interesting places and rack up hundreds of thousands of frequent flyer miles, remember these things too: If you're traveling for business, chances are you'll visit lots of interesting cities, but you'll probably only see the insides of those cities' hotels and conference rooms (along with whatever scenery happens to reside between the airport and your hotel). If it's the frequent flyer miles you're after, remember that it's pretty hard to redeem those these days anyway. You can always buy a plane ticket and visit interesting places on your own time.

Conclusion

This chapter has given you a lot to think about when it comes to honestly assessing your career interests, preferences, and aspirations. The next chapter presents concrete descriptions of the duties, work environments, lifestyle considerations, and other factors related to career paths from social services and corrections to human resources and event planning. Chances are you'll find many options that build on your academic background, pique your interest, and warrant more in-depth research.

CHAPTER 4

Free Will Exists—Career Options

Bridge work

Although your parents might see it differently, not having a job by the day of graduation is not the end of the world. You can take on a part-time job just to cover your bills during the job search or explore career possibilities through internships, fellowships, and other short-term employment options. All present great opportunities for personal growth and development and add to the repertory of skills you can tout in interviews for your first "real job." Here is a short list of exciting options:

- **Alliance of Artists Communities**

  www.artistcommunities.org

  Residency programs that foster the creative development of artists.

- **Community Alliance with Family Farmers**

  www.caff.org

  A program that promotes local economic development and social justice through support of family-scale agriculture.

- **Habitat for Humanity International**

  www.habitat.org

  A worldwide, nonprofit organization whose volunteer programs build homes for families in need.

- **InterExchange**

  www.interexchange.org

  A cultural exchange program that provides opportunities for living, working, and traveling abroad.

- **The Japan Exchange and Teaching Programme (JET)**

  www.jetprogramme.org

  An exchange program that focuses on international relations or foreign language education in Japan.

- **Peace Corps**

  www.peacecorps.gov

  A development organization whose volunteers promote world peace and understanding among diverse cultures.

- **National Park Service**

  www.nps.gov

  A government organization with several opportunities focused on preservation of natural resources and care of natural parks and outdoor recreation.

I USED TO BE YOU PROFILE[1,2,3]

Hugh Hefner

Born in Chicago on April 9, 1926

How You Know Him

Playboy, the original men's magazine

Psychology or Sociology?

Both! A Bachelor of Art in psychology and an unfinished master's degree in sociology.

His First "Real" Job

Infantry Clerk, U.S. Army

His Educational Path

Hugh Hefner (better known as, "Hef," a nickname he adopted in high school) attended Steinmetz High on the West Side of Chicago and although no more than an average student, he distinguished himself through extra-curricular activities, founding of a school paper, writing, cartooning, and serving as president of the student council.

In 1944, after graduating from high school, Hugh joined the army serving as an infantry clerk and drawing cartoons for various U.S. Army newspapers. Shortly after his discharge he spent the summer enrolled in art classes at the Chicago Art Institute. In the fall of 1946 he enrolled at the University of Illinois

1 Chris Colin. "Brilliant Careers: Hugh Hefner." Salon.com.
www.salon.com/people/bc/1999/12/28/hefner.

2 *Playboy*. The Hef Pages: Hef's Life. www.playboy.com/worldofplayboy/hmh.

3 Wikipedia contributors. "Hugh Hefner." Wikipedia, The Free Encyclopedia.
http://en.wikipedia.org/wiki/Hugh_Hefner.

at Urbana-Champaign where he majored in psychology. Hefner earned his bachelor's degree in two and a half years by doubling up on classes, all while drawing cartoons for the *Daily Illini* and editing the campus humor magazine *Shaft*, where he introduced a new feature called "Coed of the Month."

After graduating, Hef immediately enrolled in graduate school in the Sociology Department at Northwestern University. Although he didn't earn a master's degree, he did a variety of interesting research and wrote a forward-thinking mid-term paper which, being a harbinger of things to come, examined U.S. sex laws in light of the then-controversial Kinsey Institute research on human sexuality.

How This Psychology/Sociology Major Succeeded After College

After graduation, Hugh Hefner tried his hand at cartooning and, failing to sell any of his ideas for a cartoon strip, worked as an assistant personnel manager for the Chicago Carton Company (for $45 a week) to pay the bills. His future was up in the air until he landed a promising job as a promotion copywriter at *Esquire* at $60 a week in January 1951. When the magazine opted to move out of Chicago to New York, he requested a $5 raise to make the move financially worthwhile but was denied. That denial got him thinking that perhaps he could start a magazine of his own.

There were several failed attempts, but each taught him something new, and his resolve strengthened with each setback. He was certain there was a market for a sophisticated men's magazine that would reflect the views of the post-war generation. Then, lightning struck. He found and purchased an unknown photograph of Marilyn Monroe wearing not much more than a telephone (phones were larger in those days) taken before she had become famous. With photo in hand, he found a printer willing to produce the first issue and a distributor. He lured friends and family to help out financially, raising just $8,000, which included $600 of his own, borrowed from a lender using family furniture as collateral.

The first issue of *Playboy* magazine, produced on the kitchen table of Mr. Hefner's South Side Chicago apartment, was released in December 1953 and sold more than 50,000 copies. This paid off all his debt and left plenty more to finance future issues.

With success, Hugh Hefner used his power and celebrity to champion his views of sexuality in society that were likely shaped by his sociology and psychology studies. He wrote an extended series of editorials titled "The *Playboy* Philosophy," championing the rights of the individual and challenging the country's heritage of puritan repression. His views shaped the thoughts of an entire generation.

Just after the end of the 1960s, *Playboy* Enterprises went public. The magazine had a readership of 7 million copies a month and 23 *Playboy* Clubs existed around the globe with just fewer than 1 million members. The corporation also included a modeling agency, a limo service, a record label, and a TV and motion picture company run by a psychology major with a few graduate courses in sociology.

The Global Impact of This Student of Psychology and Sociology

Hugh Hefner created a publication that has been the world's best-selling men's magazine at several different times over the past four decades and obtained immeasurable global influence along the way. He has always regarded himself as "a prophet of freedom" (Hugh 36:24:36) and is an excellent example of how far force of will and a strong liberal arts education can take you. "I never intended to be a revolutionary. My intention was to create a mainstream men's magazine that included sex in it. That turned out to be a very revolutionary idea."[4]

CONSIDERING YOUR OPTIONS

You've gained new perspective on the skills and knowledge you acquired as an undergraduate, seen the relevance of liberal arts education to the workforce, and considered what you need in your first job. The next step in the process is to get a feel for the breadth of opportunities open to you given your sociology or psychology background. This chapter profiles several career paths taken by sociology and psychology majors and includes an industry overview, typical job description, resume guidance, interview tips, and career development suggestions for each entry. The "Classified Ad" section explains in basic terms what the particular career is all about, including the duties, work environment, and lifestyle that go along with it. A "Resume" section follows the ad and describes the character traits, capabilities, or experiences that are necessary for success. Next, we give you the scoop on just how to market your sociology and psychology training and other skills in an interview. The "Climbing the Ladder" section will tell you what it takes to advance through the ranks of the industry so you can plan ahead to reach your career goals. Finally, the "Related Careers" section introduces similar positions that might be up your alley.

MOB MENTALITY: CAREERS FOR SOCIOLOGY MAJORS

Career options for sociology majors are incredibly diverse. The quantitative and analytical skills you've acquired as part of your training in social research methods make you well suited for careers in a variety of different sectors. Your ability to discern how social factors impact organizational behavior is a skill that employers value highly, as the following career options will show.

---

4 Chris Colin. "Brilliant Careers: Hugh Hefner." Salon.com. www.salon.com/people/bc/1999/12/28/hefner.

Careers For Sociology Majors: Social Services

As an industry, social services promote well-being and improve social conditions for people in need. Every state in the nation has its own Department of Social Services which provides an array of valuable services and programs for the elderly, disabled persons, children, individuals, and families, which means there are opportunities everywhere, not just in major urban centers. Another critical aspect of this career path is fostering clients' independence in order to promote healthier individuals and communities for generations to come. Social services careers encompass several types of positions from counselors and health professionals to special education teachers and child care workers. The licensed social worker designation is but one extremely specific career within the wider spectrum of social services and should not be assumed to be the only career in this field.

Sociology majors are particularly well trained for opportunities in this field. Jobs in this area focus on providing practical help and support to people in times of acute crisis or permanent disability. The broad scope of most social services sectors encourages employees to gain expertise in a specific branch of the department—for example, a rehabilitation program or regional adoption services. With so many different areas in which to specialize, tasks can range from developing and running a government aid program, assessing crisis situations via direct interaction with clients, or taking care of the needs of a single challenged individual.

Focus On . . . Case Manager

The Classified Ad

Tough love is the guiding philosophy for many case managers who do whatever is necessary to get their clients' lives out of trouble and back on track. People in this field assist individuals and sometimes organizations (e.g., group homes for runaways or developmentally challenged individuals) with overcoming social problems in their environment. These problems, which affect everyone from children to the elderly, can range from health and psychological issues to financial and relationship challenges. By providing services or therapeutic interventions directly to clients, case workers not only assess problems but also help people cope with their feelings and offer feasible solutions. Karen Philips, who lives in New York, describes her role as a case manager as "ensuring the personal welfare of my clients and counseling them, as well as their families to hopefully avoid future crises."

Along with advising individuals on a daily basis, case managers also work to prevent social problems from arising within entire communities. In these positions, they promote the development of programs and services in order to prompt change that will improve general social conditions (think of the Boys & Girls Club running programs to get kids out of gangs and off the streets). With this purpose in mind, a number of individuals in this arena grow into roles in government administration and policy planning.

The Case Management Society of America defines case management as "a collaborative process of assessment, planning, facilitation, and advocacy for options and services to meet an individual's health needs."[5] A case manager is responsible for multiple cases at any given time and focuses on handling and directing unique and often complicated personal situations.

Most of this work entails a specialization or focused responsibility within the field, depending both on personal preferences as well as training. In general, though, case managers can be involved in a broad range of functions and are employed by a wide variety of institutions, including hospitals, senior centers, adoption agencies, hospices, prisons, and rehabilitation centers.

The Resume

The majority of job listings for case managers cite the need for strong interpersonal skills, active listening, and social perceptiveness, as well as analytical skills such as critical thinking and service familiarization. The social work profession is currently placing increasing emphasis on communications skills, professional ethics, and sensitivity to cultural diversity issues. Karen acknowledges that "in New York City and now almost everywhere else in the United States, knowledge of a second language is not just helpful but almost mandatory." A social worker must be capable of handling responsibility, working independently, and maintaining sound relationships with clients as well as coworkers. The *Occupational Outlook Handbook* reveals that social work employers look for people who are "emotionally mature, objective, and sensitive to people and their problems."[6] Most case managers see themselves as trained professionals who have a genuine interest in helping and working with others. A case manager must be capable of handling responsibility, working independently, and maintaining sound relationships with clients as well as coworkers.

The Interview

Your sociology degree has prepared you for the complex involvement with a large cross-section of society that is a fundamental aspect of social work and case management. Sociology majors provide valuable insight into social factors such as gender, age, race, ethnicity, education, and social class that affect every person who needs help. During an interview, emphasize your communication skills, knowledge of statistics, and experience with research design. Also, the breadth of your preparation as a sociology major is a great advantage as it heightens your potential for adaptability in any of the varied social work positions. Be prepared to discuss how and when you have demonstrated compassion and an empathetic outlook either through volunteer or previous work experiences.

5 Case Management Society of America. "Definition of Case Management." www.cmsa.org/Default.aspx?tabid=104.

6 Bureau of Labor Statistics. "Social Workers." *Occupational Outlook Handbook*. 2006–2007 Edition. U.S. Department of Labor. www.bls.gov/oco/ocos060.htm.

Climbing the Ladder

Case manager is an entry-level position in the field of social services while the title "social worker" is typically reserved for those possessing a Master's of Social Work degree. Residential counselor, group coordinator, and outreach specialist are all positions with a similar job function. People in these entry-level positions all have similar responsibilities and can advance within a social service agency or administrative department to positions such as supervisor (in-charge of a specific shift and scheduling activities and staffing coverage), assistant director (responsible for all shifts and/or other administrative functions such a managing budgets and developing grants) or executive director (the big dog responsible for the whole place). Such advancement is possible after some years of related work experience and additional training or certification (e.g., the MSW previously mentioned). Other career opportunities for case managers and social workers include teaching, research, and consulting. Some social workers also work in developing government policies through positions in government agencies and research institutions.

After gaining supervised work experience with an institution, many in this field choose to go into private practice. Private practitioners require a master's degree and they are encouraged to earn professional certifications through relevant associations and governing bodies. A network of contacts is also essential for the purpose of referrals and developing a client base. Many private practitioners opt to split their working hours between working for an agency and working in their private practice.

Related Careers

Human rights campaigner

Probation officer

Substance abuse counselor

Careers For Sociology Majors: Human Rights and International Politics

If your car has a bumper sticker proclaiming, "If you're not outraged, you're not paying attention" or "Free Tibet," then you might be a perfect fit for this socially conscious career field. Imagine sailing the high seas with Greenpeace as you help raise awareness on environmental policy or living abroad monitoring human rights violations for Amnesty International. Careers in human rights and international politics sound thrilling, and to some extent they are, but they also are physically and mentally demanding jobs (imagine the glamor of living in a war-torn area with limited food and water). For those who heed the calling, these jobs appeal to an innate impulse to advocate for social justice and empathize with all humankind. Most jobs in this area involve addressing questions of ethics, responsibility, and equity in both current and future standards for human rights. Human rights workers also reach into the realm of policy-making by reporting on their research findings and sharing suggestions for improved policies.

International politics similarly involves the study of human dynamics across nations in relation to a broad scope of social, political, economic, and civil issues. Careers in this arena extend across a wide range of fields including government, business, law, and foreign affairs. The field uses foreign policy to maintain and improve upon international relations. The domain of international politics involves several international institutions, such as inter-governmental organizations and multinational corporations, which work to ensure effective interactions among various global entities. The issues addressed by the international politics community range from worldwide sustainable development to economic growth to terrorism.

FOCUS ON . . . HUMAN RIGHTS CAMPAIGNER

The Classified Ad

Campaigners contribute to the global causes of social justice groups by developing and implementing campaign strategies, proposals, and policies. Each campaign generally involves a team of campaigners raising awareness about a specific concern (e.g., water source pollution or corporate exploitation of child labor) in a particular region of the world. A campaigner's work may also involve collaboration with external coalition partners. A considerable portion of a campaign's success depends on support from other organizations. Thus, maintaining relationships with key influential parties become a top priority for any campaigner.

Although issues, objectives, and tactics vary widely in the field, campaigners typically spend a good deal of time traveling, studying, and communicating with various constituencies. The workers' legal and scientific research ensures that the leader and other team members are well informed and prepared to develop effective campaign plans. Campaigners often engage in provocative marketing measures to increase public awareness and have assorted fundraising and advocacy duties as well.

Campaign objectives can include anything from policy changes and resource conservation to the protection of human rights and the promotion of equality. This broad range allows for a diverse group of campaign workers with varying backgrounds and opinions to unite for a single cause. Jennifer Lim, a research campaigner for an international nonprofit group, expressed a widespread opinion that "it helps to be really passionate about an issue because then not only is your work easier, but you also feel an unparalleled level of accomplishment in the end—as if your whole life's purpose is realized."

The Resume

Assuming you were the one on campus staging rallies and doing your best to raise awareness about the social issues near and dear to you, you will want to include a description of your involvement in this efforts on your resume. If you do not already have this experience, you would be well served to start getting active and volunteering for a cause (preferably one you are passionate about). This job requires a strong moral consciousness and, in some instances, the nerve to take personal risks. Even "civilized" places (college campuses) have rallies that can escalate to violent conclusions. Campaigners are also often required to go to great lengths to accomplish campaign goals and raise awareness. A campaigner should have good communication skills and be able to work effectively in groups as well as independently. Maintaining good relationships with others is crucial in this role.

Employers look for people with initiative and an innovative spirit that implies creativity and the ability to come up with new approaches to problems. John Shelley, a sociology major who now works as a campaigner but cut his teeth by organizing numerous protests at the University of California—Berkeley (not surprisingly, John's reason for going to Berkeley was because of its reputation for protests), says, "Our organization looks for experiences that demonstrate reliability in the face of danger or authority; traits like responsibility and organization are also important as they show that you can handle the hectic, but fun, environment of a campaign."

It is also important to have a basic understanding of political and legal matters in order to create effective campaigns. Familiarity with computer and research processes is very important, as is any experience in the fields of media and advertising, research, or public relations. Past work or volunteer experiences with nongovernmental organizations (NGOs) are also great preparation for a campaigning position.

The Interview

Your sociology training gave you the research and analytical skills necessary to become a knowledgeable and effectual campaigner. In addition, your experience exploring social interactions provides you with a keen awareness of issues facing people everywhere. These abilities would allow you to develop successful campaigns that focus on important ethical concerns.

Additionally, sociology training encompasses a broad span of cultural knowledge that prepares you to work with people from a wide range of backgrounds. This attribute also enhances your cultural adaptability, an important ability given the position's international travel and study requirements. During the interview, have at the forefront of your mind times when you demonstrated initiative and quick problem-solving skills and use them as proof of your capability and readiness for a position as a campaigner.

Climbing the Ladder

There are several opportunities for advancement within a campaigning organization. After only a few years of experience, you can very likely qualify for a leadership or management position. Depending on your interests and the areas in which you excel, possible advancement prospects include project leader, senior team leader, campaign director, or fundraising and development director. All of these next steps will entail supervising others and an increased load of administrative responsibility. You would also have the authority to make more strategic decisions about the direction of the organization. Generally, your track record of success within the organization is the main emphasis when determining suitability for advancement. However, many campaigners would rather stay right where they are. When asked about future plans, John Shelley responds vehemently, "I need to be on the front line effecting change. Nine out of ten times somebody 'climbing the ladder' is what I am ultimately protesting against."

Related Careers

Public relations

CIA agent

Case manager

Careers For Sociology Majors: Think Tanks

Let's be honest here—a job with a think tank is *exceptionally* difficult to land. It makes getting a consulting position with a firm like Boston, Accenture, or McKinsey look easy. Think tanks are exciting and challenging places where PhDs abound and staff members are often Mensa-level smart. But as the old cliché goes, nothing worth having is easy to get. Although this book has intentionally focused on great entry-level jobs that do not have "administrative" or "assistant" in the title, we had to make an exception here because in this career field you'll need an advanced degree to ascend the ladder. However, the lowly title could be well worth it. In the long run, you will have received the keys to a cutting-edge career surrounded by brilliant people analyzing the issues which—it is not hyperbole to say—will often affect the course of history.

So, what are these places? Think tanks such as the Brookings Institute or Rand are research organizations engaged in analysis of specific issues in order to advise and propose ideas to planning groups. For example, the Peter G. Peterson Institute for International Economics (known as the Peterson Institute for short) is a principal player in policy debates over globalization and free trade. Almost all think tanks deal with heady and complex issues exciting to only the most analytical and quantitative among us. The scope of a think tank can involve a number of areas including government, politics, economics, social welfare, or military interests. While some think tanks are strictly nonpartisan in their research, many institutes associate themselves with a particular stance on the political spectrum and receive sponsorship from the affiliated party through private donors. Think tanks can also be government-sponsored, particularly those with national security, defense, and foreign policy concentrations.

Think tanks range in size from small, minimally staffed private organizations to large, comprehensive corporations. They all require a variety of personnel to manage their involvements in policy research, publication, and public affairs. The workforce behind them typically consists of a large research faculty, research and administrative assistants, internal operations coordinators, external relations managers, fund-raising teams, and marketing staffs.

The Classified Ad

Administrative specialists work to ensure quality research and reporting methods within a think tank through resource and program development. Administrative specialists could be in charge of managing, updating, and coordinating an organization's various databases, or ensuring the smooth progress of key conferences. An administrative specialist is also frequently responsible for acting as a liaison or managing contacts and external relations, as think tanks generally consist of a large group of widely dispersed faculty and sometimes have multiple offices or partners.

An administrative specialist may be involved in planning events for a think tank, such as conventions and forums for research scholars or press and policy roundtables. The position may then call for preparing meeting materials and agendas, making logistical arrangements, managing correspondence, and working with media staff. Communications and program coordination opportunities for an administrative specialist may also include assisting with outreach to major program audiences and with research and policy materials publication processes. Much of the work required of an administrative specialist may seem mundane or tedious, but the real value of the job comes from the networking and advancement possibilities you will regularly encounter within the industry of think tanks.

The Resume

Administrative specialists for think tanks are responsible and detail-oriented individuals who are prepared to handle any task they may be given. Strong oral and written communication skills are necessary, given that an administrative specialist is often the lead contact for an organization and is frequently responsible for understanding and conveying the organization's views. An interest in policy issues and public relations is helpful when applying for a position with a think tank. Depending on the desired concentration within the position, knowledge of office software, computer applications, and research skills, and experience or previous outreach experience may be necessary. Think tanks are populated with brilliant and strong-minded people, so you will need to either be very comfortable taking direction or strong enough to push back and be heard.

The Interview

A sociology degree implies a strong understanding of multinational affairs, social theory, and both domestic and foreign relations. Sociology majors who have focused on research design, statistics, and data analysis would be ideal in a think tank. Their familiarity with research processes and data organization allows them to provide valuable assistance to an organization's research efforts or database development. Courses in economic and political sociology, cultural diversity, or racial and ethnic relations would also be worth mentioning in an interview. These and related courses demonstrate a comprehensive knowledge and concern for the social and political domains within policy-planning and thus establish a connection with a think tank's goals.

Climbing the Ladder

Opportunities for advancement within a think tank are widely available for someone in an administrative specialist position and usually depend only on one's initiative, aptitude, and relationships with other office staff. After a year or two within the organization, you could qualify for coordinator and manager positions, assuming full responsibility for operations and program coordination and related staff. With some experience in economic or financial planning, opportunities in managing a think tank's budget and allocating resources, fund-raising, and work at the senior leadership levels may become available.

Because there is not generally a lot of predictable movement at the senior levels of a research organization; advancement opportunities could emerge regularly or take several years to become available. If you are considering further education, a master's degree in a relevant area can accelerate the advancement process and provide you with a competitive edge for some positions like project associate or policy analyst. You might also consider transferring to a new position at a different organization if advancement opportunities within the firm do not come around as quickly as you would like.

Related Careers

Research assistant

Copy editor

Benefits coordinator

Careers For Sociology Majors: Corrections

Ray MacWhinnie, a correction officer at a minimum security jail in Pittsfield, Massachusetts describes the motivation behind his work simply: "I like keeping the world safe." The array of jobs falling under the corrections umbrella is a large one but the vast majority of the field's workers, somewhat oddly, love working with people—and not just the citizens they are protecting from offenders. Many are gratified by the work they do to help offenders help themselves.

Corrections is the part of the criminal justice system that seeks to rectify criminal behavior through punishment and rehabilitation. A criminal offender may be sentenced to prison, community service, or rehabilitation, among other things, and corrections officers are responsible for managing the process of carrying that sentence. Federal, state, and local corrections agencies each have their own jurisdiction over particular categories of criminals and regions of offence. These agencies are very closely tied to other groups in the legal system (other law enforcement agencies, parole offices, social service departments, etc) at their respective levels of authority.

Corrections management takes place through a variety of public and private organizations, government agencies, and correctional facilities. While the large majority of workers are employed by the federal and state governments, outsourcing to private prison companies is becoming more and more popular. Careers in the corrections industry can involve prison management, safety and security operations (e.g., security detail for wealthy individuals) or rehabilitation program management (e.g., a parole office). Correspondingly, all types of professionals can be found in the corrections system, including teachers, counselors, health professionals, security personnel, and legal specialists. Depending on the level of government and size of the corrections program, positions in corrections could involve broad supervisory roles, very specialized work, and many points in between.

FOCUS ON . . . PROBATION OFFICER

The Classified Ad

A probation officer is an agent of the court and is responsible for supervising defendants in the legal system who have been sentenced to probation as an alternative to prison. Probation officers interact directly with offenders and their families, as well as with lawyers and court officials, to become familiar with an offender's situation and ensure that the conditions of the probation are met. It is common for a probation officer to meet clients at their own homes to supervise offenders more closely and to build trust and an intimate relationship with them. Probation officers also plan rehabilitation programs for their clients, enlisting the help of community organizations, family members, and local neighbors to monitor an offender's progress and to make valuable referrals. Probation officers are generally trained in counseling methods so that they can become an integral part of an offender's rehabilitation program. They may also help their clients find employment, housing, medical care, or provide them assistance in minor legal matters. Almost anything that ensures the client's well-being and progress toward becoming a productive member of society is fair game.

Probation officers can work either with adults or juvenile offenders and are in charge of maintaining case files for each client and making regular reports to the court on a client's progress. After a certain period of observation and interaction with a client, a probation officer is required to suggest a long-term corrections course, which may include extending an offender's probation period or recommending incarceration. Along the lines of aiding the court, one component of a probation officer's work is to investigate the personal and criminal histories of accused offenders and provide advice (and sometimes testimony) in sentencing. A probation officer is usually in charge of several active cases at a time and spends, on average, 40 hours a week on casework.

The Resume

Probation officers should have a thorough understanding of correctional laws and regulations as well as of the general legal process. Course work outside of your major related to political science, law, or history can offer a very nice edge. Candidates usually must be at least 21 years of age and have no felony convictions on their record. Most employers require background checks and administer written, oral, psychological, and physical examinations to ensure fitness and readiness for the position. Candidates must also go through a training program before entering the field in a permanent position.

The job of a probation officer requires emotional strength and the ability to interact with a diverse array of people from clients to court officials to rehabilitation resources. Good communication skills are vital for these interactions as well as for the great quantity of reports, both written and oral, expected of a probation officer. Probation officers are also exposed to potentially dangerous situations, so it is important that they can handle stress and think quickly.

The Interview

Probation officer employers consistently cite the importance of knowledge of social factors and the ability to recognize and understand the sociological motives of criminals as well as the effects of incarceration as essential qualifications for this job. A sociology major is well versed in the social issues facing many offenders and thus is able to design effective individual rehabilitation programs and provide valuable and trusted assistance to his or her clients. Another useful aspect of a sociology degree is the investigative and analysis training it provides. This training has prepared you to make critical observations in stressful situations and to conduct investigations, assess findings, and prepare reports as a probation officer.

Climbing the Ladder

Many agencies place the position of probation officer into different classifications, from the entry-level position with limited assignments to the advanced position where the employee functions in a senior leadership role. In almost all cases, advancement along these classifications is based almost exclusively on seniority (e.g., "time on the job") and demonstrated satisfactory acquisition of the relevant knowledge and skills associated with the position. A higher classification means greater responsibility, a wider range of assignments, and more flexibility, along with increased pay. A probation officer can also advance to a supervisor position.

Related Careers

Case manager

CIA agent

Substance abuse counselor

Careers For Sociology Majors: Careers that focus on diversity and minority issues

An unfortunate reality of today's job market is the obvious lack of universal access to the system. Census data continues to show that women are still often paid less than their male counterparts and African Americans are underrepresented in almost all areas of American business. Many companies claim to comply with Equal Employment Opportunity standards but make no real effort to diversify either their workforce or client base. To say that diversification of the American workforce and business practices is happening at glacial speed is not an understatement.

If you find topics like gender equity, civil rights, or fair business practices interesting, you should pursue them as a career without delay. This aspect of the American job market is growing as companies and state and federal government agencies work to level the business playing field for historically underutilized businesses, particularly those owned by women, minorities, veterans, and the disabled. Large U.S. corporations like Apple Computer, Xerox, and General Mills have entire divisions dedicated to employing and buying products and services from a wider range of people. Xerox is even establishing supply lines specifically with gay and lesbian business enterprises. How serious are these companies? In 2005 Xerox states that it purchased $330 million of goods and services from minority- and women-owned businesses in the United States, which accounts for approximately 24 percent of their annual qualified purchases.[7]

FOCUS ON . . . MARKET ACCESS COORDINATOR

The Classified Ad

Market access coordinators work in supplier diversity departments which are most often found in large companies. These departments focus on outreach efforts geared toward attracting, developing, and retaining underrepresented minority suppliers for business and manufacturing operating units. Of all the careers profiled in this book, this industry and job title are undoubtedly the new kids on the block. As a result, there is quite a bit of variety in the scope of responsibilities for someone in this position depending on the product line and size of the company. While the terminology employed to describe the job functions varies widely, the underlying outreach, research, qualification, and utilization responsibilities are the same.

Market access coordinators actively seek out diverse suppliers through minority and business development organizations and participation in trade shows. This aspect of the job often requires a lot of travel. Market access coordinators also perform due diligence and research, sifting through small business filings, tax records, and a wide variety of other documents to verify the underutilized status of the potential partner. The coordinators also manage all of the paperwork that goes along with the approval process and the data that is captured to keep track of the supplier's utilization by the company. Other responsibilities include monitoring the effectiveness of the supplier diversity initiative and developing new means of supporting supplier success.

The Resume

The best market access coordinators are extroverted, patient, and detail-oriented. Sifting through government documents to verify that a business' historically

---

7 Xerox Corporation. *The Xerox Supplier Diversity Program.*
www.xerox.com/go/xrx/template/009.jsp?view=Feature&ed_name=Supplier_Diversity_Home
&Xcntry=USA&Xlang=en_US.

underutilized business status is legal and up-to-date can be tedious work. Independence and ability to work without constant direct supervision is useful for people required to be on the road visiting prospective and established partners. Basic technical skills are also required as coordinators often input information into spreadsheets and databases, use word processing to draft evaluations and reports and deliver polished PowerPoint presentations to either attract or train diverse suppliers.

Finally, enough cannot be said about the ability to communicate. Market access coordinators are the link between the company and suppliers and therefore must be able to appreciate and represent the expectations, concerns, and ultimate goals of both parties.

The Interview

Anyone considering working in this field should be able to describe why they enjoy and thrive on working with diverse populations. Any extracurricular activities related to connecting with people from different backgrounds will go a long way toward proving your sensitivity to diversity challenges. Discuss the ways your sociology training sheds light on the complex dynamics governing social interaction among different cultures, ethnicities, and genders and how this relates to day-to-day job interactions.

Climbing the Ladder

As this is a fairly new field, the ladder is still being defined. However it is safe to say that at this time, for anybody starting as either a market access assistant or coordinator, reaching the brass ring means becoming a director or vice president for supplier diversity at a major company. At this level, salaries are high (more than $100,000 a year) and responsibilities are numerous. Although in its infancy, there is also what appears to be a consulting market for people who have supplier diversity experience and are willing to teach other companies and organizations how to set up diversity initiatives or instruct minority businesses in how to land lucrative supply contracts.

Related Careers
Real estate agent

Staffing specialist

Case manager

WHEN THE INMATES RUN THE ASYLUM: CAREERS FOR PSYCHOLOGY MAJORS

Many psychology graduates before you have successfully entered the world of work in careers that don't directly relate to their college studies. In fact, roughly half of psychology majors end up working in business or finance, according to Department of Labor statistics and various education surveys. Your education has provided you with a perfect set of cross-trainers that will allow you to win on almost any playing field. As you will see, the jobs for which you qualify are exceptionally diverse. Your mission, should you choose to accept it, is to settle on just one.

Careers For Psychology Majors: Human Resources

For the discussion here, human resources refers to the overall department (it can have many divisions) within an organization that determines the firm's employment-related actions. Working in this arena means helping companies find, employ, and retain qualified personnel. The various human resources positions available involve recruiting and hiring employees, providing payroll and benefits information, and administering other work-related services (such as leadership training and professional development). A corporation's human resources staff is responsible for the delicate balance of hiring, firing, and training employees in order to craft the most effective and competent service team for the firm's growth and success.

Human resources professionals are responsible for analyzing potential and current employees' abilities (technical, interpersonal, managerial, leadership, etc.) and traits (competitive, a push-over, etc.) and/or understanding a variety of protocols (e.g., timesheets) and administrative processes (e.g., dispersing retirement benefits). Human resources workers also interact daily with the company's employees, informing them of policy changes, salary adjustments, and mediating disputes. Depending on the size of a company and its human resources staff, a position in human resources may require specialized knowledge of a single area or familiarity with several aspects of employee management.

Focus On . . . Benefits Coordinator

The Classified Ad

A benefits coordinator assists in developing and implementing a company's health care, insurance, and retirement benefits for its employees. The coordinator ensures that the company's benefits programs are implemented smoothly and run reliably, and that employees' questions and issues are dealt with promptly and accurately. A benefits coordinator is responsible for implementing updates to a company's benefits plan, and a portion of their time will involve acting as a liaison with insurance providers and negotiating new or revised policies with them. Benefits coordinators are also responsible for supervising claims for medical plans, workers' compensation, and general liability. The work of a benefits coordinator likewise involves the continuing protection and supervision of company-wide medical, dental, life and disability plans to guarantee proper insurance coverage.

As choices in insurance and benefits plans become more abundant and complex, benefits coordinators must be aware of a wide range of policy standards and regulation changes in order to effectively serve their company. Both pension plans and health benefits include numerous specific subcategories that require attention; rising health care costs make intimate knowledge of health benefits a top priority. Child care and maternity/paternity leave, elder care, nursing home care insurance, flexible benefits plans, and employee welfare programs are just a sample of the many programs a benefits coordinator must know inside and out. These and other emerging programs make benefits coordinators' jobs quite challenging as they must frequently familiarize themselves with the latest benefits options and present this information to their companies and their employees in a friendly and clear manner. A benefits coordinator is often expected to communicate and interact with a corporation's senior executives to resolve benefits issues and advise programmatic changes.

The Resume

A benefits coordinator must stay on top of a torrent of benefits-plan designs and regulations. He or she should have good analytical skills and be able to assist employees with developing their ideal benefits plan. Benefits coordinators also need strong spoken and written communication skills—customer service skills are mandatory. Any experience in retail sales or food service can be a real plus as it will have certainly provided you with plenty of customer interaction. People take their health insurance and retirement benefits very seriously and have little patience when problems occur. A benefits coordinator must be able to act calmly and considerately with a diverse array of sometimes worried and angry people.

The Interview

The inherently personal work involved in human resources careers makes a psychology degree very appropriate. These professionals have the capacity to be especially attuned to the relationships between employees and their work environments and are well equipped to decide best course of action. Stories about resolving conflict will serve you well as will examples of when you had to help others or keep track of lots of details. Both of these skills will be queried in the interview. The research and analysis skills you gained in a psychology program will enable you to employ efficient policy analysis skills and accurate identify an individual's benefits needs.

Climbing the Ladder

After a few years of experience in the field, a benefits coordinator can advance to a managerial or supervisory position within the human resources department. Outstanding work can lead to a position as the director of the department or of a related department within the company. This type of advancement could eventually lead to a senior or executive position in the firm such as vice president of human resources.

Related Careers

Substance abuse counselor

Market access coordinator

Staffing specialist

Careers For Psychology Majors: Staffing and recruiting

Staffing and recruiting are so closely related to the hiring function in human resources that many people do not realize that it is a distinct industry (and a multi-billion dollar industry at that). Even if you have not yet reached this epiphany, you probably know someone who has worked for a temporary (temp) agency on the staffing side of the equation. On the other side you have the glamorous headhunters who "place" multimillion-dollar CEOs. Beneath the surface, both concentrate on identifying, acquiring, and placing new talent for various organizations. The industry is typically categorized into generalist and specialist functions, the former involving placement in a range of fields (usually the temp agencies) and the latter including certain industries and specific positions (the headhunters).

People in this field familiarize themselves with the specific requests and conditions of the organization they represent and work as part of the process to locate, meet, evaluate, and place promising candidates. Some network via telephone and obtain leads for others to follow. Others travel near and far to meet and interview candidates. Preparation of marketing materials, such as pamphlets on the company and job descriptions, for recruiters to distribute is often another part of the job. Recruiting and staffing professionals must be aware of equal employment opportunity and affirmative action laws and guidelines, and use them to guide their recruiting activities. They must also be knowledgeable about the company they are recruiting for, including its wages, benefits, promotion opportunities, and human resources policies as they often act as the first point of contact between potential recruits and the organization.

Focus On . . . Staffing Specialist

The Classified Ad

Staffing specialists are recruiters that solicit people for positions in a single industry or specialized area. Specialists interview people and determine their skills and qualifications then place them in suitable employment opportunities. They manage the initial screening process for applicants and administer various assessment tools and interpret the results to determine a person's capabilities and appropriateness for a position.

Staffing specialists usually work as part of a company's internal staff but might also work for large employment services firms that provide external support for companies. As representatives for particular businesses, they participate in job fairs and travel to college campuses in order to procure promising job applicants. According to U.S. Army Corps of Engineers campus recruiter Cortney Kaplan, "College campuses are a huge source for our employment process. School career fairs are the most effective ways to recruit the freshest and brightest minds. This is definitely a growing trend."

Staffing specialists must also maintain a large network of contacts in order to spread the word about their company and its employment opportunities. They spend their days making phone calls (for some, cold calling is 90 percent of the job) pursuing connections to leads, harvesting resumes from applicants, organizing recruiting schedules, developing recruitment materials, traveling and attending recruiting events, and performing assessments on potential recruits.

The Resume

Staffing specialists are personable, energetic, and highly extroverted. They feel comfortable approaching others, often out of the blue, regarding their recruitment efforts. They have an eye for detail and recognize potential in others. They exhibit excellent organizational, planning, documentation, and problem-solving skills. Recruiters are also expected to have above-average negotiation skills (include bullets on your resume related to how you persuaded or sold things to others) and to be creative and resourceful when looking for and speaking with candidates. Often new methods and innovative recruiting techniques determine a recruiter's success in acquiring the best talent for his or her company. Kaplan says, "All of the progress in the recruiting industry comes through ideas from recruiters because they're the ones on site, in the field, and actively pursuing prospective employees. Some ideas are classic while others get stale pretty quickly, so a little ingenuity can really take you a long way." Recruiters must also be able to work independently with little guidance and sometimes with only loose guidelines for candidates.

The Interview

Psychology majors embrace the assessment skills that define successful and effective recruiters. These skills allow you to identify and evaluate ideal candidates for various positions. Staffing specialists must also conduct research, peruse market surveys, and examine industry competition studies. All of these investigative tasks resemble the extensive research responsibilities and education of psychology majors. Along the same lines, a significant part of a recruiter's job includes appraising past and current recruitment methods and employment trends in order to come up with new, productive recruitment solutions that enhance the accuracy and efficiency of the recruiting business.

Climbing the Ladder

Staffing specialists who demonstrate great talent in their field can advance to recruiting manager and supervisor positions. Superior positions have greater authority in determining the recruiting schedules and methods used by an organization, as well as directing the recruiting staff. Exceptional workers could even become directors of staffing departments, as executive positions become available. Some specialists, usually ones who have developed expertise and contacts in a specific industry (e.g., Silicon Valley techies or Wall Street finance types) go on to open their own recruitment consulting firms.

Related Careers
Benefits coordinator

Public relations

Case manager

Careers For Psychology Majors: Gerontology

Gone are the days of popping a videotape in the VCR of the common room and letting the old timers in the nursing home vegetate all afternoon. Nursing homes, YMCAs, community centers, and other gathering places for senior citizens now provide sophisticated programming specifically tailored for this population (e.g., yoga for elders, painting, water aerobics, etc).

Gerontology is both an academic field of study and a distinct career field. On the academic side, gerontology is not only the study of older adults, but also, and perhaps more importantly, the aging process itself. All the questions as to how and why our mind and bodies break down are of interest to researchers in this field. On the career side, gerontology involves both providing goods and services specifically for this population or working directly with elderly individuals. As the baby boomer population ages, opportunities in the field of gerontology are increasing by leaps and bounds. Census projections predict an astounding 40 million elderly citizens in the United States by the year 2010[8], and these people will require all kinds of personal health and welfare programs, recreational living facilities, and elderly care policy. Numerous disciplines can be involved in achieving this goal, including social work, nursing, counseling, medicine and recreation. People who wish to work in gerontology careers thus have a wide range of potential options.

FOCUS ON ... ACTIVITIES COORDINATOR

The Classified Ad

Activities coordinators in the area of gerontology are responsible for planning and implementing both physical well-being and life-enrichment programs for groups of elderly persons, often representing varying level of abilities. In this role, you might be responsible for planning and leading more specific, individualized therapeutic rehabilitation programs. The most common workplaces are long-term care units (nursing homes), assisted living communities (a hybrid nursing home/apartment complex) and retirement communities (essentially, a members-only living community with a minimum age requirement, often 55). In designing activity programs, coordinators must comply with certain state and federal regulations, along with rules of their employer while always keeping track of the best interests of the participating adult group. Planned activities range from outdoor sports and recreation to social gatherings and fitness programs, all, again, with the purpose of supporting and encouraging elderly persons to continue leading active and dynamic lives.

8 Arnold Goldstein and Bonnie Damon. *We the American...Elderly.* U.S. Department of Commerce. Bureau of the Census. www.census.gov/apsd/wepeople/we-9.pdf.

The Resume

Activities coordinators are tremendously upbeat people (you can imagine the enthusiasm it takes to get some seniors moving). They must be able to interact with a variety of people and maintain a motivational spirit throughout their job. It is also crucial that activities coordinators demonstrate patience and compassion. Activities coordinators often work evenings and weekends, and must possess the organizational skills to plan weekly schedules, including concurrent programming from time to time. So be sure to note any event planning or program organizing you've done on campus, in internships or elsewhere.

The Interview

Psychology students are ideal for this position because human relations are the core component of the job. You have an awareness of the individual, social, intellectual, and emotional concerns experienced by aging persons, and, if you choose this path, you will need to demonstrate your genuine concern for this population. Your broad psychological education should have exposed you to a wide range of social issues and challenges facing the elderly community, and you have the ability to talk about these from a persuasive academic perspective. The analytical and problem-solving skills you have developed will lead you to come up with innovative and effective approaches to overcoming obstacles and finding appropriate solutions. Relevant psychology course work includes classes on adulthood and aging, cognitive processes, social psychology, and human memory and learning.

Climbing the Ladder

Activities coordinators who demonstrate great enthusiasm and competency towards relevant tasks might be promoted into a role as a director of activities, which does not require further formal education but may require additional training or certification. But many elderly community living situations are privately owned, have relatively small staff sizes, and experience little turnover at managerial or administrative positions. Therefore, depending on your employer, opportunities for advancement might require you to change companies.

Related Careers
Day care provider

Substance abuse counselor

Benefits coordinator

Careers For Psychology Majors: Child Care

Any new parent can tell you that finding affordable child care is exceptionally difficult. This is great news for you if you enjoy being around infants, toddlers, and children, and have an interest in participating in their development. It's a seller's market, and with a college degree, entry-level day care positions abound. People who work in child care services attend to and care for children whose parents or guardians are at work or temporarily away. Child care workers are responsible for feeding the child, attending to basic needs, and managing the child's daily activities such as exercise and developmentally appropriate games and educational lessons. A common goal in child care is to stimulate intellectual growth through regular activity as well as social growth and independence by allowing children to interact with other adults and children outside of their families.

Jobs in child care can entail various types of responsibilities and working situations. Some child care workers care for children during an 8-hour work day while others may be permanent live-in household caretakers, and still others just supervise children for a few hours before and after school. Child care workers can work for small private groups or individuals, government organizations, large corporations, or public schools. Similarly, employers range from privately-owned day care centers, to in-house, corporate-owned day care centers or private homes.

Along with interacting with children, a child care worker regularly meets with parents to discuss progress and needs. Part of the goals of infant and preschool programs is to prepare children for school, so coordination with a child's family is critical. Before- and afterschool programs specifically aim to supplement a child's academic and social development and thus a child care worker in this type of program may ask parents to incorporate such stimulation in the home environment as well.

FOCUS ON . . . DAY CARE PROVIDER

The Classified Ad

A classic day care provider works a typical 8-hour day supervising children while the parents are at work. A provider may offer services either within a formal day care center environment or from home. In either environment, but especially in formalized child care centers, a day care provider works among other child care staff so that the child-to-caretaker staff ratio remains manageable. Some day care providers, running smaller operations, are able to care for several children single-handedly, usually after several years of experience within the child care industry. The government has strict guidelines regarding almost all aspects of day care, and infractions can be costly and may result in day care centers being shut down permanently.

A day typically begins with parents dropping off their children in the morning before they go to work. This means you are at work while most folks are just getting out the door. Once the day begins you are attending to all of the children's basic needs as well as facilitating play and interaction among children, providing outlets for creativity and intellectual development, and ideally exposing children to a wide range of new and unfamiliar situations. A good day care provider can distinguish among the interests and capabilities of each child to ensure proper growth and progress. The workday ends when the last child is picked up in the afternoon.

Providing one's own day care services is equivalent to starting a business. It requires Department of Social Service certification (which varies greatly state to state), other licenses, possession of a tax ID number, home inspections, and other qualifications relevant to operating a business. Expenses include facility leases, equipment, supplies, staffing, and operating costs. These large-scale operations usually have several staff members who take care of many children at one time.

The Resume

Day care providers are people who love being around children and demonstrate patience and maturity with their little charges. Children must be able to trust their day care provider as well as respect him or her. A day care provider should be able to maintain composure and an appropriate degree of control over their operations in stressful situations and should be detail-oriented, able to think quickly, and have good problem-solving skills. Familiarity with first aid, child development, and nutrition are helpful though not immediately necessary. A solo day care provider must be at least 21 years old and go through training and licensing programs provided by the state's department of social services.

The Interview

Your psychology degree has provided you with the skills needed to work directly with children. As a psychology major, you have a thorough understanding of brain development and early human interactions. You are therefore able to provide a valuable and effective day care program that stimulates children and promotes comprehensive development. Useful courses that you may have taken include developmental psychology, infancy and early childhood, personality, and developmental psychobiology.

Climbing the Ladder

Becoming a self-employed day care provider is the ultimate goal for many child care workers. Having your own clients and retaining all the profits, rather than earning an hourly wage is exceptionally appealing. Day care is often a "gateway" career for those interested in early childhood education. Teaching in a public school usually requires further education and certification, and some posh day care environments will require a master's degree and additional child care–related credentials. The good news is that if you do need to get further training, you can often do it part-time while still working.

Related Careers

Substance counselor

Activities coordinator

Shelter worker

Careers For Psychology Majors: Health Services

The health services industry is the largest industry in the country with more than 13 million employees, according to the Bureau of Labor Statistics.[9] Taken as a whole, the dollar value for this industry is very close to a trillion dollars. Overall, careers in the health services industry concentrate on protecting and improving health conditions and promoting well-being for all people. Jobs range from physicians and therapists to medical researchers and nutritionists. Health services agencies operate on the governmental, public, and private levels and provide a broad selection of health programs and services ranging from information on teen pregnancy to coping with and treating drug addiction. Programs target every age range, socioeconomic group, health affliction, and general public welfare.

The field of public health is also becoming increasingly popular as communal health threats like bioterrorism and disease epidemics (and how to deal with them) have gained tremendous media coverage. This aspect concentrates on protecting the health of society as a whole and includes work in planning and policy-making to ensure public safety and prevent infections. Counseling and rehabilitation services are also growing as there continues to be better understanding of social and psychological conditions.

FOCUS ON . . . SUBSTANCE ABUSE COUNSELOR

The Classified Ad

Substance abuse counselors help (through therapeutic intervention and education) people suffering from addiction to alcohol and other drugs like cocaine and heroin. They counsel individuals in both private and group sessions to help people identify the behaviors and underlying issues related to their addictions. Along with aiding in the assessment of each person's problems, counselors endeavor to help clients develop a plan that will change the behavior, lifestyle, or environments that contribute to their problems.

Much of the addict population consists of people who need help in several areas of their lives and substance abuse counselors refer patients to a variety of other information and professional services that can support their rehabilitation. The abuser may be directed to a physician or psychiatrist, financial and housing assistance agency, vocational training center, lawyer, social worker, or other professionals depending upon their needs.

Substance abuse counselors often work in therapeutic communities where substance abusers live while under treatment. They may also work for correctional

---

9 Bureau of Labor Statistics. "Health Care." *Career Guide to Industries*. 2006–2007 Edition U.S. Department of Labor. www.bls.gov/oco/cg/home.htm.

institutions, hospitals, mental health agencies, and other drug treatment centers. The breadth of employers of substance abuse counselors includes local, state, and federal governmental agencies, schools, churches, and nonprofit organizations. The typical counselor works 40 hours a week, but weekends and holidays may be necessary depending on the setting.

Demand for counselors is expected to increase over the next several years as more and more substance abusers are accurately diagnosed and placed into treatment programs instead of being sentenced to prison. As this trend increases, so will the need for treatment programs and substance abuse counselors to aid in their recovery.

The Resume

This position typically requires a Bachelor of Arts and a year or two of counseling in a related field or equivalent life experience (which can be picked up while you are still in college, by working or volunteering for a suicide or rape hotline, for example). This could include other kinds of counseling, volunteer work, or even experience as a former addict. Certification as a substance abuse counselor is voluntary and available in most states.[10] Some states may require certification in order to practice and charge a fee for services, but counselors might choose to become certified anyway as it can demonstrate competency in practice. The majority of substance abuse counseling jobs involve some sort of training program, either required beforehand or offered on-site. Training usually involves lessons on basic counseling skills, dynamics of group counseling, crisis intervention techniques, and identification and treatment of substance abuse. Substance abuse counseling requires an emotionally stable and calm personality that is able to handle emergency situations and crises. Also, it is essential for a counselor to be capable of inspiring trust and respect in their relationships with clients. Active listening and effective verbal communication skills are crucial in this position as most counseling depends on face-to-face interaction and a candid exchange of thoughts.

The Interview

Psychology majors' knowledge of the principles of human behavior makes them ideal candidates for counseling positions. Such awareness of the human psyche allows for productive and insightful interactions with substance abuse clients. Also, many students acknowledge the usefulness of their social psychology and introduction to counseling methods courses. These and other courses all contribute to a greater understanding of the issues at hand and aid in implementing interventions and communicating suggestions to patients to ensure that all information is understood.

10 The Florida AHEC Network. "Florida Health Careers: Substance Abuse Counselor." The Florida Area Health Education Centers Network. www.flahec.org/hlthcareers/SUBST.HTM.

Climbing the Ladder

For any counseling position, an advanced degree or relevant certificate program is especially useful for advancement. However, this is one field in which the work is so demanding and turnover is so high that advancement via seniority (time in the job) is very feasible. Currently, with a minimum of an associate's degree, you can advance to the position of program director in a treatment facility or other related organization. But as previously stated, this type of advancement is only made possible by years of hands-on experience. Pursuing a master's degree can accelerate promotion. Counselors can also rise to the ranks of supervisors or administrators depending on the type of agency. Some people in this field, usually after receiving additional training or returning to school, transfer into careers in research, consulting, or teaching, and some even pursue careers in private or group practice.

Related Careers

Case manager

Shelter worker

Probation officer

Every academic field and industry has its own association (e.g., The Society of Human Resource Managers versus the American Medical Association). They may appear completely different on the surface, but they share some fundamental similarities—each provides a forum for members to network, share best practices, communicate new developments, research topics and (arguably the most valuable function) share employment opportunities. Typically, all you need to do to join is be willing to pay dues (and many offer substantial discounts to students and recent graduates). So regardless of your major, feel free to explore professional associations. A list of popular psychology and sociology associations follows:

Psychology Majors:

- American Psychological Association: www.apa.org
- Association for Psychological Science: www.psychologicalscience.org
- Social Psychology Network: www.socialpsychology.org

Sociology Majors:

- American Sociological Association: www.asanet.org
- Social Psychology Network: www.socialpsychology.org
- Association for Applied and Clinical Sociology: www.appliedsoc.org

EQUAL-OPPORTUNITY EMPLOYERS: CAREERS FOR BOTH MAJORS

Careers For Both Majors: Real Estate

The real estate industry offers exciting career opportunities to both sociology and psychology majors. These include jobs with realty companies, interior design firms, property-management companies, and residential and commercial real estate developers. Careers in real estate involve helping people and firms buy and sell properties, land development (e.g., turning a neglected lot into beautiful, upscale condos), mortgage banking (providing people with home loans), urban planning (deciding what becomes a park and what gets sold to become affordable housing), property appraisal (how much is my loft worth?) and market research (what is the average rent in Malibu?) Each of these functions focuses on a specific aspect of the real estate industry and serves to optimize the local real estate market for consumers. These various subdivisions within real estate are all closely intertwined and interdependent. Brokers, appraisers, counselors, property managers, and financing experts all depend on each other. Similarly, any single person or company interested in acquiring new property or selling previous land—or many times both—must come in contact with a variety of people within real estate in order to act knowledgeably.

Because of the broad scope of the real estate industry, careers are relatively focused on even more specialized topics than those discussed above. A real estate employee may be part of a city team responsible for acquiring rural land for expansion purposes, or he or she might be involved in planning out a specific residential zone of development once a site has been selected. The real estate industry contains a huge variety of disciplines from finance to architecture to engineering to business. As such, the jobs associated with this industry can encompass a broad range of requirements and employee preferences.

FOCUS ON . . . REAL ESTATE AGENT

The Classified Ad

Hands down the most popular career in the field of real estate is that of the real estate agent. A real estate agent is a person licensed to negotiate property sales. Agents have a thorough knowledge of the real estate market in their community and strong familiarity with financing options, government programs, real estate laws and local economics. A good agent also has expert knowledge of neighborhoods, school systems, tax rates, and public transportation. Agents act as liaisons between buyers and sellers in negotiations and can represent either party. As representatives for sellers, agents spend much of their time becoming familiar with their clients' properties and making arrangements to advertise and show the property to potential buyers. For buyers, they identify desirable and affordable housing options.

Real estate agents usually provide their services to licensed real estate brokers, who are independent businesspeople selling others' property. While there is only one broker for each property, there can be several agents who represent interested buyers. Agents are then compensated by receiving a percentage of the commission earned through an agent's role in selling a property. They are also responsible for writing up contracts and finalizing agreements once a sale is made.

Working as an agent requires great flexibility; you must constantly be available to your clients, all of whom have numerous questions and concerns as they prepare to make a major financial investment. Additionally, because many people are at work from 9 to 5, Monday through Friday, real estate agents are often required to show properties (read: work) in the evenings and on weekends.

Commercial real estate agents work with corporate clients to find them ideal office spaces, buildings, or undeveloped land. This requires an agent to have an understanding of leasing practices, market trends, and the property location. They must also be aware of the area's transportation, utilities, and labor supply so that they can accurately inform their clients and locate suitable sites.

The Resume

A real estate agent is an independent person with strong interpersonal and communication skills. Honesty, integrity, and trustworthiness are important traits, and agents must be able to retain large quantities of information as they are usually working with several clients and various properties simultaneously. Alison, a California broker reveals, "We bombard a potential agent with a ton of our employee's listings when he or she first arrives, and then half an hour later, out of the blue, we'll ask him to recall as many names and details as he can in 20 seconds. If he can do it under that kind of pressure, we know he can handle all the information he'll need to know in the field." Getting licensed to sell real estate is a process regulated by each state through the department of real estate office. Even the most stringent states usually do not require much more than a passing grade in two to three real estate courses and a minimum score on a comprehensive exam. Many community colleges and for-profit vocational schools provide the necessary course work, and real estate license qualifying tests are offered quite frequently. Larger or better organized real estate offices will assist you with this process. However, it is not difficult to do it on your own, and doing so demonstrates your commitment.

The Interview

A real estate agent is a counselor, salesperson, and friend all rolled into one career. Demonstrating a knack for sales is a key to landing the job. Any part-time retail sales position will provide relevant training and stories for the interview. Both sociology and psychology majors can speak of their human relations experience and understanding of the individual and social factors that affect people's behavior and decisions. These fields of study are also comprised of intensive problem-solving experience. A sociology or psychology student is accustomed to analyzing individuals and matching their problems with specific solutions like aid services or counseling methods. The job of a real estate agent has a parallel function, as agents must identify and evaluate the needs and preferences of individual clients in order to find them a fitting home or property. The ability to excel in this area often determines a real estate agent's success and reputation.

Climbing the Ladder

Although anecdotal, it seems that the agents who truly love to sell actually avoid moving up; for them, the thrill is to be on the front line, closing deals and not taking smaller percentages from the agents they supervise. However, as a real estate agent gains experience and networking skills, he or she may move into a management position supervising other agents. Others often decide to go it alone and not share any of their commission. This entails getting a broker's license (and not much else). In almost all areas of this field, very little advanced schooling is necessary.

Related Careers

Pharmaceutical sales representative

Commodities trader

Public relations

Careers For Both Majors: Writing and Journalism

For many, the idea of writing for a living is very appealing. Perhaps it is narcissism (thinking that what we have to say is so interesting to others) or the perceived lifestyle (the whole working-from-home and writing-when-you-feel-like-it thing is a great gig reserved for a select few). Regardless of the specific reason, many flock to the field and work as novelists, correspondents, editors, proofreaders, columnists, critics, technical writers, screenwriters, and copywriters. The end result of their work varies widely, from operations manuals and press releases to news features and novels, but usually the writing process begins with extensive research and information gathering (something you're quite familiar with by now).

Writing is an exceptionally competitive industry with countless aspiring authors trying to build their reputation and get their works published. Therefore, to get their foot in the door, many aspiring authors work as freelancers and sell their works to publishers. In many ways, this career can be completely independent from your college major. If your writing is clear and compelling, who cares what you studied in college? On the other hand, a career that entails possibly working from the road or abroad, being your own boss (and, by the way, having people hang on your every word) appeals to many people. Hence, you had better be ready to work for free or, if you are lucky, intermittent pay days when you first get stared. Intrinsic motivation is mandatory.

FOCUS ON . . . COPY EDITOR

The Classified Ad

Copy editors work for such entities as newspapers, book publishers, and magazines reviewing reporters' work and editing or rewriting content. They make sure that all of the publication's editorial pieces meet certain criteria for grammar, style, length, spelling and punctuation, accuracy, and content. Copy editors generally report to an executive editor, and make suggestions for revisions, follow editorial policies, and check pieces for libel in order to prevent legal issues for the publisher. Depending on the time constraints, a copy editor might also carry out some of the research for writers and is often responsible for verifying the accuracy of facts and statistics used in the writing.

Copy editors are undeniably never given the credit they deserve because of their behind-the-scenes work. They are often the final word behind the style, technique, and final presentation of a piece of writing. Gabrielle Monroe, the editor in chief of a healthy lifestyles magazine in Florida states that a copy editor "must be able to turn a mediocre article into a compelling and intelligent feature for a national audience." At some publications, copy editors have the authority to rewrite portions of written material or send the material back to the reporter for major revisions. Most of the writing done by a copy editor involves writing captions and headlines, which must be clever and enticing snapshots of intricate stories or images. Smaller publications may also give a copy editor the responsibility of planning the layout of the publication and determining which pieces should be displayed most prominently. Many also have duties related to typesetting, such as inserting typesetting codes for headlines or complex pagination coding. Copy editors are the final reviewers of a publication's material, so they must be very thorough in their work and are frequently heralded for catching serious errors and omissions.

The Resume

Copy editors are obviously very detail-oriented, meticulous, and often considered to be what Bill Walsh calls a publication's "last line of defense."[11] They must be both decisive and flexible in the face of looming editorial deadlines, and be capable of employing common sense and natural instincts to know when a certain idea or writing structure will or will not work. Basic writing and grammar skills are essential and computer and design experience are helpful as technology continues to dominate the writing and publishing industries. Reporting experience or basic reporting skills are important for a copy editor to be effective; indeed many are former reporters.

---

11 Bill Walsh. "What Exactly is a Copy Editor?" The Slot: A Spot for Copy Editors. www.theslot.com/copyeditors.html.

The Interview

Relevant experience, demonstrated maturity, and responsibility are very important to employers in the journalism industry. They look for people who are prepared for the challenging and hectic career of a copy editor. Monroe advises aspiring editors to "Take advantage of any opportunity to get some journalism experience. Take an internship, or write a few things for your college newspaper. There are people who would shine an exec's shoes to get a job in the business, so you really have to show how much you want the job and just how ready you are for it." As mentioned in the previous chapters, you have written a great deal in college and should have plenty of writing samples in your arsenal. Additionally, your course work has provided you with exceptional research and communication skills. You can express ideas and information thoroughly, succinctly, and accurately as well as follow standard methods and guidelines. In addition, a psychology or sociology major is quite in tune with social trends and public perceptions, so you would excel at some of the creative aspects of the job, such as writing enticing headlines or determining what pieces would be principal to a reader.

Climbing the Ladder

Executive editor, or editor in chief, is the top of the pile in this world. To attain this worthy goal is as rare as becoming a vice president or chief executive officer. Most copy editors who stay in the business accumulate responsibilities over time, and advancement means more authority and a more expansive set of duties, ultimately culminating in a higher-ranking editor position. For example, at a newspaper or magazine, you may be the lead editor for a specific section of the publication (e.g., the sports or lifestyle section).

Related Careers

Hotel events coordinator

Public relations

Research assistant

Careers For Both Majors: Event Planning

The annual spending for special events worldwide is an estimated $500 billion and, the industry is only growing. In America, it seems that every year weddings get more and more extravagant and the concept of "necessary" celebrated events (e.g., doggie birthdays) expands almost exponentially. Indeed, many event planners are reaping the benefits of a universe of aging baby boomers who have a great deal of disposable income to spend on celebrating milestone birthdays, anniversaries, and retirements in record quantities.

Generally speaking, event planning involves organizing and executing events of all sizes for a wide range of clients. Special events can be business related, entirely social, or somewhere in between. Examples of events that may require the help of an event planner include charity fund-raisers, conferences, exhibitions, festivals, award events, and weddings. Depending on the size and type of any particular event, various functions within planning involve conducting industry trends research, conferring with clients, managing a budget, creating and maintaining relationships with suppliers, and networking for new clients. Planning an event requires a great deal of coordination from inception to clean-up, and each of the many tasks involved can be accomplished by firms, small teams, or individuals. The process of planning a special event can involve a variety of tasks including deciding a theme, finding a site, arranging for food, decor and entertainment options, transportation, invitations, supervising at the site, and sometimes even conducting post-event evaluations.

FOCUS ON . . . HOTEL EVENTS COORDINATOR

The Classified Ad

A hotel events coordinator supports the management and coordination of all events that take place in the facility. These could include social and corporate events in the hotel's main event rooms, weekly guest receptions in the lobby, and meetings in conference rooms or dinners in a banquet hall. These individuals are responsible for liaising with prospective and current clients, managing inquiries, meeting with patrons, and presenting hotel banquet spaces, conference rooms, and amenities. Much of the job relates to customer relations and ensuring client satisfaction as they confer with clients to discuss event set up, menus, and special requirements. Chantelle Holland, an events coordinator for Radisson Hotels and Resorts says, "You have to have a passion for getting people what they want, no matter how absurd it seems at first. It's your job to make it happen."

Hotel events coordinators also manage much of the administrative work involved in arranging an event at the hotel. They send out fee quotes to clients, draw up contracts, and guide clients through the reservation process. The events coordinator also consults with other hotel staff, such as meetings and events consultants (self-employed or "private event coordinators"), catering directors, and sales, marketing, and travel managers. He or she synchronizes the hotel's schedule of upcoming events, places orders, and plans the use of spaces and staff. The coordinator may also help with event promotion by creating signage or pursuing other marketing initiatives.

The Resume

Almost all hotel events coordinators are self-proclaimed extroverts who love meeting and collaborating with many different people and possess exceptional interpersonal and communication skills, as the job hinges on client relations. The individual must also be able to present information effectively and persuasively as well as approach clients with sincerity and tact even in the face of crisis. Chantelle shares a great example, "Between the van and the food cart, a wedding cake that was several thousand dollars dropped to the pavement. I honestly wanted to cry looking at the broken chunks and seeing the pebbles and dirt stuck to the sides. There was no hope for it. I immediately (and literally) ran to the restaurant's kitchen and told them I needed their biggest sheet cakes defrosted or baked and decoratively frosted as a stand in. Thankfully, we still had a few hours until the cutting and they came up with two different cakes, one chocolate and one yellow both beautifully presented. Of course, they were not completely happy and I did ultimately comp them a suite and deducted a significant portion from their bill but they did get their pictures and everyone had a nice piece of cake. Obviously, this is rare (if it weren't I'd be in another business), but I think it illustrates some of the necessary skills and nerves it takes to be responsible for someone else's big day."

As Chantelle's story clearly demonstrates, the career requires a knack for organization, flexibility, strong leadership and decision-making capabilities, and the ability to approach planning and deal with setbacks in innovative ways. As Holland explains, "Every Plan A has to have a Plan B, and every Plan B a Plan C, whether you've got them ready to go or you have to think them up on the spot." Any experience in sales or public relations is helpful, and several events coordinators suggest volunteer work as a great way to get a foot in the door of the event planning industry. Knowledge of media relations and marketing is also useful in events promotion.

The Interview

A psychology or sociology major is familiar with people and has profound insight into what people want and how they react to various situations. Students from these fields can approach delicate situations tactfully and influence others' attitudes to create positive outcomes. They can also effectively research and decipher marketing and consumer trends as well as event evaluations and gain conclusions from research analysis, which allow for unique and successful event planning ideas. Their experience with social settings and behaviors gives them the know-how to determine what makes a successful social gathering and, thus, a successful event. The psychology or sociology major can distinguish among clients and their needs, providing valuable perspectives on coordinating events for a wide range of clients and on diverse types of events.

Climbing the Ladder

With a few years of experience in the industry, a hotel events coordinator can advance to an events manager position with greater responsibility and decision-making authority. The events manager directs all events held at the hotel, manages event and client sales, and works with the management staff from other hotel departments to carry out events. Many events coordinators choose to start their own event planning businesses once they have built a substantial client base. The most high profile of these are wedding planners, but there are also exciting opportunities (and a great deal of money to be made) planning charity balls and athletic events.

Related Careers

Activities coordinator

Publicist

Recreation specialist

Careers For Both Majors: Sales

Careers in sales are everywhere, and they are positions for which a college major is often of little or no consequence. Sales is, fundamentally, the ability to persuade people to buy things. What better preparation could there possibly be than the study of human behavior and action? You have spent the past several years learning all of the key concepts and skills necessary for influencing people (favorable body language, understanding verbal cues, and knowing what attracts one human being to another) and you can apply this knowledge directly to the purpose of persuading people to give you their money. Sales careers include jobs in consumer, technical, media, pharmaceutical, and financial industries, and this just barely scratches the surface of the available opportunities out there.

Attracting new accounts to the company's client base is a significant component of many sales jobs. People in sales are constantly making new contacts and following leads in order to generate interest in their company's merchandise and services. Because the majority of sales positions have earnings tied to commission (you get a percentage of the sale) as well as salary, it is important for sales employees to be able to engage new customers resourcefully and make their sales targets each month. For some, a significant percentage of time is spent meeting with prospective clients, conducting sales presentations to buyer's brokers and distributors, and attending trade shows to promote merchandise. Unless you are located in a specific store, the position will involve a great deal of travel to meet with prospective buyers and clients. The upside to all this time in airports and rental cars is that most sales positions come with a healthy budget to wine and dine clients (existing and potential). Eating in the best restaurants and attending cultural and sporting events under the guise of client relations is a great perk.

FOCUS ON . . . PHARMACEUTICAL SALES REPRESENTATIVE

The Classified Ad

Out of the thousands of different sales positions out there, we specifically put the spotlight on this one because of the tremendous presence pharmaceutical companies have in college recruiting. Although there are no guarantees, it is extremely likely that one, if not many of the large pharmaceutical companies, recruit at your alma mater. Pharmaceutical sales representatives work hard to promote awareness of their company's products among medical professionals who prescribe medication. They describe their products to prospective clients, take orders, and are trained to answer questions about the product. Many sales representatives call and meet with potential clients around the world, including pharmacists, hospital administrators, physicians, and dentists. They act as liaisons between their pharmaceutical companies and clients and facilitate communication and transactions between the two parties.

Pharmaceutical sales representatives are also responsible for researching the competition and its products and then reporting their findings to their companies' decision-making groups. Additionally, they conduct valuable sales target research to determine who the potential buyers are in order to maximize the effectiveness of the company's sales efforts. They must also be up to date and knowledgeable about the latest developments in the medical and pharmaceutical industries and be able to predict what this may mean (positively or negatively) for their product.

It is an understatement to say that pharmaceutical sales is a competitive field. Prescription medications represent billions of dollars of revenue for all of the companies involved. With the ever-increasing amount of pharmaceutical products on the market, sales positions are exceptionally important to the industry. Also, once in a position, pharmaceutical sales representatives have to be tenacious in attracting clients in order to compete with other companies vying for meeting time with physicians and health care professionals. If you choose to work in this field you have to be ready for paychecks that fluctuate with your commission. However, many salespeople love this compensation structure because they believe they are always getting paid what they are worth; the harder they work, the more they are rewarded. Commenting on the aggressive nature of the business, Wyeth pharmaceutical sales representative Cristina Hernandez says, "You have to be ready for rejection—a lot of it—but it just makes every successful sale that much sweeter."

The Resume

Pharmaceutical sales representatives must be able to build and maintain effective working relationships with clients, so impeccable interpersonal, communication, and customer service skills are a must. A pharmaceutical sales representative must also demonstrate solid organizational skills and the ability to follow standards and meet deadlines as well as the stability to deal with rejection. A sales representative should be able to work independently to get clients, as well as work as part of a team to accomplish their company's sales and promotion goals. A science background and any sales experience are both advantageous when looking for a pharmaceutical sales job. Helpful college courses include psychopharmacology, chemistry, biology, economics, and English.

The Interview

The people-oriented character of the pharmaceutical sales business makes people in both majors absolutely perfect candidates for this position. The career requires the ability to employ natural tact and diplomacy with a broad range of people, build rapport with clients, and understand how people think and act. In addition, the research skills you have learned as a psychology or sociology major are also valuable assets for a sales representative job because a thorough understanding of industry and consumer trends will give you an edge in influencing new customers and developing effective sales plans.

Climbing the Ladder

Once a pharmaceutical sales representative demonstrates two or three years of consistent success in the business, he or she can advance by becoming responsible for a greater number of clients, a larger sales territory, or larger client accounts. Additionally, after several years and further training (usually provided by the company), some sales representatives advance to managerial positions (no more sales or commission) within their company and are usually titled director or vice president.

Related Careers

Real estate agent

Commodities trader

Public relations

Careers For Both Majors: Promotions and Publicity

You can have the best idea or product in the world, but if nobody ever hears about it, it will never see the light of day (or reap millions of dollars in profit). Enter promotions and publicity, a product's lifeline to consumers. Careers in these fields focus on spreading the word about new and existing products, brands, and companies. Let's tackle promotions first.

Step one of any promotion is generating a plan of attack for getting the word out, usually about a product. This can be done alone but more frequently, it involves input from many individuals and/or organizations. A career in promotions combines aspects of advertising and marketing, along with incentive plans such as sales, rebates, coupons, and contests to increase sales. Promotions groups often do thorough research to decide which tactics or combination of tactics, including television, mail, Internet, telemarketing, celebrity endorsements, catalogs, newspapers, and radio announcements, will be best suited for reaching their desired demographic.

The publicity half of the duo is typically concerned with cultivating strong relationships with media representatives that result in positive coverage. Publicists communicate updates and recent developments (generally speaking, good news) via press releases and meetings with reporters. The public values information on products and services that has been filtered through credible sources like the news media, and it's a publicist's job to make sure those channels are in place.

Focus On . . . Publicist

The Classified Ad

When famous people or companies stumble, publicists start earning their money. Publicists are professional liaisons between clients and the media and are paid to promote their client in the best possible light. The most high-profile and sought-after publicist jobs are those which involve working for movie stars and promoting (and protecting) their image. However, publicists also assist companies, politicians, corporate executives, writers, and anyone else who is concerned about their public image. Depending on the client and the desired image, a publicist controls the type and amount of information that is released to the press. Publicists also deal with damage control, remedying negative publicity and putting a positive spin on potentially damaging incidents. According to Sevahn Zargarian, a corporate publicist in San Francisco, the goal is sometimes to turn what could be a massive scandal into a little innocent gossip. As he says, "It's about expanding or minimizing, depending on what the situation calls for." It is important for publicists to effectively contain the effects of negative media coverage, whether by trivializing the incident or briskly shifting the public's focus. A publicist must think quickly and creatively in order to maintain a client's image. Understanding human perception and what influences behavior is essential to a publicist's livelihood. These are both skills that are second nature to psychology and sociology majors.

Publicists spend much of their time writing press releases, creating press packets with photos and information, and speaking directly with media contacts. They work under strict deadlines and perform other duties such as keeping track of events and important dates, and ensuring that publicity materials are completed and sent out on time. Publicists can work on their own or, more commonly, as part of a large public relations agency. They may work well beyond business hours in support of a client, and they must always be available to speak on behalf of their clients. The glamorous status of the job makes publicist positions incredibly competitive. As Zargarian explains, "When it comes to the publicity world, don't take it too hard when you don't get the first job you interview for. You'll have plenty of rejections to look forward to."

The Resume

Good publicists think and act quickly and innovatively while remaining calm in even the most stressful situations. They have the ability to organize and direct publicity plans but also the flexibility to deal with unforeseen glitches and craft alternate solutions. Superior communication skills and people skills are essential, as publicists must build and maintain relationships with a wide range of key people (usually in the media). In this way, publicists' research is extremely similar to the research and outreach done by undergraduate sociology and psychology students (as well as undergraduate research assistants). Although both majors have training in this regard, sociology majors, with their course work in mass communication and group behavior, are particularly well suited for this career. Helpful college course work for the job includes: social psychology, communications, public speaking, and group dynamics theory.

The Interview

Psychology and sociology majors are thoroughly in tune with human behavior, thoughts, motives, and responses. As it is a mainstay of the job, publicists must gauge the reaction and effect of events and either positively or negatively spin the results. Psychology and sociology majors have spent years in the classroom honing the ability to study preferred human expectations and frame circumstances to promote a given behavior. Additionally, the analytic and methodological skills learned in the classroom will enable you to approach problems and solutions systematically and confidently—all in the name of promoting your client.

Climbing the Ladder

Generally only experience (time in the hot seat successfully promoting clients) and demonstrated leadership skills are required for consideration for advancement. However, some companies do encourage participation in management training programs that improve administrative and leadership skills, and demonstrate a level of commitment and proficiency. After that, promotion to the manager level or top executive rank is quite feasible. However, some publicists find that working in a larger structure is not their forte and decide to strike out on their own. This is usually only feasible after establishing a solid reputation and a high-profile client list. Many publicists who do start their own businesses often woo clients away from their previous employers in the process.

Related Careers

Copy editor

Public relations

Human rights campaigner

Careers For Both Majors: Foreign Service

As an institution, the United States Foreign Service represents the country and its interests abroad. Those who complete the rigorous selection process with its extensive testing, background checks, and interviews (which is open to any individual with a bachelor's degree) are responsible for implementing foreign policy and aiding U.S. citizens in other countries as well as serving as liaisons between foreign governments and international organizations. Foreign Service officers are typically stationed in embassies, consulates, and diplomatic missions around the world or in Washington, DC. Just a sample of some of the tasks specific to the field include issuing passports and visas, monitoring United States influences abroad, and acting in the name of the United States during exchanges with international organizations.[12] Foreign Service Officers choose a specialized field of work within foreign affairs and are expected to be knowledgeable on a wide array of policies and current foreign affairs relevant to that area of expertise. Specialists serve more specific functions in

12 U.S. Department of State. *Careers Representing America: General Information.*
www.careers.state.gov.

support of the United States government and Foreign Service Members worldwide, holding positions like Health Practitioner or Office Management Specialist in various government offices primarily within the State Department.

Foreign Service members spend their days in a variety of roles and make observations about the state of their host countries and provide suggestions for improving policies and relations related to the country. Meriah Hudson, who recently passed the Foreign Service exam shares, "Every word reported by an [Foreign Service] associate is read and considered by somebody, whether it be positive or critical. So the position has a lot of authority in the government's decision-making process." Positions with the Foreign Service are really more of a lifestyle than a career. Living abroad for years, constantly moving in and out of little known parts of the world, and attending numerous social functions are all aspects of this career.

FOCUS ON . . . FOREIGN SERVICE OFFICER

The Classified Ad

As employees of the U.S. State Department, Foreign Service officers hold diplomatic positions around the world. They advocate for American interests in foreign countries while protecting and providing services for American citizens and foreigners who want to enter the United States. Foreign Service officers are responsible for monitoring and reporting on the state of diplomatic relations with their host countries and providing valuable input to makers of international affairs policy. They must be well informed regarding the cultural, political, and economic workings of their host countries and passionate about representing the American government to foreign entities. Sociology majors who have completed course work related to cultural diffusion and society and social institutions, as well as psychology majors who have focused on social psychology and group dynamics are perfectly prepared for this career and can choose from five career tracks linked to economy, public diplomacy, consular, management, or political matters of importance.[13]

Foreign Service officers work around the globe within an American embassy or consulate or in Washington, DC. Much of a Foreign Service officer's time is spent reading, reviewing, and writing reports related to the position. He or she must constantly provide research findings and firsthand reports recounting important occurrences that relate to American foreign policy objectives. The position is also responsible for providing explicit information and development services for specific individuals or corporations interested in conducting business overseas, and a great deal of time is spent organizing visits for government or industry officials.

13 U.S. Department of State. "Foreign Service Officer."
www.careers.state.gov/officer/index.html.

The Resume

Foreign Service officers are charged with promoting American interests around the globe and they must exhibit a passion and propensity for politics and demonstrate tact and diplomacy when interacting with others. The ability to adapt to a variety of situations and foreign cultures is critical, as is the ability to clearly and effectively communicate and resolve conflicts with citizens, local governments, and international organizations. Although knowledge of a foreign language is not mandatory, career advancement is seriously limited without this ability. Candidates must be American citizens and at least 20 years of age.

The Interview

The ideal Foreign Service officer is intensely curious about other people and interested in furthering relations among diverse cultures. Psychology and sociology majors are at an advantage with their thorough knowledge of human and cultural interactions and should emphasize this in the selection process. Psychology and sociology majors also have the experience and knowledge to make valuable observations in various environments, come to concise conclusions, and formulate new ideas for advancement. The ability to conduct useful research and make subsequent constructive suggestions is critical given the Foreign Service officer's charge to prescribe progressive foreign policy modifications.

Climbing the Ladder

Through experience in training and in the field, Foreign Service officers attain excellent foreign language skills and learn to work in a variety of unfamiliar environments. Candidates must demonstrate their capabilities in a variety of positions during a five-year probationary period before qualifying for tenure as a Foreign Services officer. After this period, officers may advance through a six-level pay-grade system upon demonstrating preparedness for greater responsibility and availability of higher positions. Eligibility for promotions is determined by supervisors' ratings and recommendations. Over time, officers gain greater control over their assignments. Eventually, officers may pursue positions as foreign ministers or ambassadors, but nearly a third of ambassadorial appointments are filled by political appointees.

Related Careers
Commodities trader

CIA Agent

Publicist

Careers For Both Majors: Recreation and Leisure

No matter who you are or where you live, people want to have fun. As an industry, recreation and leisure encompasses the wide range of activities that people enjoy in their spare time. Some of the major outlets include arts venues like museums, galleries, theaters, and recreational facilities like casinos, amusement parks, golf courses, and state parks. The wide array of entities which make up this industry includes not only actual recreational venues but also their suppliers, distributor, and the performers, athletes, and artists who provide entertainment. As you can imagine, the number of careers related to recreation and leisure is enormous and spans the entire spectrum of goods and services. A person in this field might manage a facility, supervise maintenance tasks, enlist and schedule performers, lead recreational classes, or perform any other task related to promoting the leisure industry.

Focus On . . . Recreation Specialist

The Classified Ad

Nikki Allston, a children's recreation specialist for Disney World Resorts, spends her days planning schedules, coordinating participant lists, ordering supplies, and mostly, working directly with the kids in several programs a day. "Actually carrying out the activities is the best part—I get to feel like a kid every day!"

Recreation specialists are involved in the development, organization, and operation of recreational programs within a given environment. Working environments can be quite different, from cruise ships to remote wilderness areas, and can therefore require exceptionally different skills and interests to be successful. Activities are essentially limitless but could range from impromptu limbo competitions on the lido deck, arts and crafts with children, fitness regiments, nature walks, or small-scale theatrical performances. The position may also have a significant supervisory capacity with responsibility for coordinating volunteers or other activities staff. Recreation specialists are often called upon to wear a marketing hat when promoting programs to guests of the facility or, on a larger scale, developing media to advertise programs throughout the community.

The Resume

A recreation specialist should be passionate about teaching and guiding others and should thrive in social and leadership settings. They also have to be mature and responsible enough to remain focused and professional while everyone else is having fun. Obviously, they enjoy what they are doing, but they always remember their sole focus is other people's good time, not their own. According to Allston, "Enthusiasm for the job is a must. If you don't enjoy it 110 percent, it'll wear you out in a matter of days." The job requires high energy and patience in dealing with a wide cross-section of people. Recreation specialists demonstrate exceptional organizational skills and flexibility in planning programs and directing groups. Employers generally look for experience or expertise in the subject area of the program, such as coaching or teaching experience, performance skills, athletic distinction, or musical aptitude. These are all skills and experiences which can be easily acquired through on-campus extracurricular activities such as intramural sports and performance arts clubs. It would also be appropriate for anyone pursuing this career to gain experience working with specific groups such as children, the elderly, or the physically challenged. Relevant course work includes group dynamics, business administration and management, resource management, and education. Some parks and recreation jobs may require certification—as simple as CPR and first aid,—or as formalized as the National Park and Recreation Certification Program which requires you to send your credentials to the governing body for review.

The Interview

A recreation specialist succeeds by being able to understand and cooperate with a broad range of people. Psychology and sociology majors have the requisite skills to demonstrate sensitivity and communicate effectively with all people. Their knowledge of human interactions allows them to facilitate activities in a group setting and prepare comprehensive program activities that encourage inclusive participation. Allston shares, "I really emphasized my sociology education during the hiring process. It shows exactly where my interests lie and the type of specialized group and people skills I bring to the table."

Climbing the Ladder

After some years of hands-on experience in the job, a recreation specialist can attain a managerial position in the recreation industry. Candidates for advancement demonstrate strong leadership skills and motivation. Recreation specialists may become supervisors of other recreations staff and managers of department or regional directors.

Related Careers

Hotel events coordinator

Activities coordinator

Probation officer

Careers For Both Majors: Business

The word "business" is so broad that it is difficult to speak of in useful career development terms. Business encompasses the activities of a Wall Street tycoon who initiates complex billion-dollar company buy-outs to that of a teenager in Springfield, MO, selling carpet cleaning door to door for extra spending money. It includes the manufacture, distribution, or sale of any conceivable product or service to other firms or to the public, usually for a profit. Business ventures include production and manufacturing, retail and distribution, consulting services, employment services, promotional services, and financial services, among countless other specializations. They also range from individual entrepreneurial efforts to huge global corporations.

Within each business, a huge assortment of roles and tasks exist to make sure the business runs smoothly. Businesses can be organized in countless different ways depending on their size and specific industry. There are individual departments responsible for sales and marketing, finances, purchasing, production, employment, research and development, communications and public relation, and general administration. Each department within the business usually has a hierarchy of positions with managers and supervisors at the top and assistant and support staff in their service. There is also an executive staff that oversees all business activities and controls the decision-making process of the company. A single business may execute all of its internal functions within its own walls, or outsource to other specialty firms, such as advertising agencies or employment firms, that can perform these tasks for them.

FOCUS ON ... PUBLIC RELATIONS

The Classified Ad

Similar to a career as a publicist, public relations personnel act to generate positive images for companies and promote their interests and reputations. Public relations (often referred to simply as PR) may involve reporting between a company and its consumers or communications between a company's management and personnel or between regional offices. Public relations people must create and maintain relationships with reporters, communicate their clients' views to the press, write speeches and reports and manage all inquiries regarding their companies or their products. They generally have a broad range of responsibilities and must stay informed about current affairs and industry developments. They are in charge of coming up with creative and effective public exposure strategies and may be responsible for writing press releases, carrying out marketing and advertising tasks, evaluating public opinion toward the company, organizing publicity events, and informing company shareholders, employees, and customers about changes to business practices.

The public relations industry is frequently criticized for its seeming readiness to manipulate the truth to promote a positive image for the client, and the term "spin doctors" has been used to refer to public relations specialists who can take any seemingly damaging or mundane event and "spin" it to create a constructive element for their client's reputation. According to Doug Freeman, a public relations manager for an international PR firm, "Public relations are really an art form. Not just anyone can make a sensation out of a catastrophe."

The Resume

Public relations work involves and quick, creative problem-solving. People in this profession must have exceptional communication skills, thrive under pressure, and work well as part of a larger agenda. Obviously, a keen interest in business is critical (reading *The Wall Street Journal* on a daily basis is a good idea and can be very helpful when you start going on interviews). Public relations professionals must also demonstrate tact and diplomacy as their words are very influential, and the job depends on positive interactions with the public. Be prepared to talk about times when you have had to address groups or speak publicly. The highly visible status of a public relations career makes interpersonal skills and a calm, polite demeanor essential. Course work outside of your sociology or psychology major that would be useful includes communications, economics, business administration, and English. Employers increasingly prefer participation in internships prior to seeking full-time employment in the industry.

The Interview

Public relations success hinges on being able to determine what makes people tick and how they perceive certain statements and actions. Both psychology and sociology majors have a lot of knowledge in this area and possess a thorough understanding of human behavior. They are able to influence public opinion and perceptions of a client's image because they know the types of things that register negatively or positively with the psyche of a customer. Freeman says, "One of the biggest assets I brought to the table was my psychology background. It's really given me an edge because I actually understand the reasons behind all the quirks and turns in consumer behavior, while others completely dismiss or overlook them. It's amazing how a single word or routine event can completely attract or detract the average person." Also, both psychology and sociology majors are well versed in the practices of research and analysis, and many aspects of a public relations career involve researching and evaluating public opinion as well as trends in industry and consumer behavior.

Climbing the Ladder

Public relations specialists are given more difficult and demanding assignments as they gain more experience in the field. If they demonstrate exceptional competence, they can advance to managerial and supervisory positions. This could lead to senior and executive roles, and even eventually a position as vice president of public relations. Some public relations specialists choose to start their own consulting firms once they have established solid reputations and client lists.

Related Careers

Copy editor

Publicist

Survey researcher

Careers For Both Majors: Finance

Of all the industries profiled in this book, this is probably by far the one which most people will consider unrealistic for a graduate of psychology or sociology. The reality is that it is probably one of the easier fields in which to land an entry-level position if you are really interested in the type of work it entails. The skills you have developed in either major are directly applicable and, believe it or not, will serve you well in both the interview and on the job. The finance industry encompasses a huge collection of business and economic activities that primarily fall under the three major categories of banking, insurance, and investments. The industry is based around providing services for the management of money for clients. Some of the distinct industry sectors include product sales (e.g., mutual funds) consulting (e.g., estate and retirement planning), lending (e.g., auto and home loans), insurance, and money management. Most people are not aware that there are many different types of banks, insurance agencies, private consulting firms, brokerage firms, and fund management firms that make up the general financial services industry. There is not enough space here to discuss all the types and differences. Suffice it to say that this assortment ensures that there is plenty of work for sociology and psychology majors.

FOCUS ON . . . COMMODITIES TRADER

The Classified Ad

Within the realm of investment banking, commodities traders match buyers and sellers of specific goods, or commodities. Commodities include agricultural products, foreign currencies, metals and raw materials, and natural resources, such as sugar, wheat, oil, and pork bellies. A commodities trader places orders and acts as the liaison between buyers and sellers, arranging future contracts between parties, and physically making the trades on the floor of the exchange or via computer.

Commodities traders are ultimately responsible for developing new markets for supply firms, setting prices, maintaining a large network of relationships with clients and distributors as well as trade relationships with other trading firms, and analyzing and projecting market behaviors along with associated risks. They can be involved with trading in the domestic or international market, and they usually gain expertise in a precise good or commodity group. Traders also sometimes specialize in goods in and out of a certain country or region. Before being able to buy and sell commodities, traders must meet state licensing requirements determined by state departments of commerce. They often receive training and preparation for licensing exams through their employers, and annual continuing education is required in order to maintain a trading license. Traders must also register with the National Association of Securities Dealers, Inc. (more information can be found at NASD.com).[14] Commodities traders are generally employed by banks, hedge funds (partnerships that invest in stocks, futures, options, and currencies), provider firms, trading houses, and commodity trading advisors. Such organizations are usually based in large urban hubs of financial activity, like New York, London, or Tokyo.

The Resume

Commodities traders must have excellent quantitative and analytical skills because they must study and understand the current economic conditions of their industry as well as general trends in order to speculate on future market behavior. They work independently and endure the fast-paced and often hectic trading environment. "This business is Darwin's 'survival of the fittest' in action. If you can't keep up, you'll be eaten alive in the trading world," observes Vincent Tanaka, a commodities trader for

14 Ibid.

a global hedge fund based in New York. There is no specific academic background required of commodities traders, but business, economics, and finance courses are advantageous. Any experience in sales or public relations may also be beneficial. Also, personality traits like charisma and maturity, along with sales ability and good communication skills, are much sought-after qualities in a trader.

The Interview

What is interesting about many finance careers is how few care about what you studied as an undergraduate. Much of the job is sales related and based on inter-personal skills, both of which are frequently absent from the campus course catalog. This is great news for you, as your major will rarely be held against you and may even be an asset. In the worst-case scenario, you'll be asked in the interview why you didn't pursue a business degree, but once you begin to explain your years of dealing with research and quantifying hard data (working with numbers) coupled with your well developed analytical reasoning skills, you will be in good shape. Your thorough understanding of human interactions and behaviors give you an advantage in a career where being able to read people and discover what affects their decision-making behavior will facilitate your ability to establish a wide client base and ultimately find success, which, in this field, comes with a huge paycheck. Moreover, sociology and psychology majors are trained in big-picture analyses of social patterns over time and across different demographics, which is directly related to a trader's ability to see a broad vision of economic movements and exchanges and discern future trends. In addition, because the position of a commodities trader often hinges on a strong personality, emphasizing strong personal assets like tenacity and decisiveness can genuinely help a candidate.

Climbing the Ladder

Commodities traders ordinarily achieve advancement by becoming responsible for a greater number of accounts or more sizeable accounts. According to Tanaka, most traders spend 10 to 15 years in the position and then retire or move to less active jobs within the financial services industry or in other areas altogether. "This job wears you out after a decade or so. You never lose your passion for it, but you know when it's time to move over and give an agile 20-year-old a taste."

Upon further certification, traders can become portfolio managers and increase their authority to make investment decisions on accounts. After several years of experience, commodities traders can advance to regional managerial positions or spend time supervising other traders while still handling their own accounts. Some can eventually hold leading executive positions or become partners in their firms.[15]

15 Bureau of Labor Statistics. "Securities, Commodities, and Financial Services Sales Agents." *Occupational Outlook Handbook*. 2006–2007 Edition. U.S. Department of Labor. www.bls.gov/oco/home.htm.

Chapter 4 • 91

Related Careers

Public relations

Foreign Service officer

Careers For Both Majors: Research

If you love asking questions and traveling the often-rocky path to knowledge and truth, research may be the field for you. Regardless of the field, whether it be a physicist studying the behavior of theoretical condensed matter or a marketing team figuring out what type of marshmallows (mini or coconut crusted!) kids prefer, the formal definition of research is the methodical process of studying, interpreting, and applying data in order to heighten the understanding of a subject. Major research areas include academic, financial, educational, marketing, and scientific sectors. Although the common perception of research is quantitative (based on numbers), involving experiments, observations, processing results, and analyzing data, it can also be qualitative (observational), focusing on historical information and studying past discoveries and events. The elite in the field work on a specific research topic of their choice at a research university or private laboratory. Funding is often supplied by specific organizations or federal agencies over a designated period of time. These researchers may be involved in "basic research," simply pursuing knowledge for the sake of expanding human understanding (think tenured university professor) or applied research, where investigations are made to solve specific problems or enhance business (e.g., 3M creating Post-it notes to sell for huge profits). In this case, research has been coupled with practical applications and called research and development, or R&D. Most large corporations that manufacture any type of product have a research and development group that is constantly improving or diversifying the company's products.

Of course, specific tasks that take place in research facilities vary depending on the type of research involved and the ultimate goal. The purpose of research might be to find a cure for a disease or to make nuclear energy more safe. Research in the social sciences, such as sociology, economics, and psychology have more qualitative aspects and tend to be related to specific careers involving the study of trends, behavioral observations, and/or forecasting future developments. Often, the conventional goals of this type of research are to improve policies and heighten understanding of human behavior and anomalies. Almost all researchers, regardless of focus, must write detailed reports on their procedures and findings and get their work published. Probably the only exception to this would be highly classified military research done in an environment like Lockheed Martin's Skunk Works in Southern California, a firm whose research is well beyond top secret and is not publicly revealed for sometimes 20 or 30 years after it is obsolete. Barring the military exception, published work is crucial for a researcher's credibility and allows for the general research community to review and judge the validity of the researcher's conclusions.

The Classified Ad

A research assistant is the right hand for a principal investigator (often referred to simply as the PI) or is a member of a larger research team. He or she performs a wide range of tasks and most likely does more physical work than a full research associate. Research assistants are often tasked with setting up, maintaining, and operating lab equipment, so they must be knowledgeable about numerous devices and operational procedures. They must also become familiar with the research facility's database and organizational systems, as inputting copious amounts of data points and findings is a fundamental aspect of most research jobs. Researchers are also commonly expected to perform much of the background research on procedures and past experiments and be able to promptly locate requested references and information. Higher responsibilities include developing and maintaining research databases, evaluating data and experimental results, and drawing conclusions and applying research to particular issues, under the supervision of the principal researcher. Although not always glamorous, research assistants are an indispensable part of the research process. Sonia Ahmadi, a materials research assistant at the University in Massachusetts states, "We get a lot of the grunt work, but I know the PI really appreciates us when one of the associates calls in sick. Without us, it's like a restaurant with a great chef but no waiters."

The Resume

A research assistant is a very curious person and is passionate about finding answers to questions and solutions to problems. Research assistants are also organized and adaptable to new environments and new technologies. They receive much of their practical knowledge from on-the-job training and experience. They must also be able to communicate effectively in order to explain experimental results and concisely describe complex ideas and conclusions. Helpful courses include math, various sciences, statistics, and research methodology. Of course, previous experience as an undergraduate research assistant is tremendously valuable.

The Interview

Your research methodology (the actual implementation and practice of research) and statistics courses (the quantitative analysis of various types of data) have prepared you to enter the research community. You are familiar with practices and objectives relevant to many different styles of research (cross-sectional, longitudinal, etc.) and you can analyze data and trends via a variety of statistical tools (Chi-square, Pearson-R, standard deviation, etc.) to come up with valuable data and inferences. According to Ahmadi, "All research is essentially the same. Everyone's trying to find some answer to some problem with some set of assumptions. It's just a matter of picking what kind of problem you want to solve."

Climbing the Ladder

Advancing in this career is easy to explain but difficult to do—essentially, you need to get a PhD. In almost every case, anyone seriously interested in this career path needs to be willing and able to pursue an advanced degree. Although it is possible after some years of hands-on experience in the lab to become a senior researcher or technician with responsibilities concerning the daily operations of the research facility and supervising and training new research staff, becoming a full- fledged principal investigator almost always means, minimally, a master's degree and more commonly, a doctorate.

Related Careers
Public relations

Survey researcher

Careers For Both Majors: Law Enforcement

Since the 9/11 tragedy, law enforcement, a field focused on protecting American lives and property, has gained popularity due to a ground swell of new interest and increased recruitment efforts. However, this function is carried out in vastly different ways depending on the agency. The prison guard in a minimum-security facility in Kansas and the CIA agent operating covertly in Pakistan are both protecting society, but their training and day-to-day circumstances are significantly different.

A sample of the agencies within the broad canon of law enforcement include local and state police, detectives, private investigators, and all branches of the military and government agencies including the FBI and CIA. Police officers spend their days locating and arresting criminals, investigating local crimes, resolving community problems, and enforcing traffic laws. Detectives gather evidence, perform background checks, and create reports on people suspected of engaging in illegal activity. Inspectors examine certain sites or people, and enforce specific laws regarding health, safety, and the flow of people or items in and out of the country. Special agents of the government may investigate violations of federal law, provide protective services for politicians or government officials, or enforce and regulate strict federal laws, like those pertaining to kidnapping, illegal drugs, firearms and explosives, terrorism, and espionage.

Work in any branch of the law enforcement field can be extremely dangerous and demanding, and requires a wide variety of skill sets including administration, investigation, mediation, and self-defense. The hours can be harsh and irregular. However, the people involved in these careers have a strong passion for protecting the community and make the conscious decision to risk their own well-being in the process. San Francisco police sergeant Daniel Momtaheni said, "I wake up every morning with the feeling that I was born to do this." Only that level of commitment and conviction can get you through a day as a law enforcement officer.

FOCUS ON ... CIA AGENT

The Classified Ad

The Central Intelligence Agency (CIA) gathers foreign intelligence in order to aid the federal government in forming foreign policy and protecting citizens from those abroad who wish to harm the United States. The departments within the agency for which most nonmilitary college graduates are recruited are operations (the people abroad risking their lives to gather information), analysis (the people back home guessing what the data means), and technology (the engineers who create exciting gadgets that help agents do their job more safely and effectively).[16]

CIA agents work in one of four branches. The Directorate of Operations collects human intelligence, involving fieldwork and the most "spy-like" activities. The Directorate of Science and Technology uses satellites and other technological implements to gather intelligence around the world. The Directorate of Intelligence analyzes all of the information collected by the CIA, including that from easily accessible sources such as radio and newspapers, and creates reports for the president and government officials. The Directorate of Administration handles daily logistics and personnel management for the CIA.[17]

A general requirement is that one must be a U.S. citizen to become a CIA agent. To work in the Directorate of Operations, candidates must also be under 35 years of age.[18] Day to day activities for a CIA agent vary immensely depending on current events, concerns, and assignments from the president. Most newly hired agents work at CIA headquarters in Langley, Virginia. Prospective agents are put through an intense battery of tests, including a medical examination, a polygraph interview, and a thorough background check.

The Resume

CIA agents are smart, reliable, and flexible individuals who can perform a huge variety of tasks on their own or in teams. A great amount of training takes place on the job, so a CIA agent must be able to learn and adapt quickly and follow direction well, especially as an agent often has little say over his or her assignments. Foreign language and cultural skills are essential and often the key to getting a foot in the door. Writing and communication skills are also important as you must be able to present information to others through reports. The CIA offers both internships and co-op program opportunities, so any chance to get some early experience with the organization is a plus. The CIA's rigid guidelines for resume content are available online, so be sure to review them at CIA.gov/careers/apply.html before submitting a resume.

16 Clandestine Services. "About the Clandestine Community," Central Intelligence Agency. www.cia.gov/careers/clan_aboutcomm.html.

17 SoYouWanna.com. "So You Wanna Work for the CIA." Intermix Network. www.soyouwanna.com/site/syws/cia/cia.html.

18 Ibid.

The Interview

CIA agents must be constantly aware of their surroundings and pick up on things that others do not. You have a leg up on this ability because your undergraduate work taught you the fundamentals of human perception, which you can use to make observations and come to quick, sound conclusions. Agents must be able to collect information from a diverse range of sources and often come up with spur-of-the-moment solutions in the field or in support of field officers. Plus, CIA agents must constantly work with people to extract information, so the ability to inspire trust and maintain relations with a wide array of contacts is important. The CIA appreciates the psychology major's ability to evaluate others' perspectives and the sociology major's deep cultural knowledge, both of which play very important roles in an agent's interactions with others while trying to attain intelligence.

Climbing the Ladder

New employees generally hold positions as operations desk officers or collection management officers. After one to three years of training programs and courses, an employee can work in the field or as part of the support staff for those in the field. The CIA has an internal ranking system, so as an agent gains experience and demonstrates competency and leadership skills, he or she can be considered for promotions to positions with greater responsibilities.[19]

Related Careers

Probation officer

Survey researcher

Foreign Service officer

Careers For Both Majors: Nonprofits

As a general rule, nonprofit organizations strive to aid, protect, and improve conditions to enhance the general welfare of society. But exactly how each of them goes about bettering society is quite different and encompasses agendas spanning a wide range interests from youth development to art appreciation. Nonprofits make up about 6 percent of all firms in the United States and employ 10.2 million employees.[20] They employ many of the same types of positions as for-profit businesses but also have several more specialized finance and development positions such as fundraising, grant writing, advocates, and development officers whose main goal is to solicit donations and raise money.

19 Bureau of Labor Statistics. "Federal Government, Excluding the Postal Service." *Career Guide to Industries*. 2006–2007 Edition. U.S. Department of Labor. www.bls.gov/oco/cg/cgs041.htm.

20 Bureau of Labor Statistics. "Advocacy, Grantmaking, and Civic Organizations." *Career Guide to Industries*. 2006–2007 Edition. U.S. Department of Labor. www.bls.gov/oco/cg/cgs054.htm.

It's common knowledge that positions in the nonprofit sector pay (sometimes significantly) lower salaries than those in private industry and government. As Graham Mathas, a program director for an adolescents' shelter, expressed, "You definitely don't go into nonprofits for the money. Whether it is the warm, fuzzy feeling you get or the colorful cast of people you meet, you better have another reason to take a job here."

Focus On ... Shelter Worker

The Classified Ad

Shelter workers act as pillars of support for people in need who approach them for assistance or refuge. They are frequently involved both with the daily management of the facility and its services to clients. On the client side, their responsibilities may include program administration, grant writing, advocacy, safety planning, crisis intervention, counseling, and communicating with other outlets of the organization and sister agencies (food kitchens, employment programs, etc.). Administratively, they are responsible for the maintenance of the shelter and ensuring that proper assistance is always available to those who are deemed to be in need of its services. Because shelters constantly face high demand for their services but limited space or supplies, it is a shelter worker's job to interview people seeking shelter and identify appropriate candidates, and unfortunately, turn people away on occasion. As most shelters are only meant for temporary assistance, they also assist clients with creating plans for the future and analyzing the roots of their problems in order to help them progress toward reintegration into society.

The three most common types of shelters are those for homeless people, victims of domestic abuse, and runaways. Some facilities are run by major nonprofit organizations with several facilities nationwide, or private, "stand alone" organizations, which are most commonly extensions of community centers and religious groups. As most shelters are open 24/7, entry-level workers will likely have irregular shifts and be required to work nights and weekends. Because shelters are in high demand and almost always limited in both space and supplies, it is a shelter worker's job to interview people seeking entrance and identify appropriate recipients. Ava Simpson works at a New Orleans shelter for battered women and children. She said, "Of course we want to help every single person who comes to our door. But it's unrealistic. You come face to face with reality a lot in this job."

The Resume

It goes without saying that depth of character and compassion are mandatory for this career. Sensitivity and superior interpersonal skills, and the ability to invoke trust in others are also crucial. You must be trustworthy and poised as a mentor and confidante in this role but still employ appropriate professional boundaries with clients. Cultural competence and the ability to work with a wide range of diverse people are also necessary traits for a shelter worker. Knowledge of a second language can be helpful, especially in urban environments. Due to the high demand, getting started down this path is easy: volunteer. Volunteer experience, which is abundant and available in every community or through school organizations is easily acquired during college and is the ideal way to see if this is the career for you. It will also provide you with the relevant experience perfect for both the resume and cover letter.

The Interview

Psychology and sociology majors have all the skills necessary to provide mentorship to shelter residents and ensure that they become productive members of society. Due to your thorough familiarity with human behavior and interactions, you have the ability to be empathetic to others' situations while still maintaining the professional distance needed when working with short-term clients. Your expertise, particularly in development, affords you the ability to evaluate individuals' past and provide advice focused on the future. According to Simpson, "You have to be able to recognize the potential for growth in everyone, and that involves understanding and appreciating people considerably. You have to believe you can incite progress before you can actually make a difference."

Climbing the Ladder

A shelter worker can advance to supervisory, coordinator, or management positions after only a few years of experience working in a hands-on role. Advancement means greater responsibilities and more decision-making authority, such as in the client evaluation process, as well as in advising and the development of the shelter program. After several years of experience in shelters, workers might also decide to start their own assistance programs or choose to go into other areas of nonprofit work (such as grant writing or government policy work focused on issues relating to fair employment or affordable housing).

Related Careers
Case manager

Day care provider

Human rights campaigner

Careers For Both Majors: Market and Survey Research

Telemarketers evoke a wide range of responses from people. To some, they are truly despised and evoke a level of disdain typically reserved for ex-boyfriends or a mother-in-law (just because they call at dinner time). Others relish the call and are eager to share their feelings and opinions. Personal preferences aside, our world is becoming more and more data driven, and statistics are crucial to almost every industry (from politics, with its fixation on election predictions, to food service predictions on which holidays are most likely to send people out to restaurants for dinner). Gathering data is now big business. As an industry, market and survey research involves gathering and analyzing data on the efficacy of past and current approaches in order to help institutions plan effective designs for the future. The work of market and survey researchers can be enlisted by an assortment of clients including corporations, service providers, political candidates, and government agencies. The results of market and survey research are studied and used to create successful future policies or marketing campaigns to ensure present consumer or public satisfaction, forecast future sales, or just about anything else.

Market research focuses on collecting statistical data on a company's sales, pricing, marketing, and distribution strategies, and competitors' behavior in order to make judgments on prospective sales of its product or service. They are also responsible for analyzing the data they accumulate and advising their employers based on research findings. Recommendations are made to company executives during decision-making processes and usually address the advisability of taking certain courses of action regarding the firm's marketing and sales behavior. Survey research entails gathering information on the opinions of a wide cross section of the public in order to make reasonable conclusions about general customer satisfaction, public approval, policy requirements, and future research needs. Both market and survey researchers construct and conduct surveys for their clients, assembling data through numerous methods of research and interactions with the public.

Focus On . . . Survey Researcher

The Classified Ad

A survey researcher spends his or her day designing surveys, recruiting survey participants, and investigating public opinion, preparing reports, plotting statistical data, and sometimes analyzing and presenting the findings. Parts of the survey research process are performed in small teams, such as the survey design and data collection, while others generally involve independent work to compile results and create reports. Survey researchers can work on behalf of corporations, government agencies, academic organizations, political candidates, and service providers. The conclusions of survey research are valuable factors in determining future fiscal and policy plans, current policy evaluations, customer satisfaction levels, public opinion and support trends, political approaches, and further research decisions.

Survey researchers must meticulously design surveys with formats appropriate to the participant group and content aptly reflecting the survey objectives. They conduct surveys using several methods, including telephone interviews, questionnaire mailings, Internet surveys, group dialogues, and individual consultations. They must also carefully phrase survey questions so that questions are communicated clearly to the public and responses accurately indicate public opinion on specific issues. Sophie Patel, a survey researcher for a political group in Ohio, expressed the importance of effective communication: "The survey design can determine the results from the beginning. If you ask an obscure question, you'll get an obscure answer, making it impossible to accurately analyze responses." In designing surveys, survey researchers may also confer with the recipients of data, such as economists, statisticians, and market research analysts to ensure that their survey approaches are effective and the responses will be valuable to the client.

The Resume

Aspiring survey researchers should possess strong communication skills and the capacity to interact with a wide range of people. According to Patel, "Although they'd never be asked to do it, the most successful researcher would feel comfortable walking up to any stranger on the street to get an honest opinion." Survey researchers must be able to converse and quickly establish a rapport with survey participants, maintain relations with team colleagues, and report findings to management groups and decision-making parties. In addition, survey researchers are usually required to have a couple of years of research experience before entering the career; experience conducting interviews, gathering data, and writing reports can also prove valuable. In addition to a psychology and sociology background, useful course work for a survey researcher includes economics, mathematics, statistics, and English.

The Interview

Survey researchers must be able to design effective surveys and glean practical information from survey participants. Sociology and psychology majors have an astute understanding of how people think and respond to various prompts, and they realize what kinds of issues are important to people, making them excellent candidates for survey research positions. Additionally, sociology and psychology majors have the requisite experience with research design, survey methods, and statistical analysis, and they are adept at gathering and analyzing data in order to arrive at reasonable conclusions from the general information they attain.

Climbing the Ladder

With some experience and sometimes a master's degree, a survey researcher can advance to more technical positions and assume positions with greater responsibility. Survey researchers can eventually manage their own survey design projects or find themselves in other project management or director roles in research organizations.

Related Careers
Research assistant

Public relations

Copy editor

CONCLUSION

As you can see, there are a wide variety of potential careers for sociology or psychology majors. Keep in mind that this chapter only scratches the surface—each one of the industries profiled has several other entry-level positions for which you could create a compelling application. Now that you have some specific ideas for potential career paths to pursue, when you approach a career counselor or any other interested party, tell them you want more information about a certain industry and spare yourself the "you can do anything you want" speech. After selecting a career path, the next most difficult challenge is actually winning a desirable position. Right this way . . .

CHAPTER 5

Finding and Landing the Job

NETWORKING

No man is an island—especially if he's looking for a job

Without question, the universe of liberal arts majors includes its fair share of unassuming, introverted folk. You probably already know whether or not you fall into this camp: You'd rather have dinner with one or two close friends than go to a party and face a room full of strangers (and if you're persuaded to go to a party, you'll spend the next day on the couch, recovering—alone). On an airplane, you fasten your iPod before your seat belt—just so the person next to you knows you don't want to chat. If a college professor ever gave you the choice between an individual paper and a group presentation, you didn't think twice about going solo. When people tell you that you need to network to land a job, they might as well be telling you that you have to stand on a street corner wearing a cow costume and a sandwich board, pointing passersby to the sale at Lou's Land of Leather. It just seems too vulnerable, too desperate to even consider.

Even if you're not a card-carrying member of the introvert society, the notion that you'll have to network as part of your job search might not sound that appealing—or maybe you just don't know exactly how to go about it. Either way, you shouldn't worry: For all of the negative connotations associated with the term, networking doesn't require you to interact with people in a way that's contrived or insincere—and it doesn't just take place on golf courses and at cocktail parties or in nondescript hotel ballrooms during designated networking events. It's not a process that's only effective for job-seekers aggressive enough to approach virtual strangers, give a 30-second summary of their professional accomplishments and aspirations, and ask for help finding a job. The people you'll approach as you build your own network will not—contrary to popular belief—assume you're a sycophant motivated solely by self-interest or desperation.

For the networking-phobic, it often helps if you think of networking as research, rather than as a job-hunting tactic. It's a process that allows you to leverage the richest source of information at your disposal: other people. At its most powerful, networking actually helps you decide which careers, industries, and organizations are interesting to you (and on the flip side, it can help you weed out the ones that aren't as appealing). It can also help you figure out what you'll need to do to get started and, eventually, help to frame your candidacy once you've gotten your foot in the door for a specific position.

In the following pages, we'll explain what effective networking is—and what it isn't. We'll tell you how to use the contacts you already have to begin building an extensive and powerful network that will give you a leg up when it's time to apply for the job you want. We'll tell you about the various ways you can network—from the casual power brunch to more structured informational interviews, and we'll provide guidance on the types of questions you can ask to make sure you get the most out of your conversations. And finally, we'll give you a list of do's and don'ts for networking so your experiences put you in the best possible position to land the job you want.

Hide and go seek: The hidden job market

If you hang around career counselors for any amount of time, you'll probably hear them emphasize the importance of the so-called "hidden job market"—the one you'll need to tap into to land the perfect job. The term itself implies a little more mystery and intrigue than it probably should; in reality, the "hidden job market" simply refers to the universe of available jobs that are not formally advertised. When it comes to quantifying the size of this market, different experts cite wildly disparate percentages: Some say the hidden job market represents about 60 percent of all available jobs, while other sources estimate it's closer to 95 percent. Whatever the actual percentage is, it's too big a number to ignore. If you want your job search to be successful—and by successful we mean that you not only land a great job, but that it doesn't take you longer to find it than it took to complete your degree in the first place—you cannot rely on job boards and company websites alone. You have to find out about jobs before the rest of the world does.

The hidden job market doesn't exist solely to make your life—and the lives of millions of job-seekers like you—more difficult. It arises because positions are often filled before they're ever advertised formally. Once a company identifies a staffing need, it can be weeks—even months—before the position is formally announced. It's not as though Willy Wonka woke up one morning and decided that he needed a successor to his chocolate throne, posted an ad on Monster.com later that afternoon, and then had Charlie and the other four candidates at the factory for interviews the next day. It was a much more time-intensive ordeal than that: He was probably mulling on it for some time, realizing he wasn't getting any younger and that he couldn't run the factory himself for much longer. Once he decided he needed to hire someone, he had to orchestrate the whole Golden Ticket process—and you can bet he had to get all those Oompa Loompas to approve of it. If someone would have told Willy about a good candidate before he kicked off the Golden Ticket campaign, you can bet he would have orchestrated his series of tests for *that person* first.

The real-life hiring process is also fairly slow moving. Once a hiring manager decides she needs to create a new role—or find a new person for an existing role—she usually has to obtain approval from the higher-ups first. All along, she's thinking of potential candidates she already knows who might fill the position: people who already work at the company full time, as well as any freelance, contract, or part-time workers who have expressed an interest in a full-time position. Once she gets approval, she may have to post the job internally first to comply with company policy. While the job is posted internally, the hiring manager is probably asking current employees if they know of anyone who'd be a good fit for the role. (This is where networking comes in—you need to be one of the people at the top of current employees' minds when they hear about the position!) If the well of internal candidates and employee referrals runs dry, then the position is usually posted externally—on the company's website, and/or on job websites like Monster, Hotjobs, and Craigslist.

If the job does end up seeing the light of day, you've got another obstacle to confront: Setting yourself apart from the literally hundreds of other candidates who have also seen the very same job posting and are furiously updating resumes and crafting cover letters at the same time you are. Even if you did nothing all day but hit "refresh" on your Internet browser to be sure that you're the very first one to submit your application for any new job that strikes your fancy, you'd still be one in a crowd of hundreds of applicants. Some hiring managers confess they simply just can't weed through the volume of applications the more popular job boards generate: If they get 200 resumes for a single position, they might look at the first 20 that come in, and then pick the best 5 to invite in for an interview.

All of this might seem miserably unfair to you; after all, if you have all of the experience and education the job posting outlines and you just happen to be the twenty-first person in line, why should you be out of contention? Unfortunately, the job-search process—like life—often falls short of a pure meritocracy. Hiring managers aren't lazy, but they are often overworked and eager to bring in a qualified candidate who will fit into the organization's culture as quickly as possible. In many cases, they know any number of people could do the job—even if they don't have all of the requisite experience when they walk in the door. Still, the more time hiring managers spend reviewing resumes, and the more time they spend interviewing candidates, the less time they spend on their core responsibilities and the harder their existing teams must work because they're short staffed.

When you build a network of contacts that can tell you about openings (and potential openings) before they hit the company's website or external job boards, you will have far more success than you would if you went it alone. This is true for two reasons: First, you'll be competing with a far smaller number of applicants if you express your interest before the job is even posted externally. Why would you want to compete against 200 other candidates when you can compete against a handful—or none at all? Secondly, people in a position to hire always prefer to bring in candidates who have been referred to them by existing employees. When you think about it, this makes perfect sense. Existing employees know what a firm's culture is really like better than anyone else, and they usually have a good sense of what people are likely to fit in—and thrive—in that environment. If you approach an organization through an existing employee, you've essentially made it through the first stage of the screening process. If you're basically qualified, generally likeable, and hardworking, the hiring manager would far rather hire you—or at least interview you—than sit down with a pile of 200 resumes. Wouldn't you?

Think of it this way: When you need a book to read on the beach during your summer vacation, do you go to Barnes & Noble and read the synopsis on the back of every book in the store before you made your selection? Or do you ask friends and family if they've read any good books lately and choose among those based on what sounds the most interesting? Chances are you do the latter, and it's not because you think there aren't any other books out there that would make a great beach read. You do it because considering every possible option out there wouldn't be a good investment of your time, so you rely on other people to help you narrow your options down. It's the same with hiring decisions, and it's why networking is so critical to a successful job search.

Networking "Yes, buts"

To help you overcome any anxiety you might have about networking, we've outlined the most common misconceptions about the process. We call these networking urban myths the "Yes, buts," and they're usually invoked by job seekers who are reluctant to network. When we tell these folks how important networking is to the success of their search, they usually begin their objections by saying "Yes, but . . . ." The most pernicious "Yes, buts" keep some people from networking effectively, and they prevent other people from networking at all. To help you separate networking fact from fiction, we've outlined the nine most common "Yes, buts" below, along with an explanation of why each one should be banished from your internal job-hunting dialogue—forever.

- **"Yes, but networking seems like a forced and unnatural way to deal with people."**

  Networking is essentially talking with other people and getting their opinions in order to make an informed decision about something. Chances are, you've done this already—have you ever asked someone else what they thought of a particular book or movie, or if they knew of a good dentist or tailor? Did that seem unnatural? Did people seem annoyed you asked for their advice? Remember, these scenarios aren't that different from asking for career advice. You're probably better at it than you think, and people will probably be much more eager to give it than you ever expected.

- **"Yes, but I've never been very good at schmoozing. And networking is just a more sophisticated term for schmoozing, right?"**

  Wrong. Networking sometimes involves schmoozing, but the two aren't synonymous. Think of schmoozing as the art of small talk: Without question, establishing a relationship with someone new requires some degree of small talk. But networking is more than working the room at a cocktail party. No matter how casual or informal the setting, networking has two very specific purposes: learning as much as possible about appealing career options and telling other people what you're looking for so they can point you in the right direction.

- **"Yes, but networking feels insincere and manipulative to me. People won't want to help me if they feel like I'm using them to get something."**

  By and large, people like to be helpful by sharing their experiences and expertise. Unless you give people the impression you don't value their perspectives or respect their time, chances are they will be happy to help you if they can. In his essay, "Life Without Principle," Henry David Thoreau said: "The greatest compliment that was ever paid me was when one asked me what I thought and attended to my answer." This probably rings true for you too. Think back to the last time someone asked what you thought about a class or a professor: Did you feel used? Or were you flattered someone valued your opinion enough to ask?

- **"Yes, but I hate asking for favors. What could I possibly offer them in return?"**

  There's nothing inherently wrong with asking for help. And what's more, enlisting the help of others during your job search effectively makes other people stakeholders in your success. Once someone provides you with guidance in your job search, they're personally invested in you and therefore want to see you do well. Oftentimes, this investment isn't just metaphorical: Many organizations use referral programs to encourage existing employees to bring in talent from the outside. In these situations, your contacts have more than just the warm fuzzies to gain if all goes well and you're hired.

- **"Yes, but what if I don't know that many people? I'd have to approach complete strangers and ask them to talk to me."**

  Networking does not involve approaching strangers in the vain hope that one, one day, may be able to help you land a job. In fact, it actually starts with the people who know you best: your family, close friends, professors and teachers, and current and former colleagues. Consider these—and anyone else you interact with on a regular basis—your own personal A-listers. The people your A-listers know are your secondary contacts. You might know some of them—if only tangentially—but you probably won't know most of them. It's often your secondary contacts who can put you in touch with people close to decision-makers. It doesn't really matter if you've got legions of close friends and professional contacts who know you well; all that matters is whether someone on your A-list knows one or two people who can help you set things in motion. While you're getting word out to your A-list about your job search, don't forget to ask them what's new in their professional lives, too: Talking to people you already know (e.g., family, friends, classmates) about what they do can be an incredibly valuable tool—one most people don't use enough.

- **"Yes, but networking means that I'll have to ask people that I barely know for jobs—and then 'sell them' on my skills and abilities."**

  If you're approaching it the right way, you won't be doing either of these things during a networking conversation. Networking is not about asking for a job—it's about getting advice from people who are in a position to provide it. Asking the right questions—

and actively listening to the answers—is more important at this stage than selling your skills and abilities. A wise woman (advice guru Dr. Joyce Brothers) once said that "listening, not imitation, may be the sincerest form of flattery." Author Dale Carnegie—who literally wrote the book on winning friends and influencing people—once said that you'll make more friends in two months by becoming interested in other people than you will in two years trying to get other people interested in you. Their advice rings true when it comes to networking: Your focus should be learning and listening, not talking and selling. Who knows: Maybe you'll make a friend or two along the way.

- **"Yes, but I'm an introvert. Only extroverted people are effective networkers."**

This "Yes, but" is a corollary to the previous one, so our response will sound familiar if you've been paying attention. But we'll risk being repetitive if we can make this point clear: The ability to listen to (and remember) what people say is critical to building relationships. At its core, that's all networking is: building relationships. If anything, introverts might have a slight edge over extroverts when it comes to networking conversations and informational interviews, because introverts are often better listeners than more gregarious folk. As we said before, asking someone for their opinion and making it clear you value what they have to say is critical to getting them on your side. Finally, if you really pay attention to what they have to say—and manage to retain it—you'll reap benefits during the interview stage. The ability to demonstrate a solid understanding of a given job, and a sincere interest in the organization it's with, often distinguishes a successful candidate from the rest of the pack.

- **"Yes, but I'm very qualified for the positions I'm applying for. My credentials and past performance will speak for themselves and distinguish me from the crowd. I don't need no *stinking* networking."**

We hate to be the ones to break it to you, but the real world—and this includes the job market—is far from a pure meritocracy. As a student, you're generally rewarded for what you know and how well you do your work. Sadly, there aren't many jobs where you can succeed by the sweat of your brow and the ingenuity of your ideas alone: With few exceptions, attaining professional success requires you to develop meaningful connections with other people. The importance of personal relationships applies to the job search as well. Remember that old cliché, "it's not what you know, it's whom you know"? Well, it's partly true—in reality, it's what you know and whom you know. As we mentioned earlier in the chapter, an impeccable academic record and stellar professional achievements won't mean anything if your resume never gets read.

* **"Yes, but networking involves being aggressive and pushy. I'm neither of those things."**

Contrary to popular belief, networking is actually more effective if you're not aggressive or pushy. In fact, one of the most common mistakes gung-ho networkers make is advancing their own career agendas too early in the process, which doesn't win them many friends or professional allies. Again, it's important to keep the bigger picture in mind and keep your expectations realistic. Think of networking as groundwork for a job search that will yield results later down the line. No matter how badly you want someone to pass along your resume or act as an internal reference for that dream job you've learned about, you will get much more from your conversations if you really, genuinely approach them as opportunities to learn. Your contacts aren't a means to an end; they're more like a personal "board of directors" whose experiences and perspectives you value. If this type of thinking governs your interactions with other people, you won't be aggressive or pushy—and you won't be perceived that way, either.

Start spreading the news . . .

When it comes to true love, people often say it only finds you when you're not looking for it. Does this maxim apply to finding the perfect job as well as the perfect mate? Sadly, no—not for most people. That's not to say you can't end up finding out about a great job in the course of a conversation that was never intended to have anything to do with your job search. That was the case with Alison, a 24-year-old consultant who ended up unintentionally networking when she just wanted to hear a familiar voice. "I had just moved to London from New York, and not only was I having a hard time with my job search, but I was incredibly homesick," she explains. "So I called a friend of mine back home, and I was just telling him how cold and rainy it was in London. He mentioned that a friend of his had worked in London for a few years and had experienced a similar thing. Anyway, I found out that the company his friend had worked for when he was overseas was one that I had interviewed with when I was a senior in college. I didn't know that the company even had an office in the U.K., but it turned out that my friend sent my resume to his friend who, in turn, forwarded it to my current manager. I got an informational interview at first, then a job interview, and eventually the job."

The moral of the story? Jobs won't usually find you when you're least expecting them to, but romance and job searching are similar in a different way: You're probably not going to get very far in either endeavor if you never leave your house or if you never let people know you're in the market. In fact, one of the most obvious mistakes people make when they're networking is focusing on the people they don't know and completely overlooking the people they do.

Spreading the word involves talking to the people on your A-list: Family members, close friends, current and former colleagues, classmates, teammates, professors, teachers—anyone who knows you well and interacts with you regularly. (As a general rule, anyone who couldn't pick you out of a police lineup does not belong on your A-list.) Not only should you make sure these folks know you're looking for a job, but you should let them know—with as much specificity as possible—what you're looking for. If you don't know exactly what you want to do, don't worry: The important thing is that you've let people know you're in the market. Unless they know you're actively looking, even your close family and friends won't be able to help you. Remember: Your job search might very well be at the top of your priority list, but it's not necessarily on anyone else's radar screen. We're not suggesting you send out a formal press release to inform your friends and loved ones you're looking for a job, but it's important to get the word out. That way, when an A-lister or secondary contact hears about a great opportunity, you'll be among the first to hear about it.

Don't look a gift networking contact in the mouth

You've been there, we've been there: You talk about your career aspirations during Thanksgiving dinner. The next thing you know, you're getting regular phone calls from your mother, who's suddenly playing the role of Yenta the Matchmaker in the off-Broadway musical, *Your Job Search*. You said you wanted to be a writer? Well, your cousin Mary Beth is a medical journalist who made six figures last year interviewing doctors and publishing articles on public health issues. She says you can call her and she'd be happy to talk to you. Fast-forward to a few weeks later: Have you called your cousin Mary Beth yet? She's expecting your call.

While it's tempting to roll your eyes and move on to other things, it's probably not a bad idea to call your cousin Mary Beth, even if you're not entirely sure medical journalism is your calling. At the end of the day, effective networkers leverage the resources and the contacts they're given. If someone else is willing to make an introduction or otherwise break the ice for you, then what are you waiting for? Yes, it might seem awkward at first, but chances are you'll be glad you talked to her. Maybe she has some interesting things to say about pursuing writing as a livelihood, or maybe she has some tips for becoming a great interviewer; you just never know. Motivating yourself to network when you have the opportunity is a lot like motivating yourself to go to the gym: You may dread it with every fiber of your being, but once you do it, you feel so much better about yourself and the world. Networking releases the same kind of endorphins. Will a single conversation with your cousin land you a job? Probably not (in much the same way that 20 minutes on the treadmill probably won't reshape your body), but at least you're doing *something*, right?

It's a marathon, not a sprint

Keeping with our physical fitness metaphor, we should point out that networking muscles are built over time, not overnight. Some hard-core networking books will tell you to aim for five new networking contacts per day—only you will know whether that's a realistic target for you or not. If you try to do too much too soon, you probably won't stick with it. Networking really is the job-search equivalent of a long-term fitness plan: Unless you can really make it part of your lifestyle, it's not going to do you any good. Don't start out with Atkins when you know South Beach will probably work better in the long run. Don't start by going to impersonal networking events or job fairs. Send an e-mail to one person—just one—who you've been thinking about but haven't contacted recently. Don't ask for anything. Don't tell him you're looking for a job. Just check in, see how he's doing, and ask what's going on in his life. Take the time to acknowledge people's birthdays and anniversaries, and send an e-mail congratulating them when they graduate from school, get engaged, or reach other milestones. If the reason networking makes you uneasy is that you feel as though you're getting in touch with people only when you need something, there are really only two ways to avoid that problem: Not asking for help when you need it, or being in touch more consistently so that asking for help is just a natural extension of the relationship you already have. Guess which strategy we endorse?

'Tis the season . . . for continued networking

Of course, going the extra mile to keep in touch with your A-listers is one thing, but what about the folks you know less well—the ones that you've met through referrals, informational interviews, and networking events? You can't possibly be expected to remember and acknowledge their birthdays and anniversaries (unless you want people to think that you're stalking them), right? That's right, but you can take a moment to give them a shout during the holidays—it's a thoughtful, proactive gesture that will keep these relationships current without giving anyone the impression they might need a restraining order down the line. Taking the time to maintain professional relationships means you won't have to feel awkward when you have to call a contact out of the blue about a job opportunity or ask for a reference.

To get started, dig up all those business cards you collected over the course of interviews, summer internships, job fairs, and—if you've already done some structured networking at this stage—power brunches and lunches, formal networking events, and informational interviews. Buy a pack of generic holiday cards and write short notes to your contacts wishing them a happy holiday season and offering a brief update on your professional status. Keep your tone positive, genuine, and subtle. For example, if you're still in the market for a job, your card might look something like this:

> Dear Carrie,
>
> It was great meeting you earlier this year at the Women in the Arts luncheon. Since then, I've had the opportunity to meet with some great folks about my interest in becoming a columnist with a daily newspaper, and while I'm still looking for the right opportunity, I feel excited about the many prospects. I hope all is well and that you're enjoying a wonderful holiday season. I hope to speak with you again soon.
>
> All the best,
>
> Joanna Jones

If you're employed but want to keep your list of contacts current, something like this would work:

Dear Samantha,

I know it's been a while since we last spoke, but I wanted to send a quick note to wish you and your family a wonderful holiday season. Things are going well for me at Smith Public Relations, and I've had the opportunity to work on some exciting new projects. I hope all is going well with you, and that the New Year brings you continued success. Let's stay in touch.

All the best,

Robert Yule

While the holidays are one obvious opportunity to send cards or notes like the ones above, keeping in touch doesn't have to take place between Thanksgiving and New Year's Day. The important thing is not the specific holiday or the time of year, but the fact that you're reaching out and keeping yourself visible. If there's one drawback to sending cards around the holiday season, it's that people receive so many cards yours may not stand out as much as it otherwise would. You can send out Thanksgiving cards, which makes it fairly likely yours will be the first holiday card your contacts will receive. Some people even send out networking cards around the Easter holiday (if you go this route, be sure each recipient observes the holiday). Even if there's not a bona fide Hallmark holiday on the calendar for months, there are other good reasons to stay in touch—if you see an article or news clipping you think would be of interest to someone in your circle, send it to them and let them know you're thinking of them. No matter what occasion you choose, be sure to enclose a business card with your correspondence, or write your e-mail address and contact phone number beneath your signature.

INFORMATIONAL INTERVIEWS

So what exactly do you do once you've tapped your network and identified individuals who might be able to help you with your search? In a nutshell, you ask them to share their experiences, perspectives, career advice, and professional wisdom with you—regardless of whether they have the faintest idea who you are. Officially, this is called informational interviewing, and it's the best way to glean valuable job advice from the people you've met through your networking efforts.

An informational interview is any conversation where the primary objective is finding out about a particular field, company, or job opportunity. Informational interviews are *not* job interviews (and you shouldn't approach them with the expectation they'll lead to one). Instead, informational interviews are targeted conversations with people who currently work in the industry or field that you're interested in. Targeted doesn't necessarily mean formal—oftentimes, you'll be able to glean just as much information over a casual brunch with someone you already know as you would during a more structured meeting in an office setting with someone you've never met. No matter how formal or casual, all informational interviews are the perfect forum for the following:

- **Learning about a particular organization**—how the company distinguishes itself from its competitors in the industry and how it distinguishes itself among other employers in the same field; its hiring process; its values and culture.

- **Learning about a specific job/position**—what educational background or work experience is required; which personality traits or working styles are particularly well suited for the role; what the day-to-day responsibilities are; how the role fits into the organization's broader mission; what challenges and rewards are inherent to the job; what career development opportunities are typically available.

- **Getting advice on your job search**—how your background and credentials might be viewed by hiring personnel in a particular industry or at a specific company; what factors interviewers are most likely to focus on during the recruiting process; what "barriers to entry" might exist that you didn't know about before (skills tests, writing samples, background checks, etc.); what successful candidates at a specific company have in common; which other individuals might be willing to speak with you.

- **Learning about potential job opportunities**—how a particular company fills job openings; whether there are industry-specific job boards or websites employers rely on when they have openings to fill; whether there are any industry-wide trends or company-specific developments that might affect hiring (mergers, acquisitions, restructurings, lateral movement, etc.); the most effective ways to find out about positions that have not yet been publicized.

On the approach

In order to snag informational interviews with the people who are best suited to give you advice, the *way* you ask is everything: Your request should be polite, concise, honest, and unintrusive. While there are definitely situations in which it's more appropriate to lob in a telephone call, asking for an informational interview is one task best accomplished over e-mail. You can rest assured you won't catch your contact just as she's rushing into a meeting or out the door for a dentist appointment, and you've left the ball in her court without making her feel awkward about it if she can't accommodate your request. Over e-mail, you can take the time necessary to make sure the tone of your request is appropriate: assertive yet respectful, specific yet flexible, complimentary but never cloying. You provide all of the nitty-gritty details (who you are, how you know who she is, and what you want from her) in a single, seamless paragraph. Here's an example of an e-mail requesting an informational interview:

Dear Ms. Walker,

My name is Karen McCarthy, and I'm a recent graduate of New York University here in Manhattan. I was referred to you by a friend of mine, Scott Davis, who worked with you last summer at the *Village Voice*. I am currently considering a career in newspaper journalism, and part of my research process involves speaking to people currently working in the field who are willing to share their perspectives and experiences with me. Scott mentioned that you have a very interesting professional background, and that you would certainly have some unique insights into the skills and experiences I should be building in order to launch a successful career in the industry. If you have a half-hour to spare in the next week or two, I would love to meet with you in person. If an in-person meeting isn't possible, maybe we could schedule a brief telephone conversation at a time that makes sense for you; obviously, I'm happy to work around your schedule.

Thanks so much in advance for your help, and I hope to hear from you soon!

Kind regards,

Karen McCarthy

Take what you can get

There will be times when a networking contact lets you know right off the bat that he can't meet with you in person or (for whatever reason) can't help you along in the hiring process. But if your contact is willing to share advice over e-mail or over the phone, don't discount the value of a dialogue just because it's not what you initially asked for. You can still learn a lot from these "virtual" meetings, and saying "thank you," by the way, is still in order.

The "Power Brunch"

You may have heard of a "power lunch" before, but the term "power brunch" might be an unfamiliar concept. A "power brunch" is the most casual version of an informational interview, and—especially if you're a novice networker—it's a great way to start getting the word out about your interest in a particular industry and getting advice about packaging yourself for maximum success. If you're a reluctant networker, the power brunch is the perfect way to start out; after a few weekend meals over omelets and cappuccinos, you'll definitely be more comfortable with the idea of asking for help when it comes to finding the perfect job.

Not only does the power brunch enable you to practice your informational interview skills, but you'll probably learn a lot more than you would in a more structured setting. To a greater extent than e-mail, telephone calls, or even office visits, power brunches create a relaxed environment that promotes candor; after all, you're presenting yourself as a trusted confidante rather than a job seeker on the prowl for insider information. While the focus of a power lunch is selling yourself, there's no such pressure when it comes to the power brunch: Here, the focus isn't on you but on the person you've invited. Your brunch guest might give you valuable information on breaking into the industry you want (including referrals to other contacts in your target industry), general advice on pursuing opportunities in a specific field, or insider tips on positions that haven't yet been advertised. Compared to weekday lunches—which can often be hurried and seem formal—power brunches are definitely more fun. You can show up in jeans and linger over a mimosa if the conversation takes off or catch up after you've talked shop.

The people you'll most likely invite to a power brunch are actually the people you already know best: the "A-list" we described earlier in this chapter. As we've said before, many people focus all their networking efforts on people they don't yet know while they overlook the valuable perspectives and advice of the people they already know. After a few power brunches, you'll see that there's good reason not to let this group go unnoticed. Remember, your A-list includes friends, family members, roommates, neighbors, teachers, professors, advisors, colleagues past and present—anyone you already interact with on a regular basis. To set up a power brunch, you needn't send a formal, polished e-mail like the one you'd send to someone who didn't know you from Adam: Simply call a friend or family member whom you haven't talked to in a while who's doing something cool.

The "Power Lunch"

With a few power brunches under your belt, you'll graduate to the power lunch—many times, a power lunch will involve someone a brunch date referred you to. The power lunch gives you the advantages of an in-person meeting: You get to observe the other person's body language (which will help you gauge how comfortable they are giving you the inside scoop), and develop the type of rapport only a face-to-face meeting can establish. However, because most power lunches involve contacts you don't know quite as well—and contacts slightly closer to the hiring process—the power lunch isn't quite as candid or relaxed. Though you still aren't expected to treat it as a job interview, you are expected to be professional—that means showing up on time, making sure your lunch sticks to the time you've allotted for it, and thanking your lunch partner profusely for taking time out of his busy schedule to meet with you.

Don't sweat the small talk: Specific questions to ask during informational interviews

Whether an informational interview takes place over the phone or happy-hour cocktails, you should prepare for it by developing a specific idea of what you hope to learn. Of course, the types of questions you'll ask will depend on what stage of the job-research process you're at. If you're just trying to get a sense of what a career in academia might entail versus a career in the private sector, you won't ask the same questions as someone who wants to find out what it's like to work as a research assistant for a specific university professor. The research you've done up until this point (whether online, at your career-planning office, or through other informational interviews) should also help you decide which questions to pose. Have one or two primary objectives in mind at the beginning of the conversation (whether it's finding out about a specific company's culture or figuring out what technical skills a particular job requires), and let that shape the direction the interview takes. If you get stuck, here are a few topics you might want to cover during your conversations, along with a few sample questions in each category:

- **Educational background**

  I was wondering if you could tell me a little bit about your background—what did you study in college? Did you go to graduate school? Is your educational background typical of someone in your position? Are there aspects of the job that make particularly good use of the skills you developed as an psychology/sociology major?

- **Job-search tactics**

  As you prepared for your interviews, how did you go about conducting research on specific organizations? What strategies did you find most helpful? Looking back at your interviews with this organization, were there specific things about your background and experience that your interviewers were especially interested in discussing? What surprised you (if anything) about the hiring process at your company? Is it fairly common for employers in the industry to give any job-specific tests or assessments to evaluate your suitability for the position?

- **Career path**

  How did you decide to go into this particular field? What other industries were you considering (if any), and why did you choose your specific organization? How did you arrive in the specific area/department you're currently working in? How do you see your career at Company XYZ evolving? What types of advancement opportunities are available to you? Are lateral moves—either within the company or from one company to another—fairly common? Is it realistic to expect that if I start out in an entry-level role, I'll be able to move up within the organization? How does your organization approach developing its staff and promoting from within?

- **Day-to-day responsibilities**

  What do you do on a daily basis? Can you describe what a typical day/week is like? Could you describe for me some recent projects you've worked on and your specific role in those projects? How do your specific responsibilities fit into the bigger picture of what your department does? How does your department fit into the larger organization?

- **Fit with the job**

  What do you think it takes for someone to be good at this job, and what do you think it takes for someone to really enjoy it? What have you found to be the most frustrating and the most rewarding aspects of the job? What do you wish you had known about the job before you started it? Does the job frequently require travel, relocation, or long hours? Are people in these positions supervised closely, or are they expected to work independently, with little managerial oversight? Would you describe the job as highly collaborative or not?

- **Fit with the organization/industry**

  Now that you're at Company XYZ, what has surprised you about working there? About the industry in general? How would you describe your firm's culture? What do you think is different/better about working there than anywhere else? Are there any factors specific to your experience that might influence your answer? What do you think your firm takes particular pride in?

- **Advice for you**

  In general, what advice would you give someone hoping to break into this field? Based on your experience, what advice would you give someone looking to explore career opportunities at your firm? Are there specific areas of the company that seem particularly well suited for someone with my education, experience, and background? Can you recommend other people—either inside or outside of Company XYZ—who might also be willing to share their perspectives of working in the industry? Are there any industry-specific resources (websites, trade journals) that might be helpful to someone researching the industry? Which professional associations are linked to the field, and what types of activities do they sponsor? Are there any with which I can be involved right away?

Unless your contact answers your questions with monosyllabic, one-word answers, you probably won't be able to get through all of these questions in a single informational interview, so keep your one or two primary goals in mind throughout the conversation. And regardless of how many or how few questions you ask, you should definitely be conscious of your contact's time; these individuals are not your personal career consultants, nor should you feel as though you can enlist them to support your case with recruiters. Never ask for more than a half-hour of your contact's time; if she's willing to give you 45 minutes, that's great—but be careful not to overstay your welcome. And no matter what, be sure to acknowledge that your contact has sacrificed precious free time to speak to you, and always thank her profusely for helping you out.

Compare apples to apples

If possible, speak with contacts whose backgrounds are similar to yours in some way, whether it's their educational background, previous work or internship experience, specific professional interests, geographic location, or even outside interests or hobbies. This is helpful for a couple of reasons: The more you have in common with a person, the more relevant their job-hunting experiences are likely to be to you. Also, if you're interviewing someone you haven't met before, you'll both feel more comfortable if you can find some common ground to get the conversation started—and keep it going. It's human nature, really: As a general rule, we're more comfortable with people who are like us. The more your contact can relate to you, the more comfortable—and therefore candid—they'll be when it comes to sharing the secrets of their success. Tap into your school's alumni directory and extend an introduction to alums who work in the fields that interest you. If you're a member of any social or networking clubs, ask around to see if anyone knows of a butcher, baker, candlestick-maker, or anyone who fits the career profile you're hoping to build for yourself. If there are websites or resources you regularly consult as you're doing research on your target fields, keep an eye out for specific articles that capture your interest, and contact the authors to see if they're willing to speak with you further about the topic.

Practice makes perfect

Like any other skill you're just starting to learn, informational interviewing requires time and practice if you want to become particularly good at it. The more people you talk to, the more natural the process will seem, and the less you'll feel like a 7th grader working on a research project for your social studies class. While conversations with people you've never met might initially make you nervous, you'll eventually find you look forward to them (yes, we promise). No matter how adept you become at informational interviewing, keep the following rules of the road in mind so your conversations continue to be productive:

- **Take the road less traveled.**

  Your conversations with people who aren't directly involved with recruiting might prove the most valuable. If you keep your informational interviews separate from any formal application process, you can be reasonably sure the questions you ask won't have a direct influence on a subsequent hiring decision. You'll be more comfortable asking questions you wouldn't necessarily bring up in an evaluative setting, and you'll probably get more valuable answers than you would get from a recruiter or HR contact; these folks are generally too close to the recruiting process to give you an objective perspective, and, because they're generalists, they won't necessarily be able to provide a lot of detailed information about what it's like to work in any one specific position.

  Asking contacts outside the regular recruiting process for the real scoop, however, doesn't mean you can say or do anything unprofessional—just because the details of your conversation won't necessarily get back to decision-makers doesn't mean it's outside the realm of possibility. No matter how informal the setting, you should still approach your informational interviews with professionalism.

- **Avoid the resume "balk".**

  Unless your contact has specifically asked you for a copy of your resume, don't fork one over during an informational interview. If someone has agreed to speak with you on a purely informational basis and you hand her your resume, you're essentially changing the direction of the conversation with little or no warning. In other words, you're committing the job-hunting equivalent of a "balk" in baseball (if you're unfamiliar with the term, here's the 411: In baseball, a pitcher must come to a full stop before he pitches, and, once he starts, he's got to follow through or it doesn't count. A violation of this rule is called a "balk"). You owe it to the people who've granted you informational interviews to give them fair warning, too. If you've told someone that you want to speak with them to learn more about a specific industry or job, you can't switch the rules halfway through the game by asking someone to submit your resume on your behalf. At best, your contact might not know quite how to react or what to do with it. At worst, she might question your sincerity and credibility. Of course, you are welcome to submit your resume if your contact asks for it in advance of your conversation—or during it. Have a few copies ready just in case, but don't fork it over until you've gotten the green light.

- **The favor of your reply is requested.**

  Whenever someone takes time out to help you with your job search without any expectation of getting something in return, a formal thank-you is in order. Not only is it good manners, but leaving someone with a favorable impression of you makes good business sense too. A thoughtful e-mail is sufficient, but a handwritten note makes a bigger impact—and not just because it takes a little more time and effort. "I send handwritten thank-you notes because my contacts won't wonder whether they're expected to respond," explains Carrie, a 26-year-old assistant editor. "An e-mailed thank-you note might leave the recipient wondering, 'should I send a response to say good luck? Or should I offer to keep them posted on job opportunities?' A handwritten, mailed thank-you note lets you just say 'thank you' without giving the impression that you might expect something else down the line." We think Emily Post would probably agree.

- **Mind your manners when it comes to money.**

  When you bring up the issue of money, you always run the risk of getting someone's knickers in a twist, and it's no different when it comes to researching jobs and careers. We all know that it's considered impolite to talk about money in virtually any situation, but shouldn't it be fair game as you investigate which career options make the most sense for you? It should, but it isn't. Most people (including us!) will tell you that in the context of a formal job interview, you shouldn't talk about compensation until you're offered a job. However, in order to negotiate effectively, you need to have a realistic salary range for comparable positions in mind. Salary surveys and databases are a start, but because the ranges they provide are broad, it's best to have a firsthand source to help you manage your expectations.

  How *do* you ask about money so early in the process? Very carefully. Perhaps more than any other topic of conversation you'll navigate during the informational interview, the money discussion is a little bit of a dance; the way it unfolds depends entirely on how well you read your partner.

  Some people will come right out and tell you how much they make in their current position, or how much they made when they started out in their profession. In that case, they've opened the Pandora's Box of compensation issues for you, and it's reasonable to ask whether or not the figure they've cited is realistic for the type of position you're considering. Unfortunately, most people you'll speak with probably won't volunteer this level of detail. If this is the case, you'll have to gauge how the conversation is going and how receptive your contact is likely to be if asked to provide salary information. If you save the money talk for last (and we recommend that you do), you'll have time to figure this out. If the person is reticent when it comes to discussing his company's interview philosophy, then chances are he's not going to be eager to show you a copy of his W-2. Rely on your intuition and common sense when deciding whether to broach the topic.

If you decide to ask, keep in mind that the less direct your questions, the less threatening they're likely to be. You can always cite the salary ranges your initial research has revealed and see if you get a nibble: Your contact might advise you whether your expectations should lean toward the high or low end of the range. If you haven't been able to pin down any sort of range for the job, you can see if they'll be willing to provide one. Again, the way you ask the question is critical: Saying "I'm in the beginning of my job search, and I have no idea what sort of salary range is realistic for entry-level jobs in this field" is very different from asking "Do you mind if I ask you what you make?" Asking open-ended questions that leave room for discretion are preferable to questions that require a single numerical answer. Such questions give your contact an escape route if he or she feels uncomfortable.

While we're on the subject of discomfort, we should emphasize the importance of recognizing it during the interview. If you sense that your contact is starting to bristle when the subject of money comes up, there's absolutely nothing to be gained by being persistent—and there's an awful lot to lose.

If your informational interview ends and you're no further along when it comes to salary information, remember you can consult other sources besides the salary databases we mentioned earlier: Professional associations, staffing companies, temp agencies, and headhunters can often provide salary data. Scour online job postings for similar positions and look for ones that specify salary. If you're still in school, remember that your career-planning office will probably be able to help you hone in on a reasonable range— even if they don't have firsthand knowledge of the position or industry, they're generally more adept at tapping into other resources, including alumni and recruiters who interview on campus.

- **Know when to say "when"**

We can't overemphasize the importance of not becoming "that guy" or "that girl" in the eyes of your networking contacts: The one who won't stop calling or e-mailing to check on the status of available jobs. Wake up and smell the hummus, folks: Your networking contacts are not your personal career gurus. Nine times out of ten, they don't know about every current job opening their organization has posted, and they surely don't know about all of the ones that are still in the pipeline. Usually, they have little to no influence over hiring decisions. Even if they did, they can't work miracles if you don't have the requisite skills, training, or experience for a given job. If they barely know you, you shouldn't expect that they'll be eager to provide a personal endorsement of your candidacy, so don't ask them to do it. Regardless of whether they're eligible for a referral bonus if you end up getting hired, they're not on your payroll: They have their own jobs, too.

Not only can dogged persistence backfire when it comes to your own job search, but it has the potential to create bad networking karma all around. "When I first graduated from college, I designated myself as a career mentor on my university's alumni database, which meant that current students and other alumni were welcome to contact me for career advice," says Matthew, a 28-year-old analyst at a government agency. "But I got so many e-mails and calls from people who didn't really want advice; they just wanted me to help them get a job. A lot of them just wouldn't quit, even if I told them that my involvement in the process was limited. Eventually it got old, and I took myself off of the list."

Unfortunately, many job-seekers end up misusing and abusing the opportunities that informational interviews provide. While people generally enjoy lending their advice and expertise, even the most generous, well-intentioned person will start to lose patience with someone who takes advantage of his time or just won't back off. Think about it this way: Did you ever like a song the first time you heard it on the radio, but come to despise it after a while because all the stations played it ad nauseam? When it comes to your networking contacts, know when to pipe down.

- **Don't be a one-trick pony.**

As with any single component of the job-hunting process, you can't rely on networking prowess alone to get the job you want. We said that the most impressive resume wouldn't do any good if no one ever read it, and we meant it. But the inverse is also true: No matter how savvy a networker you are (or eventually become), you won't get the job if you can't convince the person or people in a position to hire you that you'd be good at it. However, information is power: Networking allows you to figure out what you want to do in the first place, what opportunities might be available that fit your criteria, and what you need to know about a specific organization before you interview there. You can use what you've learned by networking to make your resumes, cover letters, and other application materials more targeted and effective. So while networking is an important piece of the puzzle, it's just that: one piece. You have to make sure everything else fits into place too.

RESUMES, COVER LETTERS, AND INTERVIEWS

What have I done to deserve this?

Now that your job search is underway, you may find a lot of unsolicited (but well-intentioned) advice coming your way. All of a sudden, it seems as though everyone is an expert when it comes to searching for—and getting—the perfect job. If you haven't already heard every job-hunting cliché in the book, just give it time. Chances are good someone will tell you "It's not what you know but who you know," "It's all about eye contact and a firm handshake," and "Getting your foot in the door is what really matters—after all, you can always work your way up." With all of the unsolicited guidance coming your way, it can be difficult to distinguish tried-and-true job-hunting advice from old wives' tales perpetuated solely to put anxious minds like yours at ease.

In the following pages, we'll help you separate myth from fact when it comes to landing the job you want. If there's one thing we hope you'll learn from this chapter, it's that hiring processes at most organizations are much more of an art than a science. When you're in the market for a job, you'd like to think employers' decision-making processes are—if not completely scientific—at least rational, predictable, and based predominantly on candidates' relative merits. But as a candidate for a given position, you're essentially marketing a product (that product is *you*, of course), and human beings aren't always rational and predictable when it comes to deciding what to buy. It's not enough to develop the product (by completing your degree, gaining work experience, joining professional associations, volunteering in the community, and so on)—you have to pay attention to the packaging too. In the context of a job search, cover letters, resumes, and interviews are all part of the packaging: Once you've taken the time to figure out exactly what you have to offer a potential employer, you've got to present your qualifications in a compelling, convincing way. This section will teach you how to do just that.

It had to be you: What employers look for

Before you can figure out how to present yourself—your achievements, qualifications, and experience—to a prospective employer, you need to know which specific attributes organizations will be looking for as they evaluate your candidacy. It stands to reason that every industry (and every company, and every function or group *within* that company, for that matter) uses its own unique set of criteria to inform its recruiting process and hiring decisions. Nonetheless, employers across industries mention the same qualities over and over again. According to a recent study by the National Association of Colleges and Employers (NACE), an organization that publishes research on recruiting and employment issues for college graduates, employers consider the following skills and personal attributes most important to their evaluation of a job candidate:

Skills/Personal Attribute	Importance
Communication skills	4.7
Honesty/integrity	4.7
Teamwork skills	4.6
Strong work ethic	4.5
Analytical skills	4.4
Flexibility/adaptability	4.4
Interpersonal skills	4.4
Motivation/initiative	4.4
Computer skills	4.3
Attention to detail	4.1
Organizational skills	4.1
Leadership skills	4.0
Self-confidence	4.0

(5-point scale where 1=Not at all important, and 5=Extremely important)

Source: "Employers rate the importance of candidate qualities/skills," *Job Outlook 2006*. National Association of Colleges and Employers (www.naceweb.org).

If the list of attributes above seems like a lot to remember, take heart. We're not suggesting you commit it to memory or that you convince a prospective employer you possess every single one of these traits. Instead, the list is intended to reassure you that the skills you developed as you worked toward your degree are highly relevant in the job market. In fact, many of the skills that were most critical to your success as a student are the ones employers prize most highly. Consider the list above a starting point for taking inventory of your own capabilities and strengths.

In the following pages, we'll help you turn the skills you've developed pursuing your degree into a compelling, marketable package you'll present to prospective employers during your search. And though we address the resume, cover letter, and interview separately, keep in mind that each of these is part of a single process—a process that offers numerous opportunities to demonstrate exactly what you have to offer.

RESUMES AND COVER LETTERS

If it hasn't happened to you already, it will probably happen to you soon: You've successfully landed a "Power Brunch" with a friend of a friend who has the job of your dreams. The two of you have hit it off, and after a few cappuccinos she's giving you the inside scoop on what it's like to work in the industry—what it takes to be successful, what recruiters look for when they're scouting new talent, and how she landed her job in the first place. The more detail she gives you about her work, the more convinced you are you've found your professional Holy Grail. It gets better: There's an opening in her department that would be perfect for you! She's offered to pass along your resume! Just e-mail it to her, she says, and she'll deliver it to the right person, along with a personal endorsement of your candidacy.

You think about it for a moment: You know you must have a resume *somewhere*. You can remember writing one, but it's been a while since you've updated it. You're eager to strike while the iron is hot, though; if your new best brunch buddy has offered to hand-deliver your resume to the recruiting contact at her company, you'd better fire one off to her as soon as possible, right?

Well, yes—as long as it's error-free, easy to understand, tailored (to one extent or another) to the job for which you are applying, and accompanied by a concise, well-written cover letter. If it's lacking in any of these areas, it will be worth taking the extra time to get it in tip-top shape before hitting the "send" button and setting your application in motion.

How resumes and cover letters are used

In virtually every industry and organization, employers use resumes as a way to assess which candidates should be considered for an available position. There is no way around it: You absolutely must have one; without it you will not pass "Go," you will not collect $200, and—until someone comes up with a more reliable, efficient way to screen applicants—you will not get a job. When it comes to effective resumes, there's no single magic formula that guarantees success in every circumstance. However, the best resumes have a few things in common: they are concise, results-oriented, and clearly presented. Most importantly, good resumes convince hiring personnel to interview well-qualified candidates. *The primary purpose of a resume is getting an interview. A resume alone will not land you a job offer.*

Once you've been invited to interview, your resume will shape your subsequent conversations with recruiters, hiring managers, and other employees at the company. Every person you speak with during the interview process will likely have a copy of your resume, and each person will probably look for gaps, weaknesses, and inconsistencies that they'll expect you to address during your conversation. Once you've left the office, your resume helps your interviewer (or interviewers) remember you and serves as the basis for the discussion of your candidacy.

Cover letters can play a less significant role. In general, they aren't read with the same level of scrutiny resumes are; sometimes they're read but more often they're skimmed, and, occasionally, they aren't reviewed at all. Nonetheless, you can't take any chances with your cover letter. There are many recruiters and hiring managers that will look to the cover letters when faced with several applicants that have similar resumes. You'll need to craft a cover letter that effectively introduces your resume, explains your interest in the specific position and the company, and highlights exactly what you can contribute to the role. Don't write one cover letter for several different jobs; make sure every cover letter you send out is job specific.

Together, your resume and cover letter introduce your qualifications to recruiters and hiring managers. Remember the list of attributes we mentioned at the beginning of the chapter? The person reviewing your resume and cover letter will have these qualities in mind and will be actively looking for evidence you've demonstrated them in the past. To give you an idea of how this works, we've listed a few of the key success factors below, along with the questions recruiters will most likely be asking themselves as they review your application materials:

- **Communication skills.**

  Is your resume well written? Is your cover letter (or cover message) thoughtfully prepared, tactfully worded, and customized to the position for which you are applying? Does your correspondence strike the appropriate balance between confidence and deference? Are your resume and cover letter both flawless, or are they riddled with typos and grammatical errors?

- **Teamwork, interpersonal, and leadership skills.**

  Have your prior work experiences, academic pursuits, and extracurricular activities required you to work in teams? Do your extracurricular activities and outside interests require a high degree of interpersonal interaction? Does your resume include evidence of your leadership ability? Do any of your credentials suggest you are adept at motivating and persuading others?

- **Strong work ethic, motivation, and initiative.**

  Does your resume show you've successfully juggled multiple priorities? Are you actively involved in extracurricular activities (or, if you've already graduated, do you consistently pursue interests outside of work)? Does your resume list achievements that suggest you're both self-motivated and committed to excellence? Have you demonstrated that you consistently provide a high-quality service or work product to classmates, colleagues, and managers?

The resume: Getting started

If you've attended a resume-writing workshop or picked up a reference book on the topic, you probably already know that people who receive resumes don't spend a whole lot of time reviewing each one—at least in the initial screening process. The exact amount of time and energy that's devoted to reviewing your credentials obviously varies depending on the person who's reading your resume, but a seasoned recruiter probably spends less than 30 seconds deciding your fate.

It might strike you as miserably unfair that you must spend so much time writing, revising, and perfecting your resume while the person who receives it spends less than 30 seconds looking at it—and may not even read it at all. The good news is that a thoughtfully written resume can convey an image of who you are, what you're capable of, and how you have used your capabilities to accomplish results—all in 30 seconds or less.

If this seems like a lot to accomplish, remember there are ample resources available to get you started. If you're a student, take advantage of the services your on-campus career placement office provides. Many of them compile binders of resumes from current and former students, which you can consult to get ideas. Once you've been inspired to write your own, you can schedule a resume consultation or attend the resume- and cover-letter-writing workshops offered by many campus career centers. Discussing your experiences and qualifications with an expert—particularly if you've never drafted a resume before—can help you figure out what information to include and how to package it in an effective way. Even if you already have a working copy of your resume, it never hurts to have a second (and more objective) pair of eyes on your work.

Whether you're a student or not, it's worth asking family and friends—especially those who are already working in the industry you hope to break into—for guidance. They may even be willing to send you the resumes they used to land their current positions. At the very least, they'll be able to give you an honest assessment of whether your resume is well written, error-free, and easy to understand. As a rule, successful job-seekers take all of the help they can get when it comes to "packaging" themselves for prospective employers, so don't be afraid to ask for help!

Resume content

An effective resume has—at most—three sections: "education," "experience," and (sometimes) a third section for relevant information that doesn't fit into either of the other two categories. The optional third section goes a few by different names: "activities," "additional information," "interests," "other," or "personal," depending on what you've included in the section. The order in which the sections appear usually depends on how much work experience you've got; if you are still in school or if you are a recent graduate, the education section should come first unless your professional experience is uniquely relevant and warrants emphasis (for example, you were a summer intern at the firm to which you're applying). If you're more than a few years out of school, the "experience" section should come first. The longer you've been out of school, the less resume space your education section should occupy. After a few years, you'll need to include only the basic information (institution, degrees conferred, honors awarded, and year graduated). Information on your grades, extracurricular activities, and research projects will eventually get bumped off the page in favor of a beefier experience section. If you include an "other" section, it should always appear last.

Some resume books—and career-planning offices at some colleges and universities—suggest that candidates include an objective, overview, or summary at the top of the resume, immediately after the candidate's name and contact information. However well intentioned the advice, we suggest you leave it out; your resume should already be a concise snapshot of your professional and academic experience to date, so it's redundant to summarize it even further. A career objective doesn't need to take up valuable real estate on your resume, either. If you're not applying for a particular job but are sending your resume to indicate your interest in an organization, it's virtually impossible to write an objective with the appropriate level of specificity. Resume objectives that are too broad not only end up sounding silly ("To be gainfully employed by a respectable firm so that I can afford to live in the city of my choice while avoiding incarceration and simultaneously utilizing my interpersonal, analytical, and leadership skills as well as my corporate wardrobe") but they don't really tell the reader anything useful. At the other end of the spectrum, including an objective that is too specific introduces the risk you'll be knocked out of consideration if there are no available openings that meet your criteria. If you are responding to an advertised job posting, it should be fairly obvious that your objective is getting that job—otherwise, why would you be applying for it? Your interest in a particular firm or your intention to apply for a specific job can instead be outlined in your cover letter.

The optional third section

The question of whether to include a third section ("activities," "interests," "other," or "personal") is one over which reasonable people can disagree. If you're still in school or have graduated within the past year, you're probably fairly safe including a section on the extracurricular activities you've pursued in college. Otherwise, stick to information that's relevant to the position for which you're applying or that distinguishes you in some way from other candidates (professional associations or memberships, for example, or proficiency in one or more foreign languages). The issue of whether to include personal interests or hobbies is another gray area; as a general rule, those that are fairly common (cooking, travel, jogging, and reading, for example) probably won't win you any points because they appear in resumes so frequently. Lines like "traveled extensively through Europe" almost never achieve their desired effect for the same reason. They won't disqualify you from consideration by any means, but they're unlikely to advance your candidacy either. If you're trying to choose which items to include in this section, include the ones most likely to pique the genuine interest of the recruiter. Review the resume section of this chapter profiles for insight.

Resume format

Now that you've figured out the type of information you'll include in your resume, you'll need to package it in a clean, easy-to-read, and error-free way. Keep in mind that conformity is a good thing when it comes to resume formatting: Anyone who picks up your resume should immediately be able to identify the two main sections (education and experience), and, within each of those sections, it should be easy for the reader to understand your achievements and qualifications. Adding too many stylistic bells and whistles—or packing your resume too tightly—just makes it more difficult for the recruiter to identify your credentials. To make your resume easy on the eyes, keep these resume format basics in mind:

- Keep it to one page. Writing a resume requires careful consideration of which achievements warrant mention, which can be described more concisely, and which should be scrapped altogether.

- Stick to a single, easy-to-read font (Times New Roman and Helvetica are safe choices) in a legible font size (10 to 12 points).

- Use one-inch margins on all sides; don't try to "buy" more space by shrinking the margins.

- Label major sections (education, experience, and other) clearly and leave line spaces between them.

- Write in bullets, not paragraphs. Recruiters won't take the time to weed through densely packed prose. Use the active voice rather than the passive voice, leave out first-person pronouns, use qualifying adjectives and adverbs sparingly, and keep dependent clauses to a minimum—it will help keep your writing focused, action-oriented, and concise.

- Use boldface type, italics, or small caps sparingly. Overusing these features defeats the purpose of calling attention to critical information.

- Within each of the major sections, use a reverse chronological listing Either the name of the organization or the dates worked should appear on the left (your approach should be consistent throughout the resume).

- For hard copies of your resume (these are a dying breed, but you still need to take a few copies with you when you interview), use high-quality bond paper in white or off-white.

The Magic Bullet

Make no mistake about it: Writing a resume is not the same as writing one of those family newsletters you stuff into holiday cards at the end of the year (and if you don't send these, chances are you know someone who does). You know the letters we're talking about: the ones that typically feature self-indulgent use of the third-person perspective and lots of unnecessary exclamation points. Your resume is a far more objective, achievement-driven, results-oriented summary of your qualifications in which the bullet point—not the sentence or the paragraph—is the primary component. To help you make sure your bullets hit their targets, we've consulted career-management expert and author Douglas B. Richardson, who offers these tips for making your resume stand out from the crowd:

- **Don't overdo qualifying adjectives.**

  Descriptions of "major contributions," "dynamic programs" and "significant improvements" aren't objective reality. They're the writer's opinion and are discounted as such. Use high-action adverbs sparingly, too—words like "aggressively," "proactively," and "progressively."

- **Avoid the use of "wimpy" verbs.**

  Use verbs to communicate action and achievement: Manage. Execute. Analyze. Create. Organize. Let the other drip be the one who "aidod," "participated in" or "helped bring about."

- **Emphasize your past achievements by using titles, numbers, and names.**

  Titles show that someone else had enough faith in you to invest you with responsibility. That proves something, and yet many people leave it out.

- **Quantify your achievements wherever you can.**

  Numbers serve two functions. First, they show magnitude of achievement. The person who "increased plant output 156 percent in seven months" is more impressive than the one who merely "increased productivity." "Managed technical-design staff of 350" is better proof of your skills than "headed engineering group." Second, numbers offer concrete evidence that's rarely questioned.

- **Names carry clout the same way numbers do.**

  IBM isn't a "major data processing firm." It's IBM. Working there isn't the same as working at Marty's Software Heaven. Imagine if George Washington's resume simply stated: "Played significant role in planning and implementation of major country."

- **But if you can't rely on name alone, provide a description.**

  Descriptions such as "*Fortune* 100 Company" or "world's largest shoelace maker" can make an enormous difference in how you—and the quality of your achievements—are perceived.[1]

One size does *not* fit all

If you are job hunting in more than one field, or considering different types of positions within the same field, you will need to have more than one version of your resume. For example, let's assume you are applying for two jobs: one as an account representative at an advertising agency and one as an editorial assistant at a publishing house. For each position, you need to emphasize different skills. For the

1 Douglas B. Richardson. "Skeptical Resume Reader Tells How He Really Thinks." *CareerJournal*. July 30, 2001. www.careerjournal.com.

account rep job, you'll need to emphasize your interpersonal, communication, sales, and marketing skills. For the editorial assistant slot, you'll need to stress your attention to detail, ability to work under deadline pressure, and skills as a proofreader. Naturally, there will be some overlap between the two resumes, but the thrust of each should be very different. You should also have a more generic version of your resume available, which you can use for networking purposes. This will come in handy when you meet a contact who wants to know more about your background but isn't necessarily offering you any kind of employment opportunity.

Electronic resumes

Once you've crafted the perfect resume, you'll need to save three electronic versions of it. That way, you'll be ready to send off your resume regardless of whether it needs to be e-mailed as an attachment, in plain text in the body of an e-mail, or uploaded onto an online database.

- **Microsoft Word (or other word-processing software) document.** This is the version of your resume that you'll e-mail to hiring personnel when you're instructed to send it as an attachment. It's also the one you'll print out and take with you on interviews. Though the days of sending a hard copy of your resume by FedEx are all but over, this is the version you'll use if need to send a paper copy for any reason.

- **ASCII format with line breaks:** ASCII (American Standard Code of Interchange) allows databases and data recognition software to read your resume without the confusion caused by formatting. The "with line breaks" option is critical for e-mailed resumes because there is no standard e-mail program that everyone uses; if the recipient's e-mail program doesn't automatically wrap line breaks, your resume could appear as a single line of horizontal text on the receiving end. By clicking the "insert line breaks" option, you'll avoid this potential problem. Your word-processing software will force line breaks so that no single line will exceed 65 characters of text. In Microsoft Word, use the "save as" tab, save your resume (name it differently from the first version), and save the file as plain text. When the dialogue box appears, choose "other encoding" and select US-ASCII. Also click the "insert line breaks" checkbox.

- **ASCII format without line breaks:** Use this format when you're instructed to upload your resume to an online database and to cut and paste into preset fields. Unlike the version you'll paste into the body of an e-mail, the version for web-based forms should not have forced line breaks (the text should wrap instead). Why is this? Because if you copy and paste a plain-text resume to an online application form and it has line breaks manually inserted, the end result will be a jagged effect. Each webmaster has a different default setting for how many characters constitute a single line of text, so if your resume exceeds this limit, your resume will look terrible. If you create an ASCII resume without line breaks, the text will instead "wrap," which means you won't have to manually reformat your resume once you've pasted it in the appropriate box. In order to save a version of your resume suitable for online application forms, follow the directions for "ASCII format with line breaks" above, but skip the last step.

Joanna C. Bloggs

Present address
903 Laurel Drive, Apt. #5C
Princeton, NJ 08648
609-555-7124
E-mail address: joanna@bloggs.net

Permanent address
1234 Hollyhock Lane
West Chester, PA 19382
610-555-7089

EDUCATION

Princeton University   Princeton, NJ • GPA: 3.9
- BA expected June 2005. Double major in history and English. Extensive course work (approximately 15 credits each) in Business/Management and Public Policy Departments.
- Secretary of Class of 2005. Elected by peers to plan activities that promote class spirit and unity among 1,200 undergraduates. Head publicity committee to promote major class events.

Henderson High School   West Chester, PA • GPA: 4.0
Graduated May 2001. Class valedictorian. National Merit Scholar. Completed Advanced Placement courses in English, calculus, physics, and Spanish.

WORK EXPERIENCE

Crane Communications   New York, NY
Public Relations Intern
Summer 2004
- Worked with senior account executives to manage relationships with clients in emerging high technology and health care industries.
- Assisted with the writing, editing, production, and distribution of press materials, including press releases and fact sheets.
- Conducted account-related research and compiled findings into complete coverage reports.
- Developed and maintained media lists and editorial calendars.
- Collaborated with office staff to devise publicity strategy and coordinate publicity logistics for major client events.

Chester County Community Center   **West Chester, PA**
Director of Youth Programs
Summer 2003
- Led the start-up and development of a youth volunteer program that connects 50 high schools with community organizations in need of volunteers.
- Conducted extensive research to identify participating community organizations, interview organizations' leadership, and determine their most immediate volunteer needs.
- Created a comprehensive database of area schools that enabled program to effectively match student volunteers and community groups.

Princeton University Library   **Princeton, NJ**
Library Staff
September 2001–May 2002
- Managed front desk and circulation records.
- Worked part-time while completing first year of college. Worked an average of 10–15 hours per week while maintaining a full course load.

PERSONAL

- High degree of competency in written and spoken Spanish (founded high school Spanish club; received first-place honors at State Declamation Foreign Language Championships, 2000).
- Demonstrated interest in community-service initiatives (president of high school volunteer organization; honored at 15th Annual Volunteer Awards of Chester County).

After you've spent hours tinkering with your resume to make it a visual masterpiece, you might cringe at the thought of saving it—and sending it, for that matter—in an ASCII format. Don't despair—you can minimize the damage by taking the following steps:

- Replace bullets with asterisks (*).

- Offset category headings with a row of tildes (~), a row of equal signs (=), or capital letters.

- Change your margin settings to 2 inches; 60 characters (including spaces) is the maximum line length. Setting a wider margin allows you to control where the line breaks occur.

- Select a fixed-width typeface like Courier and use a 12-point font size.

- Add white space for readability.

- Do a test run. Send a copy to a friend—or yourself—over e-mail to see how it looks.

JOANNA C. BLOGGS

Present address:
903 Laurel Drive, Apt. #5C
Princeton, NJ 08648
609-555-7124
E-mail address: joanna@bloggs.net

Permanent address:
1234 Hollyhock Lane
West Chester, PA 19382
610-555-7089

EDUCATION

Princeton University
Princeton, NJ
- BA expected June 2005.
- Double major in history and English.
- Extensive course work (approximately 15 credits each) in Business/ Management and Public Policy Departments.
- Secretary of Class of 2005. Elected by peers to plan activities that promote class spirit and unity among 1200 undergraduates. Head publicity committee to promote major class events.
- GPA: 3.9.

Henderson High School
West Chester, PA
- Graduated May 2001.
- Class valedictorian. National Merit Scholar. Completed Advanced Placement courses in English, calculus, physics, and Spanish.
- GPA: 4.0.

WORK EXPERIENCE

Crane Communications
New York, NY
Public Relations Intern
Summer 2004
- Worked with senior account executives to manage relationships with clients in emerging high technology and health care industries.
- Assisted with the writing, editing, production, and distribution of press materials, including press releases and fact sheets.
- Conducted account-related research and compiled findings into complete coverage reports.
- Developed and maintained media lists and editorial calendars.
- Collaborated with office staff to devise publicity strategy and coordinate publicity logistics for major client events.

Chester County Community Center
West Chester, PA
Director of Youth Programs
Summer of 2002
- Led the start-up and development of a youth volunteer program that connects 50 high schools with community organizations in need of volunteers.
- Conducted extensive research to identify participating community organizations, interview organizations' leadership, and determine their most immediate volunteer needs.
- Created a comprehensive database of area schools that enabled program to effectively match student volunteers and community groups.

Princeton University Library
Princeton, NJ
Library Staff
September 2001–May 2002
- Managed front desk and circulation records.
- Worked part-time while completing first year of college. Worked an average of 10–15 hours per week while maintaining a full course load.

PERSONAL
- High degree of competency in written and spoken Spanish (founded high school Spanish club; received first-place honors at State Declamation Foreign Language Championships, 2000).
- Demonstrated interest in community-service initiatives (president of high school volunteer organization; honored at 15th Annual Volunteer Awards of Chester County).

Cover letters

If you were to conduct a survey of recruiters and hiring managers, you'd probably be hard-pressed to find one who could remember a truly exceptional cover letter (or an exceptionally good cover letter, anyway). The truth of the matter is that cover letters are rarely read closely. As we mentioned earlier, they're more frequently skimmed. In fact, a cover letter is a little bit like a passport photo: Having a really good one is nice, but it isn't going to get you anywhere unless your other paperwork is in order. You can't get very far if you don't have one at all, though, and having a bad one is just plain embarrassing. In short, it's worth taking the time to make sure yours is great.

Your cover letter doesn't need to be a literary masterpiece, but it does need to be concise, well written, polite, at least somewhat personalized, and error-free. "We get so many applications from people claiming to be great writers and editors," says Diane, an HR professional at a magazine publishing company. "I'm always shocked at how many of them include poorly written cover letters with multiple typos." Not only should your resume be flawless, but it should include all the required information: the position to which you're applying, the primary reason for your interest, and a brief overview of the one or two qualifications that make you a compelling candidate. At the end of the letter, you should (politely, never presumptuously) suggest a possible next step—usually a brief telephone conversation or an in-person meeting.

By the time you've covered each of these points, you'll probably have reached the desired cover-letter length: no more than one page in hard copy, and no more than one screen shot if you're sending your resume via e-mail. The following guidelines will help you ensure that your cover letter gets the job done:

- **Address it to a particular person by name.** Be sure to indicate how you obtained that person's contact information. If you were roforrod by someone who already works at the company, mention that person's name early on; when a recruiter scans a cover letter or e-mail, he's more likely to take the time to review your credentials if he recognizes a colleague's name in the text.

- **Keep it brief.** Remember that the purpose of the cover letter is to set the stage for your resume, not to explain anything on it—or worse, repeat it. The longer your cover letter, the more likely the recruiter is to skim it (which effectively defeats the purpose of including more detail). This is not the forum to explain the genesis of every academic or professional decision you've made to date, nor is it the place to regurgitate your resume in clunky, densely packed prose.

- **While we're on the topic of regurgitating,** we should point out that the cover letter isn't the place to spit content from the company's website—or, even worse, the posted job description— back at the recruiter. While we absolutely recommend that you conduct background research on the company before making contact about a job, paraphrasing information that's readily available on the company's website isn't enough to establish that your interest is sincere. On the other hand, if you've taken the time to speak with current employees or attend an on-campus information session at your college, you can—and absolutely should—describe what in particular sparked your interest.

- **Show you're a giver, not just a taker.** No matter how brief, the cover letter shouldn't be lopsided. While you should mention one or two specific things that have attracted you to the company, you should balance your approach by describing why the company should be attracted to you. Your cover letter should imply that hiring you would be a mutually beneficial decision. Don't just talk about what the company can do for you: Explain what skills and qualifications would enable you to make a positive contribution to the company.

- **Watch your tone, missy.** We know we just told you that your cover letter should describe your potential contributions to the company, but it should do so politely. Scott, who works in the publications office of a major university, recalls an interview in which the hiring manager commended him on the polite cover letter he had sent her by e-mail. "I was surprised that it had made such an impression," he explains. "But she told me I'd be shocked at how many e-mailed cover letters she received that weren't polite or respectful." While you shouldn't be shy about mentioning your achievements and qualifications, you should never assume a presumptuous or self-aggrandizing tone. There's definitely a fine line separating confident and obnoxious—if you're having trouble deciding whether you've navigated it successfully, ask a friend for an objective, third-party assessment.

- **Take the thyme two proofread.** Because hiring managers often don't read cover letters with the same scrutiny they read resumes, you may be tempted relax a little bit when it comes to editing yours. Believe us: It's worth the few extra minutes it will take to make sure that your cover letter is error-free. Use the spell-check function, but don't rely on software alone. Spell-check is famous for letting things like misused contractions (you're vs. your, it's vs. its, etc.) fall through the cracks, and it certainly won't let you know if you've misspelled the name of the company or recruiter (and believe us, a missing comma or hyphen in the company or recruiter's name might just tip the scales against you). Spell-check also won't protect you against the famous "mismerge" that has sealed many a candidate's fate (you've described how your fastidious attention to detail will make you a valuable asset to Random House—in your cover letter to Scholastic).

Sending your resume and cover letter via e-mail

In a relatively short period of time, the prevalence of e-mail has completely transformed the way job candidates communicate with prospective employers. It's easier and faster than ever to send resumes and cover letters, but ensuring that your correspondence is flawless—and that it ends up in the right hands—is no less important. The ease and informality of e-mail can (and often does) trip up job-seekers who forget that the way they communicate—even electronically—creates a first impression that will affect how hiring managers view their candidacy. Don't let this happen to you: put the same care into e-mailed cover letters and follow-up e-mails that you would into any other type of formal correspondence. Because e-mails are transmitted almost instantaneously—and because there's no way to control how quickly or widely they're forwarded—it's virtually impossible to contain the damage the smallest error or impropriety can cause. To play it safe, complete the "To:" field last if you're communicating with a potential employer over e-mail. This way, you're covered if you accidentally click "Send" before your message is ready. Remember, there are no "do-overs" when it comes to e-mails: "Ignore last message!" and "Oops!" e-mails are ineffective and can damage your credibility.

Avoiding the recycle bin

Thanks to the havoc wreaked by both spam and computer viruses, there's no guarantee your message will reach its intended recipient. Many companies use sophisticated spam filters to guard inboxes from suspicious e-mails. Typically, these filters delete suspected spam or divert it into folders that automatically trash e-mails that go unchecked for a certain period of time. In an effort to minimize the serious threat of computer viruses, some companies restrict employees from opening e-mail attachments (including resumes) from external sources. In some cases, their servers may even delete attachments automatically as a precaution.

Overzealous spam filters and stringent external e-mail policies can definitely work against you, so it's critical that you follow the directions when responding to a job posting. If you've been instructed to e-mail your resume as an attachment, use Microsoft Word (or a comparable basic software package). Unless specifically instructed to do so, don't send it as a compressed file or as a PDF. Trust us: If the recipient can't open your file successfully the first time around, she's not going to chase you down to request another one. Make sure to include your name (at least your last name) in the name of the file (e.g., Jane_Doe_resume.doc). Many recruiters and hiring managers save all the resumes they receive for a given position in a specific folder; many also forward resumes to other colleagues or hiring personnel at their organization. A descriptive file name that includes your name ensures that your resume can be easily located and identified regardless of where it lands.

If a company has explicitly instructed applicants not to send e-mail attachments, don't do it. Not only do you run the risk that your message will end up in the recycle bin unopened, but blatantly disregarding the instructions immediately gives the recruiter a reason to eliminate you from consideration. (Trust us: He's already looking for ways to whittle down that inbox, so there's no need to tempt him with another one.) If you can't send it as an attachment, you'll need to send it in the body of your e-mail in plain-text format. It's true that plain-text resumes sent via e-mail aren't the most attractive ones out there, but what they lack in beauty they make up for in reliability. When you don't have specific instructions, sending your resume this way is the safest course of action.

If you're e-mailing your resume, the cover message that introduces it should be in plain text, too. (When you send it in HTML format, there's a slight risk the person on the receiving end won't have an e-mail program that can properly read the HTML formatting—which means they won't be able to read what you've sent. The more significant risk, though, is the spam filter: HTML messages are more likely to trip up spam filters than plain-text messages). Here's how to double-check if you're in plain text format: if you're writing an e-mail in which you can alter the appearance of text— i.e., you can italicize, underline, or change the font—you're *not* in plain text format. Some e-mail providers only allow users to write in plain text; if you're still unsure and you're using Microsoft Outlook, click on "format" in your new message window and be sure that "plain text" is the selected format.

Don't forget about the "Subject" field when sending your application materials. If you're sending your resume in response to an online job posting, you'll often be told exactly what to include in this field. If left to your own devices, remember this: The less your e-mail looks like a spam message, the less likely it will be diverted. With this in mind, never leave this field blank. Instead, include a subject line that is short and descriptive and immediately identifies you as an applicant. If you can, include the job title or requisition number in the subject line (remember that the recruiter receiving your message may be responsible for filling multiple positions). Otherwise, include only your name and the position applied for (e.g., "Zach Glass, Case Manager"). Leave punctuation marks—especially exclamation marks—out of the subject line, and don't use all capital letters in an attempt to grab the recipient's attention.

Finally, you should avoid using words in the subject line—or even in your cover message—that will convince the company's spam-filter technology that your resume belongs in the trash bin, along with e-mails promising enlarged body parts or cheap prescription drugs. You probably have a pretty good idea of what key words we have in mind (if you need a refresher course, take a break from reading this and log in to one of your web-based e-mail accounts). You're unlikely to use most of them in your cover letter or resume (if you need to, you've probably picked up the wrong guide). Still, remember that words like "free," "hard," "offer," "increase," etc. are often used by spammers, so keep them out of your correspondence if you can. If your e-mail address has several numbers to the left of the @ symbol, consider changing it: The numbers could represent something as innocuous as your birthday, anniversary, or the year you graduated from college, but, to a spam filter, they look like the type of tracking code that many spammers use.

As an added safety measure, you may want to ask any personal contact you have within the organization to forward your resume to the appropriate contact. Not only does this increase the odds you'll defeat the spam filter, but internal referrals typically boost your overall credibility as a candidate. If you don't have an internal point person who can forward your resume on your behalf, be sure to run every version of it through a few different spam filters before sending it off; send it to a few friends and family members—and include your own e-mail address or addresses in the CC field—to figure out whether it's going through. This might sound like a lot of trouble, and it is. There is an upside, though, to the omnivorous spam filter: You have a perfectly legitimate reason to follow up with the company and make sure your application materials were received.

"Power Jargon": Learning to talk the talk

Whenever you enter a new industry or company, you'll quickly find that each one has its own unique vernacular you must understand—and eventually adopt. Paying attention to the language insiders use to describe their industry and their specific roles should be part of your job-search preparation. If used subtly and judiciously, incorporating "power jargon" into your resume, cover letter, and interview can help influence the decision-maker in your favor; if you speak someone's language, they'll probably—perhaps subconsciously—consider you one of their own.

Interestingly, the purpose of power jargon is slightly different depending on the stage of the job-search process you're in when you use it. In the context of a resume, the purpose of industry jargon is getting your resume noticed—either by the human being who has the unenviable task of screening through thousands of resumes and deciding which ones make the first cut, or by the nonhuman resume scanner whose job it is to do basically the same thing by identifying and counting specific key words in resumes. In the context of a cover letter or an interview, the purpose is less to get noticed than, ironically enough, to blend in. Once you arrive for your first day of work, the purpose of power jargon is knowing what the heck you're supposed to be doing.

To illustrate the importance of understanding jargon before your first day on the job, consider the experience endured by Monica—now a 30-year-old associate editor—on her first day of freelance proofreading at a food and wine magazine. "I had no idea that in the magazine biz, the term 'hot' means that something is extremely urgent," she says. "So someone came up to my desk and asked me if I'd finished proofreading a particular story. When I said that I hadn't, she politely reminded me that it was 'pretty hot.' Not knowing what she meant—that I needed to get it done ASAP—I thought to myself, 'What's she making such a big deal about? The story's about *coleslaw* for God's sake—what's so trendy about that?'" This is why it's important to do your homework early on in the process—preferably before you make contact with a company about a job.

Understanding the importance of key words, however, doesn't give you license to use them recklessly. Power jargon can be, and often is, overused in resumes, obscuring the very credentials the candidate was hoping to highlight in the first place. If you use jargon without understanding what it means, you may use it in the wrong context and sound uninformed when you intended to sound savvy. Our advice for avoiding potential power-jargon pitfalls? Have someone who's in the know take a look at your resume and cover letter to alert you to any egregious misuses of industry or company terminology. In the interview, play it safe—your goal is to use power jargon to blend in, not stand out. Overusing jargon (or using it in a forced, contrived way) won't win you any points, especially with hiring managers who've logged countless hours interviewing candidates. Not only will experienced interviewers see right through your attempt to sound like an expert, but they'll often go to great lengths to put you back in your place. "That happened to me once," says Thomas, an assistant editor for an academic journal. "I was interviewing for my first editorial job, and I mentioned that I was familiar with the *Chicago Manual of Style*. My interviewer said, 'Oh really? Which edition do you normally use?' I was completely stumped. I had no idea which edition it was—I had to look at my copy when I got home (it was the eleventh, incidentally). Even though I had to admit that I didn't know, I got the job anyway. After a few months in the office, I eventually found out that none of the copy editors knew exactly which version they were using either. The interviewer had just been doing that to rattle my cage, I guess, and figure out whether I was bluffing."

Even though this story has a happy ending, it still offers a valuable lesson: Don't use terminology you don't understand, and if you are asked a question you don't know the answer to, just say that you don't know. If your interviewer calls your bluff, you've not only lost face, but you've potentially lost a job. It's not worth the risk.

What's the magic word?

In the 1991 remake of the film *Father of the Bride,* Steve Martin's character, George, snoops through the home of his future son-in-law's parents, only to be confronted by a pair of growling, snarling Rottweilers who seem poised to eat him alive. He knows there's a one-word command that will make them go away, but he can't quite remember what it is—only that it begins with "re." He tries a few: "Relent. Re-Recoil . . . reverse," but they only make the dogs angrier. (The word he was looking for was release). As George found out with the attack dogs, using correct keywords is important. For him, it meant he wouldn't get devoured; for you, it means your resume won't get discarded because you appear not to have experience relevant to a particular job.

Keywords are almost always nouns or short phrases. They name the characteristics, skills, tools, training, and experience of a successful candidate for a particular job. As you may already know, many organizations use resume-scanning software to identify qualified candidates among a sea of online applications; by scanning resumes for certain words and phrases, scanning software is intended to streamline the resume review process for time-starved recruiters, who may receive literally thousands of applications for a single job posting. If your target company uses this type of software as a preliminary screening tool, you'll want to be sure your resume includes the relevant key words. The number of "hits" (times the key words appear in any given resume) will often determine which resumes are actually read by a human being.

How do you know which keywords to include? Writing a resume in a scanner-friendly way is definitely more of an art than a science—and it requires common sense, good judgment, and a little bit of research. Before you submit a resume online, visit the company's website and pay attention to the language used to describe what the company does, what it's looking for in potential employees, and the job requirements it lists for specific positions; the job description and the list of qualifications associated with the position are also great resources when tailoring and tweaking the version of the resume you use.

As is the case with any job-search advice we provide in this guide, it's best to temper your enthusiasm for power jargon with a healthy dose of good judgment. Particularly if you're applying for a position through an on-campus recruiting process or through an internal referral that forwards your correspondence directly to the hiring manager, your resume may be initially reviewed by a human being—not a scanner.

A rose by any other name . . . might be something else entirely

To make matters even more complicated, there are a couple of different levels of jargon you'll need to weed through to use it effectively. There's both industry jargon and company-specific jargon. At the industry level, seemingly identical processes or functions will be described differently depending on the industry in question. For example, book publishing uses different terminology than magazine publishing, and academic and financial publishing each use a different lexicon entirely. If you looked at a "blueline" (the last version of a publication editors have a chance to review before it goes to print) at a magazine publisher, you'd be looking at the "blues," but if you looked at one at an investment bank, you'd probably be looking at a "red." If you say "blackline" instead of "blueline" because you worked at a law firm one summer and you're still in the habit of saying it, you're going to look pretty silly in your maga-zine-publishing interview.

At the organizational level, power jargon might include something as seemingly insignificant as the use of acronyms and abbreviations (and it seems the larger the organization, the more acronyms there are to remember). The names of groups, func-tions, even job titles may be abbreviated so widely within an organization that you'll stand out if you don't use them when you communicate with your potential employer.

Is your head spinning yet? Don't worry. When it comes to power jargon, there are plenty of ways to pick it up so you're at least conversational by the time you apply for a job. When you speak with industry insiders in the context of networking or con-ducting informational interviews, pay attention to the terminology they use to describe what they do and where they work. (In fact, the ability to pick up on power jargon is one of the many good reasons you should be focused on listening rather than talking when it comes to informational interviews). If your industry insider uses a term you're not familiar with, don't just nod as though you are—ask what it means! Remember, you're not being evaluated during your informational interviews or net-working conversations; you're there to learn and ask questions. And if stopping to ask what something means during one of these conversations means you actually know what it means when it comes up later in a job interview, then asking was a worth-while investment. In addition to one-on-one conversations with insiders, you can pick up power jargon by paying attention to the lingo used in trade publications, on indus-try-specific websites, and in job listings for similar positions at other companies in the industry.

When it comes time to interview with a specific company, your understanding of that organization's terminology is just as important as your fluency in industry lingo. Before you walk out the door to meet with your prospective employer, you should understand the jargon the company uses in the following contexts:

- **Its name**—Know when a company goes by its initials and when it's abbreviated some other way when its own employees refer to it. We'll illustrate our point using an example from the financial services world: If you were working on Wall Street, you would never call Goldman Sachs or Merrill Lynch "GS" or "ML." If you were an employee—or an industry insider—you'd refer to them as "Goldman" and "Merrill," respectively. However, you would refer to Credit Suisse First Boston as "CSFB."

- **Its job titles**—If everyone at a particular firm always says "RA" instead of "Research Associate," it will ever so subtly work in your favor if you refer to the job that way too (even though it still might mean "Resident Advisor" to you). The same goes for support roles—sometimes, assistants are just that: assistants. At other organizations, they're called "admins" or "PAs." If you're applying for one of those jobs, know what you'll be called (how else will you know when someone's talking to you?)

- **Its organizational structure and hierarchy**—It sounds almost silly, but pay attention to how employees and insiders refer to the specific department with which you're interviewing. Is the custom publishing department referred to as "custom pub?" Is the book publishing division referred to as "BPD" or simply "books"? Even more importantly, how are roles and job titles described? At some companies, "analyst" is a more senior role than "associate," for example, while at others, the exact opposite is true. Know which level and job title would apply to you; if you don't, your ignorance might be misinterpreted as an inflated ego.

INTERVIEWING

If the primary purpose of a great resume is to get an interview (which it is), then it seems as though the point of the interview would be to land the job. In reality, that's only half right. One of your goals during the interview process is to tell a compelling story—to present your life (educational, extracurricular, and otherwise) as an entirely logical series of decisions in which this particular job is the obvious next step. The other (equally, if not more important) objective is to learn as much as possible about the position for which you're applying, the culture of the organization you're interviewing with, and the extent to which the job fits with your personal and professional goals.

Because you're working hard to present yourself in the best possible light, it's easy to forget that interviews aren't entirely unilateral. When you're being grilled about your resume, your motivations, and your choices, it will undoubtedly seem as though your prospective employer is the one calling the shots, but the interview is also a chance for you to learn about the organization and the position you're applying for. It's the best opportunity you have, prior to your first day on the job, to fill in any gaps between the pieces of info you gleaned through networking and informational interviews. It's your chance to ask questions, to get a sense of whether or not the organization's culture is one in which you'll fit, and to figure out whether the specific position is one in which you'll be challenged and rewarded for your efforts.

In this section, we'll give you suggestions for making the most out of your interviews. We'll tell you what interviewers will be looking for during your conversations, and we'll describe the types of interview questions they're most likely to ask as they evaluate you. We'll also tell to you how to prepare for interviews—how to anticipate the topics (and questions) you're most likely to confront and how to craft compelling responses. And, along the way, we'll give you practical advice—guidance on everything from arriving on time to wearing the right shoes—so you can truly put your best foot forward.

What are interviewers looking for?

Earlier in this section, we listed the personal characteristics organizations value most in potential employees. The list is intended to be a starting point for your interview preparation; it stands to reason that the relative importance assigned to each of these attributes will vary significantly depending on the industry, the company, and the specific job you're interviewing for. You may even find, when you interview with multiple people for a single position, that each interviewer emphasizes slightly different things. Across the board, however, the people who interview you are basically trying to answer three questions as they evaluate your candidacy:

- Are you capable of doing the work?
- Do you really *want* to do the work?
- Would they enjoy working with you?

As a general rule, the less directly applicable your past experience is to the job you're hoping to get, the more emphasis your interviewer is likely to place on the first question. If you've more or less proven your ability to do the work through similar professional, academic, or extracurricular activities, your interviewer is more likely to probe the second two.

Recruiters will be on the lookout for certain intangible qualities throughout the entire interview too: qualities like confidence, conviction, enthusiasm, poise, presence, and sincerity. For example, do your eyes light up when you talk about your educational background, your professional experience, or (most importantly) the role for which you are interviewing? Do your answers sound heartfelt and impassioned, or is it obvious you've rehearsed them so many times you could recite them in your sleep? Are you comfortable and self-assured talking about your background and accomplishments, or does self-confidence quickly disintegrate into self-consciousness as soon as you step into the interview room? Interviewers don't necessarily measure these intangibles through specific questions, but rather through their well-honed intuition.

Preparing for your interview

Whether you realize it or not, you can predict the vast majority of the questions you will hear during an interview—provided, of course, you've done your homework on the industry, the organization, and the position you've got your eye on. Some questions (e.g., "Why are you interested in this job?") arise so frequently in one form or another you'd be foolish not to take the time to outline your responses well in advance. Though no amount of preparation will enable you to predict the questions verbatim, you can predict the themes the interview is likely to cover. Nine times out of ten, you're going to be asked to discuss the following:

- Why you are interested in this type of work, and why you want to work with this organization specifically
- How your academic, extracurricular, and/or professional background relates to the job for which you're applying

- The extent to which you've developed realistic expectations about the job you're considering, and whether or not you know enough about the company to make an informed decision about joining it
- Whether certain gaps or inconsistencies on your resume are likely to turn into vulnerabilities on the job

Know Your Achilles' Heel

So how do you know which part of your application is likely to be perceived as a gap or inconsistency? It really depends on the nature and level of the job you're applying for; hopefully, your informational interviews will have shed some light on the gaps that might exist between the ideal set of credentials and your own (if not, the job posting and/or description will certainly provide some clues). But across industries and jobs, there are a few common red flags that might raise questions about your ability and desire to do the work. If any of these apply to you, give some thought to how you might address them in your interview:

- **Disparity between professional/academic background and desired job**

  This is the most obvious—and perhaps the most prevalent—of all the instant red flags. If the position for which you're applying bears little or no resemblance to the work you've done in the past—or to the work you're currently doing—then your prospective employer will probably ask a few questions. They'll go something like this: If you really want to do this type of work and are so well suited to do it, then why haven't you done it already? Or, at the very least, why haven't you studied it? To be completely honest, these are perfectly legitimate questions.

- **Time gaps**

  Keep in mind that the person reviewing your resume might check to see if you've taken off between school years or jobs. Time off is not necessarily a bad thing. Recruiters know that while you're building a career, life can pull you in other directions: people start families, spouses get relocated, family members get sick, and professionals take time off to consider a career change or simply recharge their batteries. Still, you need to be prepared to explain any lapses. You needn't feel compelled to offer a lot of personal detail, but you should be honest, direct, and prepared if questions about time gaps arise. In your response, focus on what you accomplished during that time—not the ground you lost by taking a break.

- **Inconsistent or poor academic performance**

  This includes lower-than-average GPA, test scores, or grades in specific classes. If your accomplishments appear strong in one area but weak in another, you should expect questions about the disparity. The interviewer will want to know the reason behind any low grades (did you work part-time during school?) or a discrepancy between your GPA and standardized test scores. Be prepared to explain any circumstances that affected your performance, but avoid undue personal detail.

- **Job (or major-) "hopping"**

  If your resume includes seemingly disparate work experiences, or if you've been at several companies in just a few years, you risk being perceived as a job-hopper. This is unlikely to be much of an issue if you're still in school, but keep in mind that switching majors multiple times might be viewed with comparable skepticism. Frequent course changes (of either the professional or academic variety) sometimes give the impression that a person has difficulty sticking with a situation, working through problems, or committing to a job. If you're applying for a job when you've only been at your current one for a short period of time, prospective employers might wonder if you're likely to jump ship if they hire you too. If your jobs to date have been short-term by nature (because they've been summer jobs or internships), make sure you've stated that clearly somewhere on your application.

- **Geographic concerns**

  If you've spent most of your academic and professional life in one place, you may be questioned about your interest in a job that's somewhere else. Not only will a company probably question whether you're serious about relocating if you're offered the job, but they have practical and logistical issues to consider when it comes to interviewing you in person. A firm that must fly you out for an interview will probably quiz you over the phone to gauge your level of commitment before extending an invitation. Firms also know there's a good chance you may decide not to relocate even if you get the offer—and if you do, it'll probably take some time before you can physically move yourself to your new city and get settled in. All in all, an out-of-town candidate is generally considered a riskier—and potentially costlier—prospect than an applicant close to home.

You'll probably find that thinking of your interview as a conversation intended to address these themes is more effective than thinking of it as a series of questions for which scripted and rehearsed answers are expected. You'll be able to adapt quickly to different interviewing styles and formats, and you won't be thrown off when asked a question you didn't expect.

In the following pages, we'll give you a number of sample questions that tend to arise across industries and companies. Don't let the number of questions overwhelm you—you're not expected to prepare a scripted answer to every possible question, or to memorize the list of interview do's and don'ts. In fact, if you take away only one thing from the following pages, it should be this: *Knowing the job for which you are applying—and knowing exactly how your experiences and achievements relate to that position—is the single most important thing you can do to prepare for job interviews.*

Types of interview questions

Even though most interviewers will be trying to gather the same kind of information, the format of the questions will vary significantly depending on the job, the interviewing philosophy of the organization, and the person sitting across the desk from you. We've outlined the three most common types of interview questions below:

- **Resume-based questions**

  No surprises here: Resume-based questions focus on the one-page life summary that landed you the interview. It goes without saying, but we'll say it anyway: You must know your resume inside and out, and you should be ready to talk intelligently and confidently about anything and everything on it. Arrive at your interview with two or three talking points about each line item on your resume. If there's something particularly unusual on it (e.g., you wrote a novel while you were an undergraduate student, you speak seven languages), you can be sure it will come up again and again. Consider the points you'd most like to convey, and make sure you know them cold. If you're asked to summarize your resume, stick to just that: a summary. Use your response as an opportunity to connect the dots (especially if the story wouldn't be obvious to someone reviewing your resume for the first time), not as an invitation to cram in all of the information you couldn't fit onto one page.

- **Behavioral questions**

  Other questions require you to cite experiences—professional, academic, and personal—in which you've actively demonstrated specific attributes. This approach is called behavioral interviewing, and it's based on the premise that patterns of past behavior most accurately predict future performance. Advocates of behavioral interviewing report that the technique enables interviewers to most accurately assess whether a candidate possesses the requisite skills and personality for on-the-job success. The logic is appealing: Anyone can rattle off a list of attributes commonly sought by employers in their field, but successful candidates can readily substantiate these claims with examples of competency in a given area. A behavioral prompt would be: "Tell me about a time that you took on a responsibility that perhaps wasn't part of your official job description." In response, you could choose to point out that at your previous job you designed a comprehensive training program for new employees, organized guest speakers, and gathered feedback when the program was over to gauge how effective its participants thought it was. Or you might choose to highlight your involvement in a freshman-year economics study group, in which you took up the flag for an ailing team member and wrote a presentation that technically fell outside the scope of your assigned duties. Either example works, as long as it shows that you've taken initiative in the past.

With this in mind, don't simply compartmentalize your achievements into "work experiences," "educational background," "extracurricular activities," and "personal interests" as you prepare for interviews. Instead, think about each of your endeavors in terms of the skills, abilities, and attributes it enables you to demonstrate. For example, which ones helped you develop a strong team-player mentality? How about exceptional leadership skills? Which ones demonstrate your quantitative aptitude and your facility with numbers? Which ones show that you can learn from your mistakes? We've said it before, but we'll say it again: You should know your resume inside and out, and have an arsenal of experiences ready that can prove you're a rock star in any number of areas.

- **Case interview questions**

    For years, management consulting firms have used case interview questions as part of their recruiting processes. Designed to gauge candidates' problem-solving skills and general business acumen, these questions are a more highly evolved version of the word problems you were introduced to in 3rd-grade math class. But even if you're not interviewing for jobs in management consulting, you're not necessarily off the hook where these types of questions are concerned. For better or worse, companies in many industries serve up their own version of the case interview question, hoping to approximate the demands of the job to whatever extent possible in an interview setting. If it's a research job you're interviewing for, you may be asked to walk your interviewer through a hypothetical research project, explaining the steps you would take to complete the assigned task. If the position requires a great deal of public speaking, you shouldn't be caught off guard if you're asked to make an impromptu presentation on a given topic. Not surprisingly, writing, editing, and proofreading tests are often administered as part of the interview process for publishing jobs. Part of your research process should involve figuring out what those tests are likely to be.

Tips for winning interviews

In the following pages, we provide hypothetical interview questions covering a range of topics and themes. There are a few interview best practices, however, that transcend boundaries of interview question category, context, and scope. Keep the following guidelines in mind regardless of the particular questions interviewers lob your way:

- **Honesty is the best policy.**

  This little nugget is definitely one to remember during interviews. As you may have heard when you were a child, when you tell one lie, you have to tell five more lies to cover up the first one. For each of those lies, you have to tell five more, and so on. Sound advice, to be sure; interviews are stressful enough when you're telling the truth, so don't make it harder on yourself by coloring the edges of your resume with fictional experiences, skills, or interests. The truth almost always prevails in the end, so don't tempt fate by bending it—even a little.

- **Be honest, but emphasize the positive.**

  Being honest about your screw-ups and weaknesses doesn't mean that you can't spin them in a positive direction. If you're asked about a perceived weakness or mistake, you can be candid while emphasizing what you've learned from each experience. You can use the infamous "What's your biggest weakness?" question, for example, to prove that you're constantly working to overcome your Achilles' heel (or, better yet, you could provide a specific example of an instance in which you overcame it).

- **Remember the three C's.**

  No matter how much you've prepared for your interviews, make sure your responses are conversational, casual, and concise. While we can't overemphasize the importance of researching the industry, organization, and position before you arrive—and anticipating the interview questions you're most likely to confront— you shouldn't give the impression you're reading your interview responses off of cue cards. In fact, if you sound too rehearsed your interviewer may suspect you've got something to hide. Remember: "canned" is not one of the three C's.

- **Answer the question you've been asked.**

  We know it sounds obvious, but it's easier said than done (particularly if you're a rambler). If you're immersed in a full-time job search, chances are you'll have more interviews than you'd care to remember. Some candidates get so accustomed to fielding certain questions that they become robotic: They hear a few key words and they're off on their unintentionally well-rehearsed pitch. Interviews will indeed begin to sound the same, but don't forget to listen to the question!

- **Keep it short and sweet.**

On a related note, keep it brief. If you ramble, you're considerably more likely to lose your way—and more likely to exhaust your interviewer in the process! Remember, it's easier for an interviewer to ask a follow up question than it is for her to rein you back in after you've gone off on a tangent.

- **Pay attention to your interviewer's style.**

A one-size-fits-all approach doesn't work especially well during the interview process; even within the same company, interviewers adopt substantially different styles to figure out whether you're a good candidate for the job. Some are more intense, while others treat the interview as a more relaxed, get-to-know-you session. The more promptly you can pick up on your interviewer's particular style, the better off you'll be, so pay attention.

- **Don't be critical of previous employers or colleagues.**

In fact, you should be wary of sounding even the slightest bit sour on your previous work experiences. Not only would doing so suggest that you're generally negative and cynical, but if you use the interview as an opportunity to vent about a previous employer, your interviewer will wonder how you'll talk about his company when given the opportunity.

- **Keep track of the questions you're asked.**

If a question comes up in one interview, it's quite likely it will come up in another. Particularly if you feel you haven't answered a question effectively, take a minute or two after the interview to jot down the question and outline what you would say if given a second chance. You'll be glad you did when you hear the same question again in subsequent rounds.

- **Keep your audience in mind.**

This is an interview, not a confessional. Don't delve into anything you wouldn't (or at least shouldn't) discuss on a first date: your political views, religious beliefs, or anything else known to spark controversy. Along these lines, remember to temper your honesty with a healthy dose of good judgment when addressing your strengths and weaknesses—try to steer clear of anything so incompatible with the job description it'll make your interviewer head for the hills.

- **Give off a positive vibe.**

  We know interviews are inherently stressful, but interviewers simply won't rally behind a candidate who seems uncontrollably nervous or just plain miserable. Keep reminding yourself that interviews are fun—when else do you have the opportunity do talk about yourself for 30 minutes straight?

Popular interview questions

As we said earlier in the chapter, it helps to remember that your interview is nothing more than a conversation with a specific purpose: Your interviewer is trying to figure out whether you *can* do the work, whether you *want* to do the work, and whether your prospective colleagues would *enjoy* working with you. In addition, they may ask questions designed to gauge your honesty, integrity, and ability to learn from your mistakes. They may also throw in a few miscellaneous questions to lighten the mood.

Interviewers can ask any number of specific questions in order to decide whether you're a compelling candidate: The sample questions we provide are not meant to be an exhaustive list, but they'll give you a head start in your pre-interview research process. We've grouped the questions according to the qualities they're usually used to gauge. (Talking to insiders in advance of your interviews will help you figure out which specific areas your interview is likely to emphasize.) You'll have a huge leg up on other candidates if you've taken the time to research and prepare answers to the most frequently asked questions.

APTITUDE QUESTIONS (CAN YOU DO THE WORK?)

Aside from allowing interviewers to gain insight into your initiative, motivation to succeed, and your work ethic in general, questions in this category seek to answer the question, "Can you do the work?" As we mentioned earlier in the chapter, the relevance of your past work experience and academic studies typically is inversely related to the emphasis your interviewer will place on answering these questions. In other words, the less directly applicable your past experience is to the job in question, the harder you'll have to work to prove you can excel at it.

Unless you're applying for a job that's directly related to your undergraduate studies (and many first-time job candidates with liberal arts degrees are not), you should be prepared to convince every prospective employer that your achievements outside of the industry in question will translate to success within it. As we've said before, the interview is your golden opportunity to explain perceived gaps or inconsistencies in your resume so they're viewed in a different (and hopefully more favorable) light.

If your GPA is on the low side, for example, you should be prepared to talk about it (and even if your GPA is stellar, you should be ready to talk about any rogue C's or the absence of course work related to the job you'll be doing). If you don't have extensive work experience, be prepared to explain how other pursuits—extracurricular activities, sports, or independent research projects, for example—might give you an edge on the job. Whatever the chink in your professional armor, it's important to consider it in advance of your interview, rather than weeding your way through it once you've gotten there.

Questions designed to gauge your ability to do the job include the following:

- Tell me about a time when you worked on a highly quantitative or analytical project. Describe the context, the project, and the outcome.

- What is the greatest challenge you've faced to date? How did you overcome it?

- What motivates you?

- Describe a time when you achieved a goal that required significant personal sacrifice. How did you stay motivated to achieve the goal, despite the hardships that it involved?

- What classes did you find the most difficult in college? Why do you think that's the case?

- Describe any classes you've taken in college that were highly quantitative or analytical in nature? How did you do in those classes? Are you comfortable working with numbers?

- Give me an example of a project (either academic or work-related) that required significant attention to detail. Do you consider yourself a detail-oriented person?

Because your interviewers are assessing your fundamental ability to do the work, questions in this category tend to be the most confrontational. Don't be caught off guard by interviewers who ask you to explain why you chose to study Renaissance language and literature or why you spent a summer lounging in the Caribbean. There's nothing inherently wrong with either of those choices, but be sure you're prepared to convince your interviewer that they're not inconsistent with your interest in the job. Remember, no one expects all of your experiences to be directly related to the position; that said, recruiters want to be sure you're really interested in the work and not just dabbling.

Along similar lines, you should be prepared to discuss your choice of major, particularly if you're applying for a job unrelated to your degree. If you sense your interviewer is skeptical about the relevance of your academic background, your response should be respectful but not apologetic. Stand by your academic and professional decisions, and share your decision-making process with your interviewer. Don't get carried away, though: Many liberal arts undergraduates fall into the trap of saying things like, "The skills required of [whatever the job in question is] aren't that hard to learn. It's not rocket science, and I'll obviously just learn it on the job." Keep in mind that your interviewer may not have been a liberal arts major, and therefore might not agree with your assessment. So rather than dismissing the intellectual rigor required of other disciplines, emphasize that you're eager to learn things you didn't necessarily study during your undergraduate years.

Whereas the aptitude questions described in the previous section are designed to establish that you *can* do the work, commitment questions are intended to figure out whether you genuinely *want* to do the work. First and foremost, your interviewer is trying to figure out how serious you are about the job itself, and whether the company's particular culture is one in which you'll fit—and eventually thrive. By far, the most commonly asked commitment question is, "Why do you want to do this job?" followed closely by, "Why do you want to do this job at this specific organization?" Here are a few other favorites in this category:

- Walk me through your resume and tell me how you decided to pursue this job/career track.

- What are you looking for in your next job? If you could create any position for yourself, what would it look like? What do you look for in a potential employer?

- Explain your role in such-and-such job listed on your resume. What did you learn from that experience that would be relevant to you here?

- What other industries/companies/positions are you considering? Are you actively interviewing elsewhere? Are you presently considering offers at any other organizations? If you are considering multiple offers, how will you make your decision?

- Why are you leaving your current job?

- Why should we hire you? Why do you think you'd be good at this?

- What do you think you would like most/least about this job?

- Where do you see yourself in five years?

- Walk me through what you think a typical day at the office would be like if you were hired for this position.

Your ability to provide solid, thoughtful answers to these questions—responses firmly grounded in realistic job expectations—will definitely advance your candidacy. While no one expects you to have known your professional destiny since age six, or to have made every significant decision over the last two decades with this job—or any job—in your sights, you will be expected to describe your professional and personal endeavors as a rational sequence in which this position at this company is the next logical step. You should be able to articulate exactly what you hope to gain—both personally and professionally—from the experience and to demonstrate your preparedness for its challenges and demands. Keep in mind that the delivery of your message is important here: *You* have to believe your own story, or no one else will.

There are multiple "right" answers to the question of why you're interested in a specific job, there are universally bad answers, too. Don't even think about suggesting that you consider it a stepping-stone to something else, that you stumbled across it, that you're ready to take just about anything because you've been out of work for so long, or that you generally think the industry is pretty cool. If you're interviewing for positions that represent a broad spectrum of functions and industries, you aren't obligated to tell your interviewer.

If, on the other hand, the job is one you're really excited about, questions like these give you an opportunity to make that clear. Perceived commitment to (and enthusiasm for) a specific company—not just the industry in general—always influences the choice between two (or more) otherwise comparable candidates. Companies love to be loved, and with good reason: They know that if you've done your homework and genuinely want the job, you're more likely to thrive at the organization and less likely to turn around and leave once you get there. You not only present yourself as a low-risk hire, you also reaffirm your interviewer's choice of company and career (and stoking your interviewer's ego is never a bad thing).

To gauge whether you're not only enthusiastic but committed, interviewers will often ask you to describe how you see your career evolving in the long term. Give some serious thought to how you'll attack questions about what you see yourself doing one, five, or ten years from now. While no one expects you to know for certain what you'll be doing several years into the future (the earlier you are in your career, the less sure people expect you to be), you should at least be able to present a credible scenario that includes the job in question. Taking the time to consider where you'd like to be down the road isn't just interview preparation—it's an opportunity for self exploration, too. If you find you're trying a little too hard to convince your interviewer that this is a job you want—or you find it necessary to convince yourself of it—then it's probably time to reassess whether your heart is in it.

TEAMWORKING/ATTITUDE QUESTIONS (DO WE WANT TO WORK WITH YOU?)

Questions in this category are designed to assess your interpersonal skills, and—as the name suggests—your ability to work as part of a team. Through questions like these, your interviewer is trying to figure out whether she would enjoy working with you, and whether your prospective colleagues, managers, and team members are likely to enjoy working with you. The questions themselves focus on your ability to build and maintain relationships, inspire confidence among clients and colleagues, and resolve interpersonal conflict (not to mention your ability to avoid conflict in the first place). Not surprisingly, these questions reveal an emphasis on teamwork—you might be expected to describe your firsthand experience on teams, and you'll often be asked to discuss the characteristics of effective and ineffective work groups. In addition, interviewers may ask you about your interests and achievements to figure out what makes you tick and what makes you an interesting person to get to know. Here are a few common questions in this category:

- What role do you typically assume when you work in a team setting? Describe the last time you worked on a team and the role you assumed.

- Tell me about a situation in which you've had to work with some-one that you didn't particularly like or get along with. How did you overcome personal differences to achieve your goal?
- Have you ever worked on a team that wasn't successful meeting its goals? What do you think went wrong?
- Describe an occasion when you persuaded someone to do something they didn't want to do.
- How would you characterize your leadership/management style?
- What achievement are you most proud of?
- What are you passionate about?

Regardless of the specific questions you encounter in your interview, the way in which you respond to the questions is often just as important as answers themselves. When interviewers assess a candidate's interpersonal effectiveness, the intangibles we mentioned earlier in the chapter (e.g., confidence, enthusiasm, poise, polish) are especially critical. Of course, you should be ready to provide solid examples that establish your comfort and efficacy in a team-based work environment, but your ability to build a rapport with your interviewer will solidify your case. Recruiters will look for signs that you're self-assured, professional, and generally pleasant to work with.

A word about teamwork

There are definitely jobs out there that don't require a lot of human interaction, but they are far outnumbered by positions that do. If the job you're considering requires a substantial amount of teamwork, you'll want to draw your interviewer's attention to the team-oriented pursuits on your resume. Keep in mind, though, that it may not be immediately obvious to your interviewer which activities depended on your ability to interact effectively with people. For example, you may feel your experience as a staff writer for the student newspaper is highly relevant because you managed multiple deadlines for a high-maintenance editor and leveraged relationships with key contacts to obtain hard-to-find information, but "staff writer" may not scream "team player" to your interviewer. Be on the lookout for opportunities to highlight relevant experiences, and don't expect your interviewer to read between the lines. At the same time, don't overstate your team contributions or pretend you've never met anyone you didn't get along with famously—your interviewer will conclude that you're not credible.

Questions on honesty and integrity

Interviewers look for more than just teamworking ability and charisma when trying to decide whether you'll fit in. They place a great deal of emphasis on your honesty and integrity too (as the list of attributes most commonly sought by employers at the beginning of this chapter attests). They'll sometimes ask questions regarding your mistakes and failures to determine whether you're honest and accountable when you screw up (and we all screw up from time to time, so knowing when to admit it—and knowing how to mitigate the damage—is key). Questions like these also examine your ability to learn from past experiences and continuously improve your perform-ance—a skill that's crucial for professional success whether you're part of a team or not. Popular honesty and integrity questions include the following:

- Tell me about a time you made a mistake. How did you handle it?
- Tell me about your biggest failure.
- What is your biggest weakness?
- Describe an ethical dilemma you faced in the past. How did you resolve it?

The way in which you answer these prompts will say a lot, as questions regarding mistakes and failures require diplomacy and tact—two qualities employers value highly. Of course, you should be honest when you answer questions such as these. We all want to present the best possible image of ourselves during job interviews, so it stands to reason that none of us particularly enjoys talking about our faults. Still, if you're asked about your past mistakes or biggest weakness, you have a unique opportunity to distinguish yourself. If you can demonstrate your maturity, humility, and sense of humor about your foibles, your likeability (and credibility) will skyrocket.

Miscellaneous questions

In an ideal world, all organizations would approach their recruiting processes with the same level of thoughtfulness and sophistication we're advising you to bring to your interviews. Sadly, this isn't the case. In fact, we'd be remiss if we didn't point out that some interview questions will have little or no relevance to the job. At best, these questions are intended to put you at ease, to give you a breather in the midst of an otherwise stressful interview, and simply to get to know you a little better. At worst, they can reveal your interviewer's inexperience in a recruiting role. Only you will be able to guess which one applies to your interview. Elisabeth, now an alumni relations officer at a West Coast business school, was asked the following question when she interviewed for an administrative position on campus: "If you were stranded on a desert island and could bring three CDs, subscribe to three periodicals, and order three television channels, which would you choose and why?"

Make no mistake about it: There's very little an interviewer stands to learn about your ability to do the job by asking you a question like that. "I got the impression that she had never interviewed anyone for a job before, and she got a kick out of being on the other side of the desk or something," Elisabeth told us. You may encounter novice interviewers who enjoy throwing curve balls your way. If you do, be a good sport and humor them—at the very least, the questions might spark some interesting conver-sation at a future cocktail party.

When it's your turn to ask questions

Toward the end of the conversation, your interviewer will probably ask if you have any questions for her. There are a few different schools of thought on how candidates should approach this part of the interview: Some insiders insist that you should always ask a question when offered the opportunity, and that your question should prove to your interviewer how much research you've done on the industry and the specific firm.

Although this advice is well intentioned, it can easily backfire (especially if you come across as a know-it-all trying to challenge your interviewer). If you approach the interview as a learning experience, then it follows that you should stick to those questions you'd genuinely like answered. Make the most of the opportunity to ask the questions that require insider insight. If you really want to know why your interviewers chose to work at the company you're interviewing with, ask away. You're not likely to lose points for asking questions that aren't insightful or penetrating enough, provided your questions don't display blatant ignorance regarding the industry, the company, or the specific position. The list of informational interview questions in the previous chapter includes topics that would be appropriate to explore if you have the opportunity. The following list may also prove helpful:

- I wondered if you could describe your own career path to me. How did you arrive at this organization, and how did you end up in the specific role/department you're currently in?

- What do you think it takes for someone to be good at this job, and what do you think it takes for someone to really enjoy it?

- What are your three most important strategic objectives for this year?

- I want to be sure I have a clear understanding of how this role fits into the organization as a whole. How would the specific responsibilities of this position fit into the bigger picture of what your department does? How does your department fit into the larger organization?

- Can you tell me how job performance is evaluated with regards to this position? How do you assess whether someone is on track and meeting expectations? Do you have a formal review process? Could you describe it to me?

- Is this a new position or would I be replacing someone?

- What is a typical career progression for someone in this particular role?

- Can you outline the organizational structure in this department? Division?

- What are your company's key competitive concerns?

- How would you describe your firm's culture? What do you think is different/better about working here than anywhere else? What things do you think the company's leadership team takes particular pride in?

- Are there a lot of opportunities for training and development here? Are rotations into different functional or geographic areas fairly common?

Danger ahead: Proceed with caution

Even though it's generally safe to ask questions you'd sincerely like answered, there are some you should probably avoid, no matter how badly you'd like them answered. (At the very least, you shouldn't ask them in an evaluative setting such as an interview). Stay away from questions in the following categories:

- **Presumptuous questions,** such as "How quickly will I be eligible for a pay increase?" or "When can I expect to have my own clients?" Questions like these will give your interviewer the impression that you consider the job offer a done deal, which could make her predisposed to prove you wrong.

- **Questions that suggest you have underlying concerns about the job,** such as "I heard that this job involves a lot of late nights and weekend work. Is that true?" You may have legitimate concerns about the position, but it's probably best to ask someone other than the person evaluating your candidacy for the inside scoop.

- **Questions that imply you've already got one foot out the door,** such as "What do people typically do once they leave your firm?" Unless you're interviewing for a contract job or a position that has a specific start and end date, you should probably avoid giving your interviewer the impression you've already got your sights set on bigger and better things.

While crafting questions of your own, keep one last thing in mind: Most of your interviewers will be on a fairly tight schedule, either because they've got other candidates to speak to or because they have their own jobs and schedules to get back to. Learn to read your interviewer: If it's clear that she is trying desperately to wrap things up, don't feel pressured to ask your questions simply because you've prepared them. If you sense she's trying to move things along, a diplomatic response might be, "Thanks. I'm sure you're on a tight schedule, so if it would be better to contact you later with any questions, I'd be happy to do that." This way, you've left it up to her— if she's indeed at the end of her interview tether, she'll take you up on your offer. If she's got plenty of time, she'll invite you to ask away (and she'll be impressed that you respect her schedule, which will win you extra points).

Learning from your interview

As we said at the beginning of the chapter, the interview process will usually leave you feeling as though your prospective employer has the upper hand. And, quite honestly, they probably do. But that doesn't mean you shouldn't be evaluating the company just as rigorously as they're evaluating you—you just can't do it as overtly. As the conversation evolves, ask yourself if your interviewer is someone you would like to work with—does it seem like he would make a good mentor, teammate, or manager? As you learn more about what you'd be doing on a daily basis, do you feel yourself getting more or less jazzed about the job? In general, does the company's approach towards the recruiting process seem organized and professional? We spoke with one job-seeker who recalled an interview experience that quickly changed her impression of a particular firm. "I was supposed to meet with three different people during a single office visit," she explains. "But one of my interviewers just never showed up! I was left sitting in a lobby for an hour and 25 minutes until the third person came to meet me. They ended up scheduling a phone interview a week later, but no one ever explained or apologized for the no-show. It didn't leave me with the best impression of the company."

Though such egregious breaches of interview etiquette are pretty rare, you can still learn a lot about an organization by the way it approaches its recruiting efforts. We know it sounds a little bit *Oprah,* but listen to your inner voice when it comes to your interviews. If your enthusiasm for a job starts to wane as you learn more about it, pay attention to those feelings. As a general rule, people are never quite as enthusiastic about a particular job as they were before they were offered it; if you become less excited about a position as you learn more about it, chances are it won't grow to be more appealing once it actually starts. One of the few downsides of cultivating exceptional interview skills is the risk of talking your way into jobs that don't necessarily match your skills or interests. So while it absolutely pays to do your research, know your resume, and invest time preparing for each individual interview, it's equally important you trust yourself when all is said and done.

Thanks for the memories

It's true in tennis and golf, and it's true in job interviews too: Once you've taken a swing at the ball, it's essential to follow through. Whether you interviewed in person or over the phone, and whether it was a first-round screening interview with HR or a final-round cross-examination by the senior vice president of Global Widget Marketing, you need to send a thank-you note at the completion of the interview process. Sending a thank-you note isn't just a polite way to recognize the time and courtesy someone's extended to you, but it's a way to reiterate your interest in the position, jog your interviewer's memory of your conversation, and highlight one or two specific things that make you a compelling candidate for the job. Apply the same sensibilities to your thank-you note that you would toward your cover letter: Think polite, concise, personalized, and absolutely error-free. Make sure your proofreading efforts extend beyond spelling and grammar; after all, you worked hard to establish your credibility and interest during the interview—you don't want to undo it all by making an embarrassing slip-up in a thank-you note. If you were introduced to multiple people during your office visit, make sure you get their names and titles correct. This is important whether you're sending them individual thank-you notes or mentioning them by name in the note you send your primary contact. "I once sent a thank-you note to a hiring manager after a series of interviews with multiple people," says Sarah, a 26-year-old research associate at a consulting firm. "One of the people I met with was named Edwin Famous. But I hadn't taken his business card or written down his name immediately after the interview, so when I sat down to write a thank-you note to my primary contact, the name that stuck out in my head was—for some reason—'Amos,' rather than 'Edwin.' I thanked the hiring manager profusely for not only taking the time to speak with me, but for introducing me to Miriam and Amos as well.

Unbeknownst to me, the entire office—including the person whose name I botched—found out about my error and found it extremely entertaining. It didn't cost me the job or anything—not only did I get an offer, but I accepted it. But from the day I started until the day I left two years later, I was the one who got the name wrong in the thank-you note. I'll never do that again." When you were little, you may have been told that if you couldn't think of something nice to say, then you shouldn't say anything at all. Well, when it comes to writing thank-you notes to interviews, the rule is this: If you can't get all of the names right, then it's better to not to include them at all. Of course, the best approach of all is to collect business cards from every person with whom you meet—and to proofread your thank-you correspondence diligently before sending it.

While your thank-you notes should always be flawless, they don't have to be written by hand and sent via snail mail to be effective. It was once considered gauche to send anything other than a hand-written note on quality stationery, but most hiring professionals these days agree that a prompt, well-written e-mail (sent no more than two business days after the interview) generally gets the job done. We've said it before, but it bears repeating: Don't let the ease and informality of e-mail give you a false sense of security. Like your cover letter or resume, your thank-you note is an opportunity to convey a confident, competent, and professional image to potential employers; don't waste that opportunity by regurgitating the same spiel you used in your cover letter. If anything, your thank-you note can be a more powerful tool for advancing your candidacy because you can use what you've learned in your interview to write a personalized, targeted note. In it you should mention one or two specific topics discussed during the interview that reinforced your interest in the position. If your interviewer described the specific attributes or qualities the position requires, mention one or two achievements that prove you possess them. Finally, offer to send any additional information the hiring manager might require in order to make a decision. (Chances are they would have asked if they needed anything, but it's nice to offer nonetheless.)

Cultivating a Professional Appearance

You've put a lot of time and energy into preparing for your interview, so wouldn't it be great if you could rely solely on your impressive achievements and your sparkling personality to get you the job of your dreams? Sadly, you can't. Putting your best foot forward means not only proving you have the academic and professional chops for the role, but looking and acting the part too. According to a recent report by the National Association of Colleges and Employers (NACE), a candidate's professional appearance does influence hiring decisions. "Job candidates need to remember that their overall grooming and choice of interview attire project an image," says Marilyn Mackes, the organization's executive director. "They are marketing themselves to the employer as a potential employee, and part of marketing is the packaging." The two most important appearance-related factors, according to the NACE study, were personal grooming and interview attire.

- **Grooming**—Nearly three-quarters of NACE's survey respondents said that a candidate's personal grooming would strongly influence their hiring decision. The term "grooming" might sound a little Kennel Club, but it means that your hair should be clean, neat, and appropriately styled. The same goes for your teeth—no one should be able to tell that you had a Caesar salad for lunch. If you're concerned about your breath, you can pop a breath mint or chew a piece of gum—but nothing should be in your mouth by the time you meet your interviewer. If you share your house with a furry friend, be sure the evidence isn't all over your suit; invest in a lint-roller and give yourself a once-over before heading out the door. Your nails should be clean, trimmed, and not brightly painted. Be sure your clothes are clean and neat, without any missing buttons, wrinkles, tears, or stains (check under the arms).

  Speaking of underarms, remember that decades-old deodorant commercial that advised, "Never let them see you sweat"? That's good advice for your interview too: Gentlemen, wear a short-sleeved white cotton t-shirt under your dress shirt to mitigate any possible sweat effects. For women, a nice sweater shell underneath your suit jacket instead of a button-down dress shirt will achieve the same thing (you won't have to worry about ironing that way either). Remember that natural fabrics like wool and cotton are generally more breathable than synthetics, so keep that in mind as you select your interview duds.

  If you choose to wear perfume or cologne, don't overdo it; your personal fragrance shouldn't arrive at the interview room before you do. While we're on the topic of odor, don't ever smoke outside before you walk into the office building. One of the many drawbacks of this habit (don't worry, we aren't here to lecture you) is the lingering smell.

The "less is more" guideline applies to makeup, ladies. Candidates of either gender should steer clear of flashy or excessive jewelry.

- **Interview attire**—Approximately half of all employers who responded to the NACE survey indicated that nontraditional interview attire would strongly influence their opinion of a candidate; another 38 percent said it would have a slight influence. For women, traditional interview attire means a well-tailored suit in a neutral color (black, gray, navy, and dark brown are all safe choices) and conservative shoes (no stilettos, open toes, or even peep-toes). For men, it means a suit in a dark, neutral color (black, navy, or dark gray), a white or light blue dress shirt (no flashy stripes or patterns), a silk tie with a conservative pattern, socks that match the trousers (no white!), and conservative, polished dark shoes.

While a suit is definitely a safe choice, keep in mind that relatively few companies observe a business-attire dress policy these days. You shouldn't assume that the rules that will apply once you've gotten the job will pertain to you when you're interviewing for it, but it's entirely possible that the person scheduling your interview may let you know that a suit is not *de rigeur* for your office visit. If this happens, consider yourself freed of the suit requirement. You should still err on the side of conservatism, though. The personal grooming guidelines still apply, and even a more casual ensemble should be clean, pressed, and well tailored.

Source: National Association of Colleges and Employers. "Employers Say Appearance Counts for Job Candidates" (www.naceweb.org/press/display.asp?year=2006&prid=236): May 10, 2006.

Arriving on Time

Whether the setting is an urban jungle or a corporate park in the 'burbs, and whether you're driving or taking public transportation, you'll need to do some planning to make sure you arrive on time for your interview. Try to arrive at least an hour in advance—that way, you've left ample cushion time in case you run into traffic, encounter public transport delays, can't find a parking place, or get lost en route. In the event your journey goes smoothly and you arrive an hour in advance, you can visit the closest coffee shop and use the extra time for focused interview preparation. You can review the company information you've collected and take one last look at the questions you hope to ask during the course of the interview. Not to mention, if the trip has left you looking a little less pristine than you did when you left home, you can use the time to tidy up your appearance before you walk in the door.

NEGOTIATING THE OFFER: A CHECKLIST

Congratulations! Your thorough preparation and solid credentials have landed you a job offer. Now what? Well, the same truth that applies to marriages applies to job offers: Just because the ring's on the finger doesn't mean things can't still unravel. You still have more preparation and work to do to ensure that you live happily ever after. You may have heard the age-old wisdom that when it comes to negotiating salary, the first one to cite a number loses. There's some truth to this nugget, but negotiating a pay package that's both attractive and fair is a little more complicated. Here are our top tips for making sure your employment offer is a win-win proposition:

- **Wait your turn.**

  Until you've actually been offered a job, it's not appropriate to initiate a discussion of salary or benefits. If you're asked in preliminary conversations or early-round interviews what salary you're hoping to earn (or what salary you've made in the past), try to keep it vague; mentioning a specific figure too early in the process is a no-win situation. If you name too high a figure, they'll question whether you're likely to accept the job if it's offered to you; if you name too low a figure, you'll leave money on the table. To continue with the poker metaphor, play your cards close to the vest and don't show your hand too early.

- **Know your worth.**

  When you apply for a job, you're essentially selling services to a prospective employer. You can't possibly negotiate an offer if you don't know the going rate for those services. Take the time to figure out what people in positions comparable to yours are earning. Web-based tools such as Salary.com and SalaryExpert.com make it easier than ever to obtain a baseline figure for a given job title in a specific geographic area. This should only be a starting point, however (as we said before, the ranges these sites provide are necessarily broad). If you can, check with your contacts in the industry—friends, acquaintances, networking groups, professional associations—to hone in on a salary range you can reasonably expect.

- **Know your bottom line.**

Base salary is only one component of the total-compensation picture, but (particularly early in your career) it can be the most important piece. If that's the case for you, have a bottom line—in other words, the lowest base salary at which you'd be willing to accept the position—in mind. Other compensation-related factors (performance-based bonuses, paid time off, company-sponsored retirement plans, paid relocation expenses, and employer-paid health insurance, to name a few) can help you evaluate the offer, but give some thought to the relative importance you assign to those factors *in advance* of your discussions.

- **Manage your expectations.**

The strength of your negotiating position is determined by supply and demand. The more specialized your skills—and the higher the demand for those skills—the more leverage you'll have. In general, the more entry-level the position, the larger the pool of qualified candidates the employer can choose from. The sector you're considering plays a role, too. If you're considering jobs in academia or the public sector, there's usually room to negotiate; if the hiring manager must work within established pay-grade levels, he will have less discretion when it comes to deciding how much to pay.

- **Manage *their* expectations.**

If you ask for more money and get it, remember that you'll be expected to make a proportionately greater contribution to the organization you're joining. This isn't necessarily a problem—provided you keep up your end of the bargain. If your performance is less than stellar, however, you'll have damaged your credibility—and your subsequent pay increases and advancement opportunities will probably suffer as a result.

- **Take a long-term view.**

Whether it's getting the job offer in the first place or negotiating your salary and perks, it's easy for "winning the game" to become your top priority. Know, however, that the best job opportunity isn't always the one with the fattest paycheck—it's the one that offers the best experience. Consider whether the position will enable you to develop skills that will make you more marketable down the line. Consider the position's promotion potential, learning opportunities, and the extent to which it makes good use of your skills and abilities. Your career is an investment; don't give up long-term career opportunities for short-term financial gain.

- **Keep the big picture in mind.**

Know, too, that while paying rent is important, compensation is only one piece of the pie when it comes to your job satisfaction (and your overall mental health, for that matter). Other factors—such as work/life balance, job security, and geographic location—should influence your assessment of the job offer, too. Don't forget that the company's culture—and the quality of your managers, mentors, and colleagues—will have a significant impact on your experience. If you can't stand the thought of going to work every day, no amount of money—either now or five years down the line—will make it worthwhile.

- **Mind your manners.**

One of the things that makes negotiating a job offer different from negotiating the price on a used car is the need to preserve the relationship with the party you're doing business with (in this case, your future employer). With that in mind, your negotiation approach should never be confrontational—nor should you give the impression that you're unreasonable or greedy. Even if the initial offer falls short of your expectations, be polite and gracious about it. Begin any counter-offer discussions by saying you're sincerely appreciative of the offer and the opportunity.

- **Play fair.**

There's no doubt about it: Negotiating your compensation is tricky business. Aim too high and you run the risk of damaging your credibility or pricing yourself out of the market entirely. Settle for too little and you'll always be playing catch-up (and you'll probably feel undervalued and unappreciated down the line). When it's time for negotiations, keep "fair and reasonable" in mind as you evaluate specific terms. It's in your best interest to earn fair compensation, and it's in your employer's best interest for you to feel you're compensated fairly for your efforts.

Thanks, but no thanks: Learning from rejection

As a matter of personal and professional pride, we'd all like to get an offer for every job we apply for. But, in reality, most of us don't. Sometimes, you know exactly where you went wrong: It's usually the point in the interview at which the room starts to get really hot, the walls seem to close in around you, and everything starts to happen in slow motion. "I've had interviews where I knew things were going downhill right from the start," says Paul, who recalls an on-campus interview for a research job at a university. "For some reason, I thought my interview was at 10:30 A.M., and I left myself plenty of time to find the building on campus where my interview was taking place. But, when I walked in, my interviewer introduced herself and said, 'You know, we were expecting you at 10:00 A.M. Did you get lost?' It turns out I had gotten the interview time wrong. Five minutes into the interview, my cell phone started ringing because I'd forgotten to turn it off. So within 10 minutes I was completely distracted and flustered, and I felt I couldn't recover. It wasn't entirely surprising that I didn't get the job."

In situations such as these—where you know your interview didn't go exactly as you'd hoped or planned—the best thing you can do is value the experience as an opportunity to learn. It might not be much consolation at the time, but you'll be far less likely to make the same mistakes (in Paul's case, showing up late and leaving his cell phone on) again, and you'll only refine and improve your approach as you go along. The interview process shouldn't be a game you're determined to win. Instead, it's a unique opportunity to learn about yourself, polish your presentation skills, and explore one of the literally thousands of career possibilities available to you.

What do you do when you've been passed over for a job and there's no "smoking gun"—you knocked every question out of the park, got along famously with every person you met, and still didn't get the offer? How do you figure out what went wrong so you can learn as much as possible from the experience?

First, understand that there are times when even the most meticulous research and thorough preparation aren't enough to land an offer with a particular company. It's entirely possible that you did do an outstanding job during the interview process—it might just be that another candidate did it a little bit better. Maybe the successful applicant went to the same college as two or three of the people who interviewed him. Maybe you felt there was chemistry between you and your interviewers, but one (or more) of them didn't feel the same way. There are dozens of possible reasons, and it's just not worth the emotional energy to figure out which one it's most likely to be.

However, if you decide to ask for feedback after you've gotten a "no thank you," do keep a couple of things in mind:

- **Accept that you might not get what you're looking for.**

  Even if you ask nicely, you might not get constructive feedback. No one likes to be the bearer of bad news—not even HR folks or hiring managers, who have to deliver it on a daily basis. And in the overly litigious society we live in, no one wants to get sued either; so it's really no surprise that employers are typically reticent when it comes to justifying their hiring decisions. You need to be prepared for the stock answer, which is "We were overwhelmed by the number of qualified applicants for the position and have offered the position to the candidate whose experience and background most closely matched our hiring needs."

- **Remember that timing is everything.**

The best time to ask for feedback is when the decision maker (or, in many cases, the messenger) calls you to tell you you're not getting the job offer. Of course, rejection phone calls are more the exception than the rule these days; in many cases, companies will choose a more passive-aggressive route and send you an e-mail or letter, or not get back to you at all. If you get a rejection e-mail, the best time to ask for feedback is immediately after you receive it.

- **Cross-examinations are not appropriate.**

  You're far more likely to get meaningful feedback if you steer clear of questions such as "Why aren't you hiring me?" which immediately puts the other person on the defensive. Though it might seem as if you're beating around the bush, you're probably best served saying something along the lines of "Thanks very much for getting back to me and letting me know. Since I'm still in the process of interviewing with other organizations, I was wondering if you could give me any advice or feedback that might help me with future interviews."

- **Don't ever argue — ever.**

  If your HR contact or recruiter does give you feedback that you disagree with, it's never appropriate to engage them in a debate about the merit of their decision. No matter how watertight your argument might be, it won't change the outcome; it will just protract an inherently awkward and uncomfortable conversation. You want to keep the conversation short, sweet (or at least bittersweet), and polite. Most employers have zero tolerance for confrontation in this scenario.

- **Take a hint.**

  If you leave a voice-mail or send an e-mail message asking for feedback and you don't get a reply, leave it at that. Don't send follow-up messages or phone-stalk your contact trying to get them to speak with you. If they don't want to give you feedback, they don't have to—and you've got nothing to gain by trying to beat it out of them.

It's not you, it's me: Declining an offer

If, on the other hand, you receive an offer from an organization but choose to decline it for any reason, you should be just as gracious turning it down as you would be accepting it—or negotiating its terms. Let your prospective employer know as soon as you've decided it's not the right opportunity; as a candidate, you may already know how frustrating it is not to receive word after you've invested a lot in an application process. While it may be tempting to delay a potentially unpleasant conversation, letting your contact know promptly about your decision is the gracious, professional thing to do, especially since the organization still has a position that needs to be filled.

Just as the first step in negotiating an offer is thanking your contact profusely for extending the opportunity, the first step in declining the offer is also expressing your appreciation. Then, offer a brief explanation—in however much detail you feel comfortable—why you have decided to decline it. As far as personal information is concerned, leave it out if you're at all in doubt. Feel free to stick to the basics—i.e., "It's just not the right opportunity for me at this particular time."

In some instances, the employer may probe you for more specifics, so be prepared to politely say enough but not more than you feel is appropriate or judicious to reveal. Of course, never bad-mouth any organization, individual interviewer, or employee with whom you met. Again, thank them for the time they spent speaking with you about the position and tell them you very much enjoyed meeting with them and learning about the role and the organization.

Though it's never quite as much fun to decline a job as it is to accept one, remember that it's okay to decline a position that's not right for you. It's also perfectly acceptable to decline an offer if you just want to wait to see what else is out there in your job search—it's better to be out of a job a few extra weeks or months than quit one six weeks after you started because it's just not working out. Trust your gut as well as your evaluation of the job's criteria. If something just doesn't seem right for you, follow your instincts. Even if your friends, parents, and significant other are telling you what a great opportunity it is, you're the one who's got to go to work every day.

CHAPTER 6

Advanced Degrees and Fellowships

GETTING STARTED

Still not ready for the world of work? You're not alone. According to a recent study by the Council of Graduate Schools, more than 1.5 million people enrolled in its member institutions in the fall of 2005. Education and business enrolled the largest numbers of students—about one-fifth of the grad school population pursued advanced degrees in education, and approximately 14 percent studied business. Humanities disciplines (including English, history, and others) accounted for about 7 percent of graduate students, and social sciences (a category that includes both sociology and psychology) accounted for slightly more than 7 percent of the total.[1]

If you've enjoyed yourself as an undergraduate student, the notion of returning to the safe cocoon of campus life might seem appealing. We should point out, however, that even if you pursue an advanced degree in the same subject that you majored in in college (and many people study something different), graduate school will hardly seem like a continuation of your undergraduate education—the purposes of the two degrees are very, very different. Even though you specialized in college to some degree simply by declaring a major, the real purpose of your liberal arts studies was to obtain a body of knowledge in a wide range of fields. The purpose of graduate school, on the other hand, is to explore the body of knowledge in a particular field.[2] The two most common types of advanced-degree programs—master's programs and doctoral programs—are explained below.

The Master's Program

As a master's candidate, you'll spend about two years at graduate school. The purpose of this program, in the university's eyes, is to give you a solid education in a specialized field of scholarship. At many universities, you may be able to study part-time while working to support yourself. You'll receive less financial help than declared doctoral candidates do (in fact, it's possible you won't receive any financial assistance at all). In a typical two-year master's program, your academic experience will look something like this:

- **Your first year:** You'll take courses much as you did in college, fulfilling the course work requirements of your degree. The workload is heavier, the course topics are more specific, and much more is expected than was in college. You'll either be assigned or choose an advisor at the beginning of your program. With your advisor's help, you'll begin to develop an academic focus. A number of professors will supervise the work you do.

- **Your second year:** You may take further courses to complete your degree requirements. Deciding on your research focus, you'll direct more and more energy toward your concentration.

1 Council of Graduate Schools. *Graduate Enrollment and Degrees Report: 1986 to 2005*. September 13, 2006. 3–5. www.cgsnet.org.

2 John A. Goldsmith, John Komlos, and Penny Schine Gold. *The Chicago Guide to Your Academic Career* Chicago: University of Chicago Press, 2001: 20.

Taking one semester or an entire year, depending on the program, you complete your master's thesis. The purpose of this thesis is to demonstrate mastery in your field. If you show promise, you may be encouraged to continue toward the doctorate.

The Doctoral Program

The doctoral candidate spends five or six years at graduate school. From the university's perspective, the purpose of the program is threefold: to give the candidate extensive knowledge of the field; to train him or her to do original and meaningful research; and to prepare him or her to function as a member of a teaching faculty.

In a typical six-year doctoral program, your academic experience will look something like this:

- **Your first three years:** You'll take courses to satisfy your degree requirements and gain a broad knowledge of the field. If you're fortunate, you'll gain valuable experience by snagging a research or teaching assistantship. (Most appointments are filled with fourth- to sixth-year grad students.) You'll gradually focus your research interests, working with an advisor who is usually appointed at the beginning of the program, and you'll develop your working relationships with professors prominent in your areas of interest. At the end of your second or third year, you'll complete a thesis or take comprehensive exams, or both. The thesis or exams will help demonstrate your qualification to continue with doctoral work.

- **The last three years:** Course work becomes a much smaller part of your academic work, and may end altogether as you work at conceptualizing your doctoral dissertation. Your dissertation must constitute a new and meaningful contribution to knowledge in your field. You'll teach more and more classes, and may even teach a course of your own design. You'll collaborate increasingly with faculty members, who may rely on you for research and who will inform you of their own work. You will probably become closely associated with a single professor who will become your dissertation director. You'll devote more and more energy to your own research. Your program culminates in the completion of your dissertation, which may include an oral defense of your work before a faculty committee.

Why me? Reasons to go

The decision to attend graduate school isn't one that should be made lightly. "Over the years, I've come to realize that many, if not most [graduate students] seriously underestimate the enormous investment of time and money that graduate school will require," says Tom Thuerer, Dean of Students in the Humanities at the University of Chicago.[3] If you decide to go to graduate school, you don't want to fall into this camp. As with any investment, consider your goals and objectives well in advance to ensure you get the best possible return.

We'll discuss the financial realities of attending graduate school later in this chapter, but, suffice to say, it can be an expensive proposition. Pursuing an advanced degree also requires significant personal and professional sacrifice—at least in the short term. And while you may have been encouraged to explore several different academic paths as an undergraduate—trying on various majors to see if they fit with your skills and interests—graduate school doesn't offer the same level of flexibility. In graduate school, the stakes are higher and the cost of changing your mind is much, much higher. True, just because you've started working toward your degree doesn't mean you're obligated to finish it, but investing the time and money in a program and not having a degree to show for it is a scenario you'd like to avoid.

To ensure you get as much as possible out of the investment—and the experience itself—be sure to give serious thought to whether grad school is the right choice for you. Pursuing an advanced degree can influence your personal and professional life in a big way, so your decision to attend should involve some honest self-assessment and good, old-fashioned soul searching. Grad school isn't the right choice for everyone. Sure, you could probably get through it (you wouldn't be offered admission if you couldn't do the work), but do you really want to white-knuckle your way through a program that's not only expensive and time-consuming, but one that's supposed to be intellectually stimulating and enriching? There are numerous reasons people go to grad school; if you're like most people, these are the ones most likely to apply to you:

- **Because you have to go**

   In many fields, graduate-level studies are part of the drill if you want to obtain the licenses and certifications necessary to work in your chosen profession. Medicine and law are two obvious examples of this—if you want to be a doctor, there's no way around medical school (which is a good thing for everyone), and if you want to be a lawyer, law school is in your future. Teaching often requires a graduate degree, though the educational requirements will vary depending on the subject and grade level you hope to teach, you'll probably need to complete some level of postgraduate work, whether it's a required teacher-training program, or (if it's a tenure-track college professor career you're thinking of) a masters' degree or PhD.

3 John A. Goldsmith, John Komlos, and Penny Schine Gold. *The Chicago Guide to Your Academic Career.* Chicago: University of Chicago Press, 2001: 30.

- **Career advancement**

  In some industries and organizations, graduate studies are required—either officially or unofficially—for upper-level or management positions. Even if it's possible to get in the door of an organization without an advanced degree, you many find that you can only move so far up without one. In some cases, an advanced degree is actually a prerequisite for a step-up in seniority; in others, it's more of an unwritten rule. Either way, think of an advanced degree as a type of currency—depending on where you work (or where you'd like to work), you might just have more purchasing power when it comes to getting promoted. And it's not necessarily because the skills or knowledge you picked up in grad school are directly applicable to the everyday responsibilities of your job. "I enjoyed my master's program immensely," says Mary, a 28-year-old analyst with the U.S. government who obtained her master's degree in public policy. "But I wouldn't necessarily say I'm using what I learned in my job every day. Even so, I probably wouldn't have this position if I hadn't gone to grad school. The department that I work for is pretty stringent about its master's degree requirement." The good news is that if you're considering grad school as a possible way to move up within your current organization, there's a good chance your employer will foot at least part of the bill. Many companies offer generous tuition reimbursement programs.

- **Because you're switching careers**

  You probably already know that people switch jobs more frequently today than they ever have before—and not just across organizations or functions either. In fact, not only are job changes becoming more frequent, they're becoming more dramatic, too. It's not uncommon to see dancers and artists become journalists or doctors, bankers become small-business owners, teachers become therapists, or investment analysts become CIA operatives. As we've said before, careers don't always evolve in a linear fashion. Sometimes, the position that we once considered our "dream job" becomes less satisfying over time. Other times, our personal priorities or circumstances change, making the career path we're currently on seem less appealing. For some folks, taking a class, attending a lecture, or getting a part-time job transforms a one-time hobby or interest into the focus of their professional aspirations. The reasons behind peoples' career changes are as varied as the occupations that they move in and out of. In many cases, pursuing an advanced degree provides a bridge between two disparate careers. Graduate school provides much more than just expertise when it comes to establishing your credibility with future employers; the very fact that you took the time to pursue an advanced degree proves you're committed to building a career in the field.

- **For the love of money**

When it comes to graduate school, there's no money-back guarantee. In fact, the only thing that earning an advanced degree guarantees is a few extra letters at the end of your name. And while U.S. Census Bureau data supports the notion that earnings increase with higher educational levels, there's no question that some letters are worth more than others—at least when it comes to salaries. According to Census Bureau research, people with professional degrees (MD, JD, DDS, and DVM) earn higher salaries on average than any other segment of the U.S. workforce. For the rest of the working world, progressively higher education levels correspond to higher earnings, all other things being equal. These salary trends make sense; like any other market, the labor market is driven by supply and demand. Higher demand for your skills—and/or a scarcity of supply when it comes to your particular skill set—will drive up the "price" that employers will pay for your efforts (in other words, your salary). In general, the higher your level of educational attainment, the higher your level of specialization—and the more scarce your skills, knowledge, and experience generally becomes.

However, depending on the specific graduate degree you're pursuing, the dollar increase in your new salary might not be enough to offset the cost of obtaining the degree in the first place. With the cost of higher education increasing each year, students are carrying more debt upon completion their undergraduate degrees than they ever have before. Tack on the cost of funding a graduate degree, and you'll quickly find that all of this learning comes at a steep price. If your interest in graduate school springs primarily from the promise of a fatter paycheck, proceed with caution: You'll need to conduct a thorough cost-benefit analysis to figure out whether the enhanced earning potential justifies the substantial costs. The Bureau of Labor Statistics' website, BLS.gov, includes hiring projections in addition to salary ranges for various occupations; by reviewing resources such as this one, you'll learn what factors influence the job market in your field and what the landscape might look like by the time you graduate.

- **Network connections**

As we discussed in detail in Chapter 5, networking will be an important part of your job search whether you have advanced degree or not. The connections forged in grad school could potentially give you a leg up when it comes to learning about job opportunities in your field. Even if they can't hook you up with a full-time job, grad school classmates will often be able to provide you with professional advice that's just as valuable. "Not only did the 23 other people in my MFA program become some of my closest friends, but they've become a powerful network of professional contacts that I continually rely on," says Lisa, currently a senior travel writer with a consumer lifestyle magazine. Lisa, who earned her MFA in fiction writing, recently co-edited a collection of anthologies and is currently working on a book scheduled for publication in the spring of 2007. "The people who were in my writing program were able to put me in touch with agents and publishers who would be able to help me put a book deal together," she says. "I don't know if I would have been able to get that done without them." Connections like these will pay off whether you're intending to stay in academia or not; as always with job-hunting, it pays to know people and to have them know you, too.

- **You just can't get enough . . .**

. . . of school, that is. Many people pursue graduate studies purely because they're absolutely fascinated by their chosen field of study, and they want to develop a highly specialized area of expertise. Whether you eventually want to teach at the college level, or you just want to breathe, eat, and sleep your academic passion for a while, graduate school will enable you to fan your intellectual flames. Those who go all the way with their studies and earn their PhD are a unique breed—a species of intellectual omnivore that enjoys learning for its own sake. Such individuals are visibly charged by scholarly debate and discussion and have the patience and single-minded focus to endure a half-dozen years or more in an academic environment.

- **Because it's the path of least resistance**

Just because there are many perfectly legitimate reasons to go to grad school doesn't mean there aren't a few bad ones too. Pursuing an advanced degree as a default option (i.e., you still haven't decided what you want to do and are hoping to postpone the inevitable transition into the real world) isn't a great idea. If you're simply frustrated with the way your job search is going, or hoping to use graduate school to wait out a downturn in the economy, think again. Graduate school is hardly a quick fix for a broken job search, and the economy may very well pick up long before you've even made a dent in your student loans.

So how can you tell if you're using grad school as a stall tactic? Well, only you know for sure, but if you find yourself contemplating graduate school but haven't really narrowed in on a field of study, that's definitely a warning sign. It's possible that the relative security of being a student—and not necessarily a commitment to a particular field—has captured your interest.

That doesn't mean that you shouldn't explore grad school as an option, but you should consider your other alternatives, too, to be sure that fear isn't the only factor motivating your decision. Trust us, there are other ways to bide your time, and most of them require far less time, energy, and money than graduate school. For the grad school experience to be worthwhile for you, it should make sense as part of some larger plan for your career.

Do you have what it takes?

When deciding whether grad school is something you'd like to do, it helps to consider the skills and attributes successful grad students consistently demonstrate—not just the attributes that make them capable of doing the work grad school requires, but the personal qualities that make them gush with enthusiasm when they describe the experience 10 years down the road. Across disciplines and institutions, graduate students who both succeed in their programs and seem to genuinely enjoy them typically have these four things in common:

- **Compound interest**

  Far and away, experts say a genuine passion for the subject matter is the single most important factor determining which grad students thrive and which become frustrated and disappointed with their decision. A genuine passion is very different from a peripheral interest. In other words, pursuing a masters' degree in linguistics because you took a single English literature class probably doesn't represent the most well-informed choice. In order to make the most out of your graduate school experience, you need to have a deep, enduring interest in the subject, the profession, and its literature. When you apply to programs, admissions staff will examine your transcript and resume not just for evidence of academic achievement (though the importance of solid grades and test scores can't be overstated), but for classes and extracurricular activities that demonstrate an interest in—and a commitment to—the field.

- **Not-so-idle curiosity**

  In addition to an inveterate desire to study the field you've chosen, it helps if you're an intellectually curious person in general. In other words, do you enjoy exploring concepts and ideas, whether or not they specifically relate to your chosen field of specialization? Do you enjoy the process of pulling things apart—literally or metaphorically—to understand how they work? Are you intrigued by the challenge of understanding—and expressing—two or more seemingly contradictory perspectives on the same issue? Is your pursuit of knowledge driven largely by your interest in the question more than the practical application of its answer? Whether you're pursuing a two-year masters' program, a six-year PhD program, or a full-fledged career in higher education, you'll enjoy your time in academia a lot more if you're excited by the *process* of learning and not just the degree you'll have in hand when you graduate.

- **Perfect timing**

  Well-honed time-management skills are another prerequisite for graduate-school success. If you're attending school full-time, you'll probably be balancing competing academic priorities within the classroom walls and possibly the demands of extracurricular involvements, a part-time job (whether it's related to funding your studies or not), a family, and some semblance of a social life. Samantha, who completed a master's degree in English, juggled a couple of different jobs in order to finance her graduate education. As part of the fellowship she was awarded during her first year, she participated in a program known as "Artists in the Schools," where she taught writing to elementary, middle, and high school students throughout the state. "I also worked as a reporter for the university press office," she says. "And I did freelance work for the daily paper, doing book reviews. And I also worked part time at a café serving lattes. Thinking about it now, it's no wonder I didn't produce as much writing as I would've liked." If you're pursuing your degree on a part-time basis, the demands of a full-time job are most likely in the mix. Either way, you're likely to have a lot on your plate, so understanding how to prioritize is key if you want to finish your program with your sanity intact.

- **Eyes on the prize**

  Somewhat paradoxically, the ability to work on a single task for an extended period of time—whether it's a dissertation, thesis, or any long-term research project—is just as important as the ability to juggle multiple tasks at once. The research and writing required in graduate school is highly focused—much more so than in undergraduate studies—so grad students devote a seemingly inordinate amount of time exploring a highly specialized area of interest within their field of study. By its very nature, work like this requires a great deal of autonomy, not to mention a better-than-average attention span. Successful degree candidates are therefore highly motivated, unusually self-disciplined, and comfortable working independently. A good dose of patience doesn't hurt either, since even the most exciting and groundbreaking research projects usually involve some fairly monotonous tasks. In general, the road to completing an advanced degree and seeing it pay off is long and arduous. If instant gratification is important to you when it comes to your academic pursuits, a professional degree might be a more suitable choice than an advanced degree in the liberal arts.

Ask and it shall be answered

We know what you're probably thinking: "Of *course* I have all of those skills and attributes! I am literally bursting with excitement about my field of study, I can handle multiple competing priorities, I love monotony, and I have the self-discipline and patience of a saint!" If you have a killer transcript, and a resume full of related extracurricular activities, and work experience to boot, then it's time to sign you up. All you need to know is where to send the check, right?

Not so fast. We said that considering graduate school required a great deal of introspection and honest self-assessment, but we didn't say that was all that was required before you jumped on board. In Chapter 5, we stress the importance of networking and conducting informational interviews to make informed decisions about your career—and just because you're thinking of applying your talents to academia for a while doesn't mean you're off the hook where this type of legwork is concerned. You need to ask questions before you decide to apply to school. Not only will this type of research make your applications more compelling, but, more importantly, you're far more likely to choose the right program—and the right field of study, for that matter—if you've taken the time to look before you leap. In the *Chicago Guide to Your Academic Career*, the book's three authors (all distinguished professors and scholars themselves) emphasize the importance of seeking advice from as many informed perspectives as possible before you apply. Here are some specific questions they suggest you ask as you begin to gather information:

- **To professors (past or current) who know your work well:** Do you think graduate school, in this particular field, would be a good choice, given my level and kinds of talents? Do you think I would have a contribution to make?

- **To professors in your field who have completed graduate school within the last five years or so:** What are the current issues in the field? Where do you see the field going? What is graduate school like these days?

- **To graduates of your own college or university who are now in graduate school in a field close to yours or who have recently obtained jobs (your undergraduate teachers, the Career/Placement Center, and/or the alumni office should be able to provide you with names and contact information):** How have you found the graduate school experience? Were you well prepared for the program you entered? Is there any advice you wish you'd received before entering graduate school?[4]

---

4 John A. Goldsmith, John Komlos, and Penny Schine Gold. *The Chicago Guide to Your Academic Career*. Chicago: Univesity of Chicago Press, 2001: 22.

Two words: Manage expectations

Even if you've determined that you'd probably succeed in graduate school—meaning you'd not only do well academically, but you'd probably really enjoy it—you may not be entirely convinced you should go. If you're trying to decide whether the investment would be a worthwhile for you, you're not alone. Formulating realistic expectations—in terms of the graduate school experience itself and its expected payoff in the long run—is one of the best ways to assess whether attaining an advanced degree is the best possible next step. If you take the time to speak with current grad students, recent alumni, professors, and other prospective grad students (like yourself), you'll probably find that people's objections to graduate school fall into two categories: the practical and the personal.

- **Practical Concerns**

  The practical reasons all relate to two things: the cost of school and the likelihood of getting a job afterward. Together, these two factors will determine whether graduate school makes sound practical sense for you. It's possible to land a job easily after earning an advanced degree and still struggle to pay back your loans. It's also possible to complete a graduate program with no debt and still have trouble finding work. Many people would find each of these scenarios unacceptable. To avoid any nasty surprises, spend some time researching the probable cost of your graduate program, and study the state of the job market in your field. The most important aspects of the job market are the availability of positions and the salary range. Together, these pieces of information give you some idea of what your professional future (and loan-paying power) might look like. The more information you dig up, the better you'll be able to appraise the practical obstacles to graduate education.

- **Personal Concerns**

  The personal pitfalls of graduate school are a little more complicated. They depend on your likes, dislikes, and powers of endurance. Many people begin graduate programs and never complete them. This is especially true for those pursuing doctorates: Some of these people quit for financial reasons, but many leave because they find that the life they're living is unacceptable. Beginning a graduate program you never finish is the worst-case scenario. Investigating graduate programs should involve not only research into the broad academic outlines, but also research into what your daily life as a graduate student will be like. In an informal survey of hundreds of graduate students, these are the top five lifestyle complaints students made:

  o   It's hard to make ends meet financially.

  o   There is little or no free time.

- There is not enough socializing in the department/school.
- There is nothing to do in the university community or surrounding area.
- Fellow graduate students are neurotically competitive.

- When making your decision, be sure to consider these aspects of graduate life as well as anything else that could have a substantial effect on your quality of life. Once you can clearly articulate why you want to go to graduate school, you'll be able to make an informed decision as to whether the advantages of an advanced degree outweigh the sacrifices you'll need to make in order to get one.

Timing is everything: When to go

When you started thinking about college, you probably knew when you were going to be attending (about three months after you graduated from high school, most likely). With graduate school, there's a little more variation in this regard. Some unusually focused college grads pursue their advanced degree immediately after obtaining their bachelor's degree (which means, of course, they're going through the application process while they're still in school). Most graduate students, however, have taken at least one year off between their undergraduate and graduate programs—usually to work, sometimes to travel or volunteer, occasionally just to take a break. In fact, more often than not, practical experience—particularly as it relates to the advanced degree you're hoping to pursue—makes you a more desirable applicant than one who has little to no work experience to speak of.

So when should you go to grad school? Well, the short answer is: It depends. On one hand, many people find the years between college and graduate school to be an extremely valuable time for exploring professional options—and for doing some important self-exploration too. Because you've had a few years in the workplace, you'll probably bring a more informed perspective to bear on your academic pursuits. You might also have saved a little bit of money during your working years or at least been able to pay down some of your undergraduate debt, if you had any. But more important than any nest egg is the greater sense of clarity and purpose you'll have since you've had some time to consider what you really want to do and what's especially important to you in your career. No matter how much you enjoyed college or how much you excelled there, perhaps there wasn't ever really a question you would go. When you enroll in graduate school—particularly after you've taken a few years off to work—you're usually there because you want to be there. If the pure love of learning isn't enough, the fact that you've taken out loans or depleted all of your savings to finance your higher education will probably motivate you to squeeze every last drop of value out of the experience.

On the other hand, taking time to work in between your degrees means you'll have to adjust to life as a student again, which can be difficult for some folks who have been out of an academic routine for several years. If you've been earning a regular paycheck, you might find it difficult to give up that income and learn to live as modest graduate student. The longer you wait, the more likely it is that personal commitments—a spouse, a significant other's job, children, or mortgage—may complicate your decision of what program to attend (or whether to go at all).

There's no magic formula when it comes to deciding whether to take time off between your undergraduate and graduate studies, or (if you decide to work for a few years) how many years you should work (or travel, or do whatever it is that you're doing between degrees) before you go back. The only absolute guideline is that you should go to graduate school when you're absolutely certain it's what you want or need to do. As we've belabored in the preceding pages, pursuing an advanced degree isn't something you should take lightly, so you shouldn't apply until you're sure it's right for you. The option to go to grad school will always be there, and spending time in the "real world" can actually make you more interesting to graduate schools once you decide what you want to do and are ready to apply. The richness of your life experiences will cause the most difficult part of the application—the personal statement—to write itself. You will have cultivated a sincere interest in a particular degree that you need in order to advance your career or gain more influence in a particular field. Your enthusiasm and ability to convey how the degree fits into your long-term goals will leave Admissions Committees inspired and ready to offer you a spot in their next class.

That said, finding out what's typical for other students in the programs you're considering doesn't hurt. Most of the time, graduate programs will post statistical information about their current students on their websites, and often times, the average age of entering students is listed. Again, you shouldn't feel discouraged to apply if you're a few years off the mark (these numbers are averages, after all), but they can help to shape your expectations of what your experience will be different. Kurt, who recently began a MFA program in writing after working as a teacher for nine years, was surprised how old he felt on the first day of school. "Not only have I been working for a while, but I've been married for three years, and my wife and I are expecting our first baby. A lot of my classmates are 23 or 24. I feel so old!" Conversely, if you're attending grad school right after college, you may find that you're the only 22-year-old single person in your class. Again, the extent to which you do or don't fit into the prevailing demographics is only one data point, but it's one that will definitely shape your experience in and out of the classroom.

What to consider when deciding where to apply—and where to go

Like deciding whether or not to go to graduate school, selecting target schools is more complex than it first seems. Filling out applications is a huge demand on your time and energy, and whether you're taking undergraduate exams or holding down a job, you probably can't afford to spend weeks dealing with a large pile of applications.

Applications are a financial drain as well: Grad school application fees range from $20 to $90, and average about $50. These high fees are no accident. Many universities, with admissions committees swamped by record numbers of applications, have raised their fees in order to prevent less-motivated applicants from applying and reduce the number of incoming applications. Given today's fees, you can expect 10 applications to cost you about $500—and that's before you figure in postage, transcript handling fees, photocopying, and so on. It can really add up.

Economically speaking, you can see the saturation-bombing technique that a lot of people use to apply to college isn't very practical for grad school. It pays—in time and money—to narrow your field down to four or five good target schools. To figure out which institutions make the cut, you'll probably want to consider the following six factors:

- **Academic fit**

   In selecting schools, the most important aspect of any school is its academic fit—that is, how well suited the school is to the research you want to do. If you're a prospective grad student in, say, psychology, then it's certainly a good idea to find out where the leading psychology departments are; but to have a really good graduate school experience, you need more than just a respected department. You need individuals on the faculty who share your research interests, and who will become involved in your work and involve you in their own.

   The importance of finding professors to work with varies according to your degree ambitions. If you're looking for a master's degree to round out your education or give you that professional edge, then the overall quality of the faculty may be more important to you than finding the ideal mentor. Because your grad school experience will probably involve more course work than research, you'll want to make sure the classes offered are relevant to your interests and will give you some background for your research. If you are decided on doctoral work and an academic career, however, the specific research interests of professors become much more important. If you already have an area of academic specialization in mind, you need to find out whether that subspecialty is well represented in the departments you're considering. In any case, graduate work will always be more profitable and enjoyable if there are professors in your program who will take a personal interest in what you're doing.

   As you gather information about your prospective professors, remember that the most brilliant scholars in the world are not always the best teachers. No matter how celebrated the scholars are that you'll work with, it won't really matter if teaching isn't their scene or if they're rarely accessible to students. Make no mistake about it: The quality of teaching can make or break your experience. "I was surprised by the lack of professionalism exhibited by some of my well-paid teachers," laments one recent master's grad. "Overall, I'd give the experience a 6 out of 10. I wish I had gotten an MBA." To avoid any nasty surprises, talk to other students (see below) to gauge their level of satisfaction with the teaching. Also, try to schedule interviews with the faculty members you are most interested in working with.

- **Reputation**

  To a greater extent than our undergraduate education, graduate schools represent an affiliation with a specific department, just as much (if not more than) an affiliation with a specific university. Keep this in mind as you consider which programs you'll apply to. When it comes to reputation, the excellence of a particular program doesn't always correspond to the institution's overall reputation—or the strength of its undergraduate programs. Harvard, Princeton, and M.I.T. might vie for the tops spots of the various undergraduate rankings each year, but, when it comes to department-specific rankings, there's a lot more variety.

  Most of the people we spoke to relied—at least to some extent—on department rankings, which are published annually for graduate programs in much the same way they are for undergraduate institutions. (Keep in mind, though, that rankings aren't available for every advanced-degree program you might consider). While rankings can provide some useful information as you make your choice, remember that they represent just one data point. Be sure to read the fine print about research methodology as you interpret ranking information. Consider the following excerpt from the 2007 edition of *U.S. News & World Report's America's Best Graduate Schools*: "Rankings of doctoral programs in the social sciences are based solely on the results of peer assessment surveys sent to academics in each discipline."[5] There's nothing inherently wrong with this approach, but you should be aware that that these particular rankings do not incorporate the quality of teaching (mentioned above) or the availability of job-placement resources (mentioned below). If that information is relevant to you, you'll need to obtain it through additional research.

- **Job placement**

  When you're considering which programs to apply to—and, eventually, when you're deciding which school to attend—be sure to visit the career center and ask what resources are available to graduate students. While some universities have excellent, program-specific career-planning resources devoted to their

5 "Social Sciences & Humanities: PhD Programs Ranked Best by Department Chairs and Senior Faculty." *U.S. News & World Report: America's Best Graduate Schools*. 2006: 65.

graduate students exclusively, others do not. Talk to students currently enrolled in the programs you're considering and ask if they've found the resources available to them to be satisfactory. Many students enroll in programs assuming job placement—or at least career counseling—is part of the deal, and they're unpleasantly surprised to find out how few resources actually exist. Regardless of whether you're hoping to snag a position in private industry or make a career in academia, ask questions. Find out whether employers visit the campus to recruit graduate students in your program. If you're going the academic route, ask whether recent grads have gotten academic positions, how long their searches took, and where they're working. In the end, you may not lean on the resources your program provides. In fact, you may not use them all. As we've said before, though, it's important to develop realistic expectations before you sign up.

- **Students**

  To really figure out whether a particular program might be a good fit, you need to talk to the students currently enrolled in it. As you make your final decision among programs, you'll ideally visit each campus and talk to current graduate students. Ask them about the faculty's level of commitment to the graduate program, whether they enjoy working with their professors, and whether they feel they've been given enough guidance and opportunity to develop their own research. Ask them to describe the good points and the bad points of the department and the school. If you can, schedule time to speak with a graduate advisor; ask how well the program is organized, and what the ratio of graduating students to entering students is. If you take the time to gather qualitative and quantitative information like this, you'll make a much more informed decision than you would if you relied on rankings alone.

  While you're on campus, be sure to ask students about their quality of life too. Your lifestyle will not necessarily resemble the one you enjoyed as an undergraduate student. ("Grad school is mostly devoid of the cultural and social atmosphere that is so intoxicating about undergrad life," says Scott, who recently completed a two-year master's program in urban planning. "And the football was worse in grad school too.") Still, you want to enjoy your experience as much as possible, and that means taking the time to consider what your life will be like outside of the classroom as well as in it. Ask whether there are opportunities to socialize and whether there's a strong sense of community among graduate students. As you talk to people who are attending the programs you're considering, give some thought to whether you can see yourself fitting in at each place. Not only are you going to grad school to advance your formal education, but you're going to be building a network of friends and supporters, too—your fellow students should ideally be people you like and respect. The impressions you get as you visit different campuses are a valuable part of this decision-making process.

- **Geography**

  This one's pretty straightforward: The geographic location of the university should influence your decision to attend. If you have a particular aversion to rain, then you might prefer not to spend the next few years of your life in Seattle; if you're especially claustrophobic, New York City might not be the place for you. But the question of geography isn't just about personal preferences: There are practical implications, too. For example, depending on your field of study, it might be considerably easier to secure part-time jobs (or jobs between academic years) in some parts of the country than in others. If you have your heart set on settling down in a particular region, then you'd probably be best served attending graduate school there (or somewhere close by). If you have a spouse or significant other who's going to accompany you, your partner's career prospects in each of the locales you're considering will also influence your decision.

Making the Most of Your Experience

In 2001, about 32,000 graduate students participated in a survey conducted by the National Association of Graduate-Professional Students (NAGPS). When asked what specific advice they would provide to entering students, getting a head start on career planning was the suggestion that survey respondents offered most frequently. Building a network of personal and professional contacts—by attending professional conferences, joining student organizations, and actively seeking the support of professors and advisors—was another popular recommendation.

Source: Adam Fagen and Kimberly Sudekamp Wells. "A Little Advice from 32,000 Graduate Students," *The Chronicle of Higher Education.* January 14, 2002. http://chronicle.com/jobs/2002/01/2002011401c.htm.

"Rapunzel, Rapunzel": Getting into the ivory tower

While you might think the graduate school application process begins when you start trawling around various schools' websites and committing program rankings to memory, it really begins months earlier—albeit only informally. The process starts when you begin to consciously seek out and nurture relationships with your undergraduate professors and advisors as well as professors or researchers at your target graduate institutions. It continues when you prepare for and then take the GRE, a topic discussed in more detail below (while not a required application element for every program, the GRE is compulsory for admission to most programs). Whether you start thinking about your applications six months or six years before they're due, one thing is certain: With all the pieces that go into a graduate school application, it's definitely not something you can whip up over a weekend or two.

Many universities have a single application form for all their graduate programs and a set of basic application requirements to which individual departments may add. At some schools, individual departments have their own applications. At these schools, you will have to request an application from an individual department rather than a central office.

Once you've accessed and reviewed the admissions materials, it's time to complete the applications to your target schools. Before you dig in, take some time to consider all the application pieces (we discuss these below) and set a schedule with self-imposed deadlines that are possible to meet. The applications themselves typically require a general information form, GRE scores, transcripts, recommendations, and a personal statement. Some programs may have additional requirements, such as an interview or portfolio.

Due to differences in departmental requirements, it is difficult to make generalizations about applications. Still, application processes across institutions and programs usually involve the following.

- **Deadlines.**

    First things first: Meeting your schools' deadlines is one of the most important details of the application process. You don't want to be rejected from a school for which you might otherwise have qualified simply because you were late in filing your application. Check with each individual department to which you are applying to find out their specific deadlines. Also be aware that there may be separate (usually earlier) deadlines for those students seeking financial aid. Get your applications in as early as possible.

- **Test Scores.**

    Almost all graduate schools ask applicants for applicable standardized test scores, such as the GRE General Test, a GRE Subject Test, or the Test of English as a Foreign Language (TOEFL). Here again, you must check with individual departments to ensure you meet their specific requirements. Although there are a few programs that don't require the GRE General Test, most do. Only a few programs require a GRE Subject Test. All foreign students from countries where English is not the native language are required to take the TOEFL.

    Preparing for the GRE may require the single biggest investment of time when it comes to applying for graduate school, so get started early. Ryan, who recently completed a two-year master's program, says he prepared for the GRE by completing a single section of a practice test "maybe every other day at work. My boss was very encouraging." (If you are currently working full-time, we should point out that few managers are likely to be as supportive of practicing for the GRE while you're on the clock).

No matter when and where you prepare for the test, however, make sure you've budgeted enough time for it. The weight placed on your GRE score in relation to the other factors Admissions Committees consider (e.g. undergraduate GPA, letters of recommendation, relevant experience in your chosen field, etc.) will vary from school to school and from program to program, but it's never insignificant. The scores from these tests (like SAT scores when you were applying to undergraduate schools) are one of the few objective metrics that help Admissions Committees evaluate candidates with very different academic and professional backgrounds. In addition to influencing admissions decisions, GRE scores are an important factor in the awarding of teaching and research assistantships and merit-based financial aid.

- **Transcripts.**

A transcript is a certified, official copy of a student's permanent academic record. All graduate schools require official transcripts of your grades from any colleges you attended. Most schools ask that transcripts be sent directly to them, but some ask that you collect the information and send in a complete application package. Contact the Registrar's Office (at every undergraduate institution you have attended) to request that your transcript be sent either to you or directly to the school to which you are applying. If your school used an unusual grading scale, you will often need to translate your transcript into the requested format.

- **Application Fee.**

Application processing fees range from moderate (around $30–$45) to expensive (over $75). As mentioned earlier, these high fees are no accident—they are designed to discourage less serious applicants from bombarding busy Admissions Committees. Fee waivers are occasionally offered by a school for applicants who can prove financial need. A good rule of thumb: If you failed to qualify for a fee waiver for the GRE, you are unlikely to qualify for a fee waiver from an institution. Check with the graduate Admissions Office of the schools to which you are applying to find out if you qualify for a fee waiver.

- **Letters of Recommendation.**

These letters are one of the most influential aspects of your application to a graduate program. Committee members use them to get a more personal perspective on an applicant. Keep this in mind when choosing your recommenders. Their words will (hopefully) be what set you apart from the other applicants. A borderline student is often pushed into the acceptance pile because of excellent recommendations.

Some application packets include recommendation forms that ask a recommender to rate your abilities in various categories; such applications generally also provide blank spaces for open-ended comments on an applicant's personality and potential. Other applications simply ask recommenders to write their own letters. Most schools require two or three letters. Try to get three or even more, in case one is lost or submitted late. Some programs require more recommendations for PhD applicants than they do for master's degree applicants. Others require additional recommendations for students applying for funding. Be sure you know the specific procedure for the department to which you are applying. If there's any doubt in your mind, call the Dean's Office or the admissions contact for that department.

If you've been out of school for a few years, you might find it difficult to approach professors from your alma mater and ask them for recommendations and understandably so: their recollections of your academic performance aren't exactly fresh. Jessica, who applied to master's programs three years after she completed her bachelor's in sociology, asked for a few recommendation letters before she completed her undergraduate course work even though she wasn't sure exactly which degree programs she'd eventually apply to. If you're still in school, you might consider this approach: This way, even if the specific applications require that your recommenders fill out additional forms, your professors will have some record of all the nice things they said about you when your academic prowess was still fresh in their minds. If it's too late for that, consider drafting a sample letter (or even an outline) that can serve as a map for the person writing your recommendation. In it, you'll want to include the points you'd most like your recommender to cover, including any specific academic achievements—in his class or otherwise—and the topics of any research projects you undertook during the class. Also provide your recommender with a copy of your transcript.

No matter what your circumstances and no matter whom you approach, give your recommenders plenty of warning when you ask them for letters! If you ask the week before the letter is due, chances are your professor (or manager or coworker) won't be able to devote enough time to crafting a compelling recommendation.

- **Personal Statement.**

  While applicants to medical, law, and business school are often asked to submit fairly lengthy essays about their motivations, goals, greatest achievements, character flaws, and/or solutions to hypothetical problems, applicants to other graduate programs are usually asked to submit a personal statement only. The personal statement may be called anything from the Autobiographical Statement to the Letter of Intent. Whatever its name, if you are required to write one, do it well. No matter what type of graduate program you are applying to, Admissions Committee members will evaluate the following: how clearly you think, how well you have conceptualized your plans for graduate school, and how well your interests and strengths mesh with their programs.

- **Interview.**

  Of major importance for admission to some graduate programs, interviews are not required for entrance to others. However, many schools encourage you to visit the campus and set up appointments to speak with Admissions Officers and individual faculty. It's a good idea for you to check out the places at which you're thinking about spending the next several years. You'll get insight into the school and the programs that you just can't get on paper. If an interview is optional, take advantage of the opportunity to make a personal impression.

Tips from a faculty member for getting letters of recommendation:

- Get to know the professor early on. Get to know the professor early on. Get to know the professor early on.

- Thoughts on how to hold a conversation with your professor in office hours:

  o   Tell me that you like the class.

  o   Tell me a thought you had about the lecture.

  o   Recommend a book I might like.

- Just show up so I can get an idea of who you are. I need to speak to your personality a bit—is he energetic? Does she talk in class?

Your unwritten application

As we've said several times now, the application process begins long before you start filling out all of those forms (and paying all of those fees). A large part of your application is never put down on paper. It consists of the contacts you've made with faculty at the programs you're applying to, your conversations with them, and the impressions you've made. Put this "unwritten application" on your checklist right beside "Bother Professor So-and-So for a recommendation" and "Study for the GRE." It's that important.

With all the piles of paper involved in applying to graduate schools, it's easy to conclude that paperwork is what it's all about. You spend weeks poring through faculty listings, course offerings, and graduate bulletins to choose your schools, and then you start filling out application forms, requesting transcripts, and writing essays. Of course, all of these documents are important. But in the graduate admissions game, you have a big advantage if you talk to people.

Unlike undergraduate schools, a typical graduate program receives hundreds—not tens of thousands—of applications each year. From this applicant pool, a program might extend offers of admission to a few dozen, expecting some of those admitted to choose other schools. It's a group of applicants small enough that the Admissions Committee can reasonably expect to meet—or at least talk to—a fair number of them. Some graduate programs receive fewer than 100 applications annually, making an individual applicant's chance of making personal contact better still. At the same time, some popular graduate programs do receive several thousand applications each year, and the Admissions Committees in charge of these programs won't necessarily have time to chat. In general, however, there's a lot of room in the graduate admissions process to talk with professors and other members of the department.

To put together the strongest possible application, you've got to be a go-getter—or at least pretend you're one. This means talking to professors in a way that makes your research interests and career intentions clear to them. If you've done some thinking about what you want from a graduate program, professors will sense your clarity and direction and get a better feel for you as a prospective student.

There are two steps to developing personal contacts within a department: First, know what program you hope to enter and what field you want to work in, as well as what you want to learn from your conversations with faculty; and second, pick up the phone and making some calls—even if it makes you nervous.

Footing the bill

Okay, now it's time for a pop quiz to see if you've been paying attention: Do you remember what the average starting salary was for a recent graduate with a degree in the liberal arts? In case you don't remember, it's approximately $31,000 per year. According to *U.S. News & World Report*, $31,000 also represents the average cost of attending graduate school for one year.[6] While that figure includes tuition and living expenses, it doesn't include the cost of being out of the workforce if you're attending graduate school full-time (and according to the Council of Graduate Schools, more than half of graduate students—around 55 percent—attend full-time).[7]

When considering the cost of graduate school, you can't ignore the implicit costs as well as the explicit ones: You're not just foregoing a real income, but you're also delaying possible career advancement opportunities. Even if your graduate program is related to the job you left behind—or the job you aspire to get—you're out of the workforce to one degree or another while you're in school. Depending on your degree program, you may not be getting any on-the-job training that's directly applicable to what you'll be doing once you finish.

The simple truth is this: Whether you're hoping to attend grad school before the ink has dried on your undergrad diploma, or whether you've been out of school for several years and would like to return to school as a way to improve your earning potential or even change careers entirely, grad school is an expensive proposition.

That said, the cost of attending graduate school alone shouldn't deter you from pursuing a graduate degree. The fact is, you have many options for financing your education, and, if an advanced-degree program is where your professional and personal stars align, then the investment will eventually pay off. However, it's important to understand how the investment will influence other decisions in your life: It's not uncommon for graduate students to postpone major milestones—like purchasing a house or starting a family—in order to fulfill their educational aspirations (and the ensuing financial obligations). While only you can decide whether choices like these are worth it—or whether they're even necessary, you need to research the implications of attending school so that you're not unpleasantly surprised once you've got your hard-earned degree in hand. To help alleviate some of the financial pressure of graduate school, the primary ways of financing a higher education (other than calling a wealthy relative, of course) are listed below:

- **Earn it.**

  For many graduate students—especially doctoral candidates—fellowships and assistantships go a long way toward paying the graduate-school tab. At the graduate level, grants like these are usually awarded based on merit. The most generous award packages not only cover tuition and fees, but also pay a stipend and provide health insurance coverage. Not all awards represent a totally free ride; while fellowships usually have no work requirement, graduate assistants typically work up to 15 hours a week

6 Kristin Davis. "The Hunt for Money." *U.S. News & World Report: America's Best Graduate Schools.* www.usnews.com/usnews/edu/grad/articles/brief/GBFinAid_brief.php.

7 Council of Graduate Schools. *Graduate Enrollment and Degrees Report: 1986 to 2005.* September 13, 2006: 3. www.cgsnet.org.

teaching, grading papers, leading discussion groups, supervising lab courses, or assisting faculty with research. If your financial aid package involves an assistantship, teaching responsibilities will place significant demands on your time. Completing your academic work will already take a major amount of time and energy, so consider whether the academic intensity of the program you choose—not to mention your time-management capabilities—will enable you to get everything done.

The amount of fellowship and assistantship aid available to you depends on the field of study you're pursuing. In the humanities, for example, only about half of full-time PhD students and 40 percent of full-time master's degree students have assistantships, and the stipends awarded are usually lower than they are in other disciplines, such as engineering, math, and computer science. To make the financial picture even more sobering, keep in mind that high-paying internships between academic years (par for the course in professional degree programs) aren't as commonplace in liberal arts fields.

The first step toward getting a fellowship or assistantship is to indicate on your admissions application that you want to be considered for all forms of financial aid. The choicest awards are often made by departmental committees on the basis of application materials and sometimes supplemental recommendations. To find other awards or assistantships, check with your school's Financial Aid Office, Graduate School Office, and Fellowship Coordinator (if there is one), or seek out faculty members in your department who are directing research funded by outside grants. Several government agencies and private organizations also sponsor outside fellowships that students can apply for on their own.

As part of the process of researching individual schools and programs, ask what percentage of students in the program are funded through fellowships, grants, and assistantships, and ask whether that changes after the first year. Some programs fund only a small percentage of students during the first year and provide funding in subsequent years based on academic performance (it's definitely worthwhile to ask whether the programs you're considering employ this approach, since it inevitably creates competition among students).

- **Borrow it.**

Most graduate students will borrow money to pay some or all of their graduate school costs. According to the National Center for Education Statistics, 69 percent of full-time master's degree students borrow to cover their expenses; on average, they carry a total of $32,500 of debt (including remaining undergraduate debt) once they finish their master's program. Some degree candidates have no choice but to finance their degrees with savings or loans; for those who earn their degrees part time while continuing to work full time, assistantships are impractical, and their income typically disqualifies them from subsidized student loans.

Of the borrowing options available, subsidized Stafford loans represent the cheapest type of student debt available. Interest rates are currently 5.3 percent, and you can borrow up to $8,500 per year ($65,500 in total). The federal government pays the interest on your loan while you're in school and for six months after you graduate or drop below half-time status. Even if interest rates rise significantly by the time you need to repay, they can't exceed 8.25 percent.

Students qualify based on financial need, so it's necessary to file the Free Application for Federal Student Aid (FAFSA) to get subsidized loans. If your need is high, you may also be offered a subsidized Perkins loan, with an interest rate of 5 percent. You can borrow an additional $10,000 a year in unsubsidized Stafford loans (and up to $138,500 in Stafford loans overall). Rates are the same as for the subsidized Stafford, and you can defer making payments, but interest begins accruing right away.

If your school participates in the Federal Direct Student Loan program, you'll borrow directly from the federal government. Otherwise, you can choose your own lender. Rates are usually the same no matter where you go, but some lenders waive upfront fees or offer attractive repayment incentives that make loans even cheaper. Student loan giant Sallie Mae, for instance, rebates 3.3 percent of your loan amount after you make 33 on-time payments.

For students who own a home, a home-equity loan or line of credit is another choice. Many banks were recently offering lines of credit at 6 percent or less, and the interest you pay is generally tax deductible. (So is up to $2,500 a year in student loan interest if you earn less than $50,000 as a single taxpayer and $105,000 if you file a joint return. A lesser amount of interest is deductible if you earn up to $65,000 or $135,000, respectively.)

If loans like these don't entirely meet your needs, keep in mind that many commercial lenders (like Citigroup and Bank of America) typically offer private education–related loans at rates only slightly higher than those for federal loans. Not only are the rates competitive, but you can typically borrow substantially more money with private lenders than you can with government lenders, whose maximum loan amounts may not provide you with the funding you need to cover all your expenses. For information on connecting with private lenders (and for general advice on financing your graduate education), check out the

"Scholarships & Aid" section of the Princeton Review's website—PrincetonReview.com/grad/finance.

However much you borrow, make sure you know exactly how much it will eat into your monthly expenses once you graduate. Several websites—including FinAid.org—provide online calculators that will let you know how much debt you can afford to take on in order to fund your master's or doctoral program.

- **Ask your employer for it.**

  If you're currently working and can make a compelling case that your advanced degree is job-related, it's possible that your employer may be able to foot at least part of the bill. According to *U.S. News & World Report*, approximately 49 percent of private firms offer tuition-reimbursement programs for job-related educational expenses as an employee benefit. About 14 percent will help employees pay for courses that aren't job related. The percentages are significantly higher for professional and technical employees and for employees of large and medium-sized firms. While employer-sponsored funding is more common among business-school students financing their MBA, it's often a compelling option for employees of colleges and universities too. Educational institutions often offer significant tuition breaks for employees—so if you're currently working at a college or university (as a research assistant or an administrator, for example), remember that your employer might help fund your advanced degree. Even if you're not pursuing an advanced degree, many schools allow their employees to take a certain number of credit hours—or continuing education classes—for free, which is something to keep in mind. No matter who your employer is, be sure to read the fine print before you tap into this kind of funding, because you typically can't just take the money and run—there are usually restrictions on how long you must stay with the company once you've obtained your degree.

- **Tell Uncle Sam about it.**

  Students paying out of pocket for tuition and fees can take advantage of the federal Lifetime Learning tax credit, worth up to $2,000. The credit equals 20 percent of the first $10,000 you spend in tuition and fees each year. If you file a single return, you're eligible for the full tax credit if your income is $45,000 or less and for a partial credit with income up to $55,000. For married couples filing jointly, the tax credit is fully available with income up to $90,000 and partially available with income up to $110,000. You can use the credit even if you don't itemize deductions, and it reduces your tax bill dollar for dollar.[8]

8 Kristin Davis. "The Hunt for Money." *U.S. News & World Report: America's Best Graduate Schools* www.usnews.com/usnews/edu/grad/articles/brief/GBFinAid_brief.php.

Careers in Academia: The PhD Option

In order to complete a doctorate degree, you will need to be able to conduct independent research resulting in the creation of new knowledge. Including the time it takes to write and defend a dissertation, this degree can take anywhere from five to seven years to complete. Progress towards the degree can be slow, and a few major hurdles need to be overcome early—qualifying exams, course work in the first couple years, and the defense of a dissertation idea before a self-selected panel of professors.

If you want to tackle the hard problems in society and have activist instincts, you may want to go elsewhere (like Capitol Hill). Academia may not be the agent for social change it used to be, but you can expect to make a very positive difference on a small segment of the academic community and your students. As one graduate student told us, "I would encourage anybody who is thinking about going to graduate school with the intention of pursuing an academic career to try something else for a while and see if your passion for the subject leads you back to it. If it does, then you are in the right place."

You may have gotten to know the graduate teaching assistants in your psychology or sociology classes, but life as a graduate student involves quite a bit more than teaching undergraduates. Once you enter a PhD program you are not a "student" in the same way you were as an undergraduate. You are part of the academe, and you are treated by professors as a colleague. There is no pressure for grades and you probably won't take tests, but the workload is very demanding. The general absence of hard and fast constraints means that self-discipline is essential for finishing the degree. However, you are still a "student" in some ways, and as such, you'll enjoy all the rich opportunities for culture and fun that are part of campus life. Most graduate students we talked to agreed that, despite the many challenges, the path is vastly rewarding.

Going all the way: An academic career

The traditional employment objective of PhDs is a tenure-track faculty position. While these positions aren't impossible to obtain, landing one is far from a sure thing—and the path toward getting one is arduous. A master's degree may be sufficient to qualify to teach in a two-year college, but a doctoral degree is required to teach in four-year colleges and universities. While the PhD dissertation is the most important element of the search for a first job as a professor, postdoctoral experience—teaching or research done by PhDs *after* they've earned their doctorates but *before* they've landed tenure-track teaching positions—is also crucial. For the coveted tenure-track positions, virtually every successful job candidate now boasts at least one and usually two "postdoc" years, and these are necessary to remain competitive, which means gathering a sufficient backlog of publications and writings in progress. Personal relationships with faculty are also critical in this hunt for a first job, as teaching positions in many areas (particularly the humanities) can be scarce. While approximately 80 percent of college jobs are in four-year institutions, about a third of all college faculty are employed part-time or in non–tenure track positions, and this percentage has risen in recent years as colleges attempt to control costs.

It's worth noting that landing your first job after you've completed your PhD is far from the end of the road. You'll spend at least five or six years as an assistant professor. In your seventh year, you'll be evaluated for a tenure position on the basis of teaching and research (which almost always means published work). Institutions vary in the relative importance they place on these criteria, but it's always some combination of the two. Those who earn tenure are—for the most part—virtually guaranteed job security until they retire. Tenure also effectively separates junior faculty from senior faculty at most institutions. Senior, tenured faculty members have far more discretion when it comes to deciding what to teach as well as when (or whether) to conduct research than do junior faculty.

Folks who are jazzed enough about their studies to go this route aren't necessarily motivated by money or the certainty of getting a job—and that's a good thing. Not only do most doctoral candidates live pretty frugally while they're working toward their degree, but, unlike advanced degrees in business or medicine, there's no guarantee of recouping the financial investment. According to a recent article in *U.S. News & World Report*, roughly 30 percent of PhDs who earned their degrees in 2004 were still seeking employment or planning further studies in 2006, thanks in large part to a perennially tight job market for tenured professors. According to the same article, PhDs in the humanities and liberal arts face a particularly formidable challenge when it comes to landing a job. In 2001, for example, there were more than twice as many newly minted PhDs as there were available tenure-track teaching positions. Of course, non-academic jobs are an option, too; in fact, approximately 4 out of 10 PhDs go the private-sector route. Still, the relative scarcity of available jobs—especially when compared to the investment of time and money that a PhD requires—leads to a fairly high attrition rate among doctoral candidates. Roughly 40 to 50 percent of matriculating students never earn their PhD.[9] And some master's degree candidates who toy with the idea of pushing forward for a PhD decide against it when they take a hard look at the job prospects.

The good news, however, is that the job outlook for future professors is considerably brighter than it was even a few years ago. According to the Bureau of Labor Statistics, employment of postsecondary (i.e., college and university) teachers is expected to grow much faster than the average for all occupations through 2014. That's good news if you're in for the long haul since the BLS also predicts that "PhD recipients seeking jobs as postsecondary teachers will experience favorable job prospects over the next decade."[10]

9 Silla Brush, "Beyond the Ivory Tower." *U.S. News & World Report: America's Best Graduate Schools.* 2006: 54–55.

10 Bureau of Labor Statistics. *Occupational Outlook Handbook,* 2006–2007 Edition. U.S. Department of Labor. www.bls.gov/oco/ocos066.htm.

11 Ibid.

Though job prospects will vary significantly depending on the field you're in, there are a few demographic trends working in your favor if you want to be a professor. First of all, significant numbers of current professors (many of whom were hired in the late 1960s and the 1970s) are expected to retire over the next few years. Not only is the supply of professors expected to shrink, but demand for professors is expected to increase. The BLS predicts higher enrollment numbers at colleges and universities, which stems mainly from the expected increase in the population of 18- to 24-year-olds (who make up the majority of the college-student population).[11]

Even with the decreasing supply and increasing demand for college-level professors, however, it's important to remember that a significant proportion of the resulting job opportunities will be part-time positions. The BLS predicts that while competition will remain tight for tenure-track positions at four-year colleges and universities, there will be a considerable number of part-time or renewable, term appointments at these institutions and positions at community colleges available to them.[12]

And now the good news . . .

While a career in academia isn't the right choice for everyone, it can prove to be an immensely satisfying, rewarding profession for many people. (If there weren't an awful lot to recommend it, why would so many people be clamoring for it?) If you love reading, observing, and figuring things out then there are few careers that offer greater opportunities for indulging your unique intellectual interests. As a professor, you're not just developing an area of expertise—a significant portion of your time and energy will usually be devoted to knowledge creation. The profession is therefore best suited for motivated self-starters, and its highest rewards are given to those who can identify and explore original problems in their fields.

You're also paid to teach that material to people who are interested in learning it— and for many professors (hopefully including the ones you'll be working with) the opportunity to contribute to other people's learning and growth provides the greatest source of professional fulfillment.

There's also a lot of variety in an academic career: Many full-time faculty engage in outside professional activities. Economists consult with governments and corporations; engineers and academic labs develop products for private industry; humanities professors write articles which appear in newspapers and magazines. Many find this ability to work professionally on terms they define, while remaining in their institutions, to be among the most satisfying aspects of the profession. In addition, the significant administrative positions in colleges and universities are usually filled by former and current professors, and it is not uncommon for careers in university administration to develop from teaching careers.

Aside from the career satisfaction many professors enjoy, there are other—more practical—perks that come with the job. In addition to the time spent teaching in the classroom (which amounts to as few as 3 hours a week in graduate schools, up to 12

12 Ibid.

to 16 hours a week in undergraduate schools), professors spend time meeting with students during designated office hours, sitting on committees, and completing any number of administrative duties associated with teaching a class or running a department. But they can allocate the rest of their time as they see fit. Professors get summers off too—or they at least get a three-month break from their teaching and administrative responsibilities. In actuality, few professors spend three months on the beach every year; many devote the majority of that time to conducting their own research, catching up on journal reading, and planning the courses that they'll be teaching the following semester. Still, they can complete that work whenever—and wherever—they choose.

Job security is another big draw. A tenured-professor gig isn't the guaranteed job for life it once was (post-tenure review is now required at most universities, and those who fall behind on teaching and independent scholarship may not be as secure as they would have been 10 or 20 years ago). Still, once professors earn tenure they have considerably more job security than their counterparts in the private sector. Of course, they typically don't earn the same fat paychecks, either. In 2004–2005, salaries for full-time faculty averaged $68,505. Specifically, the average salary was $91,548 for professors, $65,113 for associate professors, $54,571 for assistant professors, $39,899 for instructors, and $45,647 for lecturers. Educators in four-year institutions earned higher salaries, on average, than did those in two-year schools. In fields with high-paying non-academic alternatives—e.g., medicine, law, engineering, business—professors tended to earn higher-than-average salaries, while professors in others fields—e.g., the humanities, education—typically recorded salaries on the lower end of the range.[13]

FELLOWSHIPS: KEEPING THE DREAM ALIVE

Imagine being paid as a student to do research and produce articles on the Arctic National Wildlife Refuge, to present your dissertation at a conference on developmental psychology surrounded by intellectual luminaries, or being courted for editorial positions at various well-known newspapers due to a summer spent right in the belly of a newsroom. Ah, the innumerable and diverse joys of a fellowship. A true acknowledgment of your professional potential, fellowships allow you to pursue your research interests and learn directly from some of the most prominent leaders in your field. More importantly, they can help fund your graduate education. Essentially, fellowships are like scholarships that provide undergraduate, graduate, and postgraduate students and professionals with short-term intense learning experiences lasting anywhere from several months to over a year, and specific professional development opportunities that will have a direct impact on the fellow's future career path. Most fellowships are sponsored by the academic department to which you're applying and

13 Bureau of Labor Statistics. *Occupational Outlook Handbook,* 2006–2007 Edition. U.S. Department of Labor.

are intended to provide particularly gifted students with the time and resources to immerse themselves completely in their areas of study. Some of the most prestigious fellowships are privately funded. See Appendix A for information about fellowship opportunities that may be of interest to you as a psychology or sociology major.

CHAPTER 7

Popular Advanced Study Options for Psychology and Sociology Majors

I USED TO BE YOU PROFILE[1]

Dr. Ruth Westheimer

Born in Germany, 1928

How You Know Her

Sexually Speaking the first radio talk show about sexual literacy

Psychology or Sociology?

Both! A Bachelor's Degree in Psychology and a Master's Degree in Sociology

Her "First" Real Job

Kindergarten teacher

Her Educational Path

When she was 10 years old Ruth Westheimer was sent to Switzerland to avoid the rising Nazi regime and attend primary school. The school quickly became an orphanage as more than 95 percent of the German Jewish students' (including Ruth Westheimer's) parents were killed while Hitler terrorized Europe. Since only boys were allowed to participate in academic pursuits in Swiss schools, Ruth was taught to be a maid. At 16, she fled the school and its low expectations, moving to Israel where she helped in the struggle for independence. Although there is some debate as to her role (several reliable sources claim this sex therapist was trained as a sniper) it is confirmed that she was wounded in action and unable to walk for more than a month. Following her military service, Ruth moved again, this time to France. Here she enrolled at the Sorbonne in Paris and graduated with a degree in psychology and taught kindergarten for several years after graduation.

Once again on the move and with only her psychology degree to her name, Ruth immigrated to America in 1956. Soon after her arrival, she was accepted into the Columbia School of Social Research and earned a Master's Degree in Sociology. Wanting to put her academic understanding of psychology and sociology to more practical purposes, she decided to stay in New York and get a Doctorate of Education (EdD) in the Interdisciplinary Study of the Family from Columbia University Teacher's College. While writing her dissertation, she studied human sexuality with Dr. Helen Singer-Kaplan at New York Hospital—Cornell University Medical Center and became an expert on the subject.

How This Psychology and Sociology Major Succeeded

With her EdD, Dr. Ruth began working for Planned Parenthood and imagining a day when she would use mass media to help spread what she called "sexual literacy." The public adored this 4' 7" ball of fire who could

---

1 Wikipedia contributors. "Ruth Westheimer." Wikipedia, The Free Encyclopedia. http://en.wikipedia.org/wiki/Ruth_Westheimer.

communicate effectively across multiple media platforms. However, it wasn't until Dr. Ruth was in her mid 50s that real fame hit when she began her radio show with frank, no-holds-barred talk about sex. No one had ever done this before, and by accepting the challenge, she skyrocketed from relative obscurity as a college professor to world renown as Dr. Ruth. Her books have been translated to 23 languages. Her television career has spanned both broadcast and cable. Her first TV show aired locally in New York and soon went national on Lifetime's *The Dr. Ruth Show.* Both her TV and radio shows have been syndicated nationally and internationally.

Advice From This Fellow Psychology/Sociology Major

"No matter what degree you are receiving today, it doesn't lock you into any one path. If you feel like trying your hand at something else, I say go ahead and take a chance."[2]

—May 2004 Trinity College commencement address

I USED TO BE YOU PROFILE[3]

Ronald Reagan

Born February 6, 1911 in Tampico, Illinois (in an apartment above a bank)

Why You Know Him

The fortieth President of the United States (the oldest ever elected at age 69) 1981–1989

Psychology or Sociology?

Bachelor's Degree in Sociology

First Job Out of College

Radio announcer at station WOC in Davenport, Iowa

His Educational Path

President Reagan graduated from Eureka College after double-majoring in sociology and economics in 1932.

How This Sociology Major Succeeded

In 1937, while in California covering spring training for the Chicago Cubs as a radio announcer, Reagan decided to take a screen test at Warner Brothers

---

2 Ruth Westheimer. "2004 Trinity College Commencement Address." Trinity College. www.trincoll.edu/AboutTrinity/commencement/releases.

3 "Discover Reagan." www.ronaldreagan.com/index.php.

Studio. His clear voice, easygoing manner, and athletic physique, all which would endear him to the public in his future political career, helped him land a seven-year contract.

His first major political role was president of the Screen Actors Guild, an influential labor union, which he claimed was being infiltrated by Communists. In this position, he testified before the House of Representative's Un-American Activities Committee on Communist influence in Hollywood. He also kept tabs on actors he considered disloyal and informed on them to the Federal Bureau of Investigation under the code name "Agent T-10."

Entertaining political aspirations, Reagan entered the 1966 race to be the thirty-third governor of California and won, defeating two-term incumbent Pat Brown. He was re-elected in 1970. Reagan made the leap to national politics by winning the Republican presidential nomination in 1980. Sixty-nine days after taking office, Reagan was shot by a would-be assassin. When his wife Nancy arrived at the hospital, Reagan told her, "Honey, I forgot to duck."

The Global Impact of This Sociology Major

A recent Gallup poll on the most popular presidents in U.S. history indicates that Ronald Reagan was chosen by 87 percent of Americans polled, followed by John F. Kennedy, Dwight D. Eisenhower, and Franklin D. Roosevelt.

BACK TO SCHOOL

You've carefully considered your career goals and objectives, and weighed the personal, financial, and career implications of pursuing an advanced degree. Now dive deeper and explore your options for graduate study.

How the programs are presented

The entries in this chapter provide a comprehensive overview of some of the most popular graduate programs (with popular areas of concentration) attended by both psychology and sociology majors. This list is neither exclusive nor exhaustive and merely highlights a significant range of graduate school options. Like any graduate course, we begin with "The Syllabus," a discussion of the common overall curriculum, specific course work and the usual types of degrees offered. After describing the particular field of study, we introduce you to "Your Classmates" with an overview of the skills and personality traits commonly held by individuals in this area. While it does not constitute a mandatory list of abilities, these suggestions define the kind of person most likely to possess the motivation and interest to complete an extra year or ultimately pursue a PhD in that particular area of study. Next, we present the "Only in Academia" section, which highlights a few quirky topics of interest to some in the field. Hopefully this will provide a better idea of some of the exciting features and latest developments in the discipline and demonstrate that the sky is the limit when it comes to possible thesis work. The "After Commencement" section discusses what you might be doing—you guessed it—after graduation. Finally, the list of "Related Programs" details a few of the many other options you might want to consider if that particular graduate program piques your interest but is not exactly where you see yourself as a graduate student.

SOCIOLOGY PROGRAMS

Anthropology

THE SYLLABUS

Anthropology is the study of humanity, with an emphasis on cultural evolution and comparison. The discipline is traditionally divided into four fields: physical, cultural, linguistic, and archaeology. Each subdiscipline concentrates on a certain cluster of civilization's history such as human evolution, social behavior, language, and historical remains. Anthropologists are typically concerned with human development either over time or across cultures. Most of their time is spent studying past evidence, researching information, or searching for new sources of evidence.

Because of the broad subject areas encompassed by anthropology, a graduate program in this discipline will most likely require some form of specialization within the field. In addition, many graduate programs in anthropology will require or suggest knowledge of a second language. A PhD program will involve years of research culminating in a dissertation in the final year of the program. The first portion of the program is thus dedicated to course work in anthropology and the chosen specialization, while the remaining time is allocated for research and development of the dissertation. The PhD program typically involves about three years of course work and various requirements, and then an open-ended period in which to complete the research and dissertation. An MA program is usually a truncated version of the PhD program, covering the first one or two years of the PhD track. An MA degree will most likely still involve a specialization and a thesis supported by hands-on research carried out as part of the program.

YOUR CLASSMATES

Anthropology students have a genuine interest in culture and society and in learning about different philosophies as well as developing new theories through research. They exhibit sensitivity and curiosity regarding matters of diversity and cultural distinctions. Graduate students are well-rounded individuals with backgrounds in statistics, quantitative methods, language skills, and written communication.

Some of the more unusual areas of specific interest include:

- How we think with animals (otherwise known as anthropomorphism)
- Human influence on natural disasters
- Influences of cross-cultural issues (e.g., circumcision) on adoption
- The logic behind environmentalism

AFTER COMMENCEMENT

People interested in pursuing their PhD are most likely attracted to careers in academia, including teaching, researching, and writing. Those who receive an MA can find careers in the social sciences or health fields. Anthropologists can apply their knowledge and research in institutions such as government, industry, and museums. As Jan Cochran, an anthropology graduate student and certifiable optimist notes, "Every single job involves some interaction or study of humans, so an anthropology degree makes you an expert in everything."

RELATED PROGRAMS

Public, Urban, and Regional Affairs

Higher Education and Student Affairs

Public, Urban, and Regional Affairs

THE SYLLABUS

Cities are complex organisms that require daily management and planning by a host of individuals to run smoothly. Public, urban, and regional affairs are key parts of this process and a logical next step for sociology majors who are interested in the ways in which laws and policies affect specific communities. Attending city council meetings, acting as representatives for entire populations, and liaising between the public and the government or business organizations are just a few of a public affairs official's almost daily interactions.

Graduate programs in this area delve into topics in human development, community design and planning, finance, economics, and research. Programs usually involve research projects and a mentor-mentee relationship with faculty members. A graduate education will most likely result in a Master of Public Administration (MPA), but other degree tracks like the Master's in Urban and Regional Planning or Public Policy are possible. Each master's program contains specializations. Obtaining a PhD in Public Administration is another option. Typical course work for PhDs includes microeconomics, statistics, research methods, demographics, public policy and law, ethics in public policy and administration, public budgeting and finance, organizational dynamics, and leadership and managerial effectiveness.

YOUR CLASSMATES

Graduate students in public, urban, and regional affairs programs are quite diverse and range from mild-mannered environmentalists with visions of lush green spaces to future politicians hungry for power and influence over lucrative city contracts. Overall, however, most are looking for a leadership role and a platform from which to spur progress and develop new social and policy strategies.

ONLY IN ACADEMIA

Some of the more unusual areas of specific interest include:

- The homeless and their role in public spaces
- Waste management issues
- How electric power markets communicate
- The comparison of yearly income to those who drink bottled or public (tap) water

AFTER COMMENCEMENT

Graduates find work in the private, public, and nonprofit sectors. They work in a variety of influential positions within public affairs, as city and county managers, public safety managers, law enforcement positions, policy analysts, humanitarian organization directors, school administrators, and military officers. Some choose to devote their careers to teaching and research in the field.

RELATED PROGRAMS

Anthropology

Political Science and International Affairs

Criminology and Forensics

THE SYLLABUS

Do you love watching *CSI*? Are *The Silence of the Lambs* and *Manhunter* two of your favorite films? If so, this is the field of study for you. Criminology and forensic science (also known simply as forensics) involves the investigation of crime and focuses on the scientific phenomena behind crime and the analysis of residual evidence. But while criminologists focus on the theories and research behind crime and study crime as an individual and social production with distinct causes and consequences, forensics is the more hands-on dissection of a crime, combining the tenets of science, criminology, and law through evaluations of physical evidence and criminal laboratory analyses.

Graduate programs related to these wide ranging fields are numerous. Possible degree programs include the MS in Forensic Science, MA in Criminology, and various criminal justice programs with concentrations in forensics or criminology. Master's programs take approximately two years to complete, and certificate programs in related fields are an option as well, often requiring one year of study. Internships in the field are considered important aspects of most graduate programs, and lab and research experience is frequently a significant component of the curriculum. Course work covers topics such as crime scene reconstruction, physical analysis in forensic science, biomedical methods in forensic science, justice administration, psychological applications in criminal justice, toxicology, research design and statistics, race and crime, law and society, and sociology of law enforcement.

YOUR CLASSMATES

Students in criminology and forensics programs are exceptionally inquisitive and are, usually, also strong willed and comfortable taking risks. These are important traits to have since people in this profession often interact with front-line law enforcement. Additionally, most practitioners have an avid interest in law and in supporting the legal and justice system. Most participants are fascinated by the physical science behind social behavior and the applications of investigative principles and methods. Concepts in chemistry and laboratory sciences, as well as criminal justice and the law, appeal to these students, who are often very interested in integrating these related fields.

ONLY IN ACADEMIA

Some of the more unusual areas of specific interest include:

- How to identify bodies using nothing but an ear print
- The specific cause of death for individuals discovered in wells and sewage systems
- Age-based determinants related to femicide
- Self-mutilation

AFTER COMMENCEMENT

Graduates find positions within the criminal justice system in all areas of law enforcement including courts, corrections, juvenile justice, and crime scene investigation. Employers include government organizations, regional police departments, corrections facilities, and private research organizations. Some graduates may choose to pursue a doctorate in order to provide teaching and consulting services in criminology or forensic science.

Survey Methodology

Anthropology

Political Science and International Affairs

THE SYLLABUS

If you were intrigued by the idea of pursuing a career in a think tank or some other behind the scenes position in politics, this is the graduate field for you. No doubt about it, a graduate degree in political science or international affairs will prepare you for a run for office. However, if you aspire to be an elected official, you are probably better off going out and running for a low-level office in your hometown to see if the career and lifestyle meet your expectations. Graduate study in political science and international affairs prepares students for careers in public policy, energy regulation, social security administration, and political action research. Political science and international affairs concentrates on the origin and operations of politics including relations between countries or the politics of individual towns and cities. This graduate field integrates the theory and practice of political systems and public policy.

Some of the more popular degree subfields under the umbrella of political science are American government and politics, comparative politics, international relations, and political theory. They can be studied alone or combined, and students can pursue a doctorate in many of these fields. Regardless of the program or concentration, all emphasize broad theoretical concepts as well as practical applications of policy analysis through course work, internships, fellowships, and research projects. Typical courses in the areas of political science and international affairs include international economics, research methods, advanced statistical techniques, international relations theory, U.S. foreign policy, globalization and social change, contemporary political thought, causes of war, political geography, military strategy and policy, and politics of revolution and change.

YOUR CLASSMATES

Graduate students in this area are intrigued by the prospect of enriching foreign relations and political developments domestically and abroad. They have wide interests in government, law, history, economics, policy, international relations, and research, and are quick to debate almost any political position or development. They also share an avid interest in creating effective global progress in the political realm and promoting cooperation and understanding among parties.

Some of the more unusual areas of specific interest include:

- The moral implications and ethics of torture and exemplary assassination
- How ethnic movements are effected by non-ethnic support
- The influence of corporate greed on global governance
- The history behind why people in the Middle East are distrustful of Americans

AFTER COMMENCEMENT

Just a few of the jobs that political science and international affairs graduates are well prepared to leap into are policy researcher (or, as they are often called, "wonks"), Foreign Service officer, political action lobbyist, and CIA, NSA, and FBI analyst. These careers share an emphasis on researching governments and political trends, policy making, analysis, and advising.

RELATED PROGRAMS

Public, Urban, and Regional Affairs

Conflict Resolution and Mediation

Survey Methodology

THE SYLLABUS

Are you a nitpicker? Do you make lists every day to keep track of what you need to get accomplished? Did you teach yourself Excel just because it's a great way to keep track of things? If so, then look no further: This is the graduate program for you. Survey methodology is the study of sources of error in surveys that compromise the quality and accuracy of results. Those in survey methodology seek to intertwine the concepts of design, collection, processing, and analysis of surveys and come to conclusions about their relationships to error. They work to produce the most effective survey methods and the most accurate data for any type of research.

Survey methodology students are educated in the theory and practical applications of the field. Programs result in a Master of Science or Doctorate in Survey Methodology, and the core courses include statistical methods, cognition, communication, survey measurement, questionnaire design, and sampling methods.

Your Classmates

Many hard-core researchers lean toward introversion and prefer the solitary nature of programming and poring over data. Undoubtedly, your classmates will excel in mathematics, statistics, and science, and be interested in contributing to quantitative research endeavors and furthering the effectiveness of survey methods. Although primarily from the liberal arts, practitioners in this field come from a variety of undergraduate backgrounds. Regardless of previous study and training, graduate students in this field must be familiar with survey design and its application, including how it is perceived both scientifically and publicly.

Only in Academia

Some of the more unusual areas of specific interest include:

- The effects of non-response household surveys
- Modes of inference for finite population sampling
- Biometric responses to web surveys
- Why people do not like telemarketers

After Commencement

Survey methodology graduates come out prepared to work in all aspects of the survey process—from creation to fulfillment. They develop new survey methods and test the limits of their applications, select samples, and create new administrative procedures that enhance the efficacy of surveys and heighten accuracy. In a laboratory setting, survey methodologists work with focus group subjects and scientists to develop specific methods to improve sample selection and data collection. Out in the field, methodologists train survey distribution staff and generally supervise survey operations. Employers range from government agencies to universities to private firms. Countless government agencies at the local, state, and federal levels employ survey methodologists as they receive much of their statistical data via surveys. Academic institutions employ survey methodologists at numerous survey research centers. Private firms seek thoroughly trained survey methodologists to work on their data collection and research staffs. Graduates hold positions at a variety of research think tanks, from assistant to project director.

Related Programs

Criminology and Forensics

Anthropology

Conflict Resolution and Mediation

If you enjoyed your sociology courses focused on group dynamics, gender equity, race relations, or social psychology, then graduate work in conflict resolution and mediation might be for you. Regardless of the industry or the environment, professionals in this field spend their days settling arguments among various parties whether they are individuals, groups, companies, or even nations. Mediators work to understand the origin of the conflict and to promote understanding and negotiation among all peoples with the objective of reaching a mutually agreeable solution. John Wall, a former regional manager for Arbitration Forums, a company that settles claims between insurance companies out of court, describes what it takes to work in the field: "In almost every case, both sides of the table believe that they are 100 percent right and the other side is crazy. This makes for sessions which are both exciting and sometimes funny, but the element of anger, which sometimes has turned into true hatred, can make for some pretty tense sessions that are no fun at all. Patience is a key and keeping the discussion civilized and rooted in facts is the highest priority."

Graduate programs educate students on the theory and methods of successful mediation, and students learn to use the principles of conflict resolution to analyze disputes and generate reasonable solutions. Curriculum focused on clarifying morals and the ethical behavior necessary to approach conflicts is a major component of the program. Another large segment is devoted to mediation practice via internships in a hands-on environment such as an ombudsman office, which is a specific department charged with solving internal disputes, often between colleagues or between workers and management. Graduate students might attain a master's in conflict analysis and resolution, conflict transformation, or in social and public policy with a concentration in peace and conflict studies. Other programs can range from graduate certificates which are just a single year of introductory graduate training in conflict resolution, to a doctorate degree for those interested in becoming consultants, educators, or researchers in conflict resolution. Some typical classes for a graduate student in any of the focus areas include culture and conflict, violence prevention and intervention, theory and practice of mediation, negotiation and facilitation, and nonviolent social change.

YOUR CLASSMATES

People in this field value equity and want people to get along. Many were the peacemakers in their home while growing up, settling arguments between siblings and relatives in an effort to maintain harmony. John Wall describes other necessary attributes: "In addition to patience, you must at least appear exceptionally thoughtful, love details, and be process oriented. People only respect the mediation process if it is orderly, it is based on an understandable protocol, and the final outcome reflects logic and/or precedent. If the client doesn't understand your process, any conclusion you make will be suspect and, most likely, unacceptable." More broadly speaking, students are prepared to provide innovative and resourceful additions to the methods of conflict resolution and to put their educations into practical applications. These students are flexible and adept at working with diverse people in crisis situations, and they demonstrate patience and compassion while negotiating with others. It is important for students to gain a true understanding of fairness and justice in order to evaluate situations properly and equitably.

ONLY IN ACADEMIA

Some of the more unusual areas of specific interest include:

- E-Negotiations: Using the web and e-mail to speed up getting along
- Will the world's religions ever be able to get along?
- How to promote positive community growth after (literally) being bombed
- Negotiation between long-standing adversaries

AFTER COMMENCEMENT

Graduates find themselves working in a variety of settings providing consulting, mediation, and negotiation services for a wide range of parties. Clients include communities, businesses, nonprofits, international committees, and government organizations, and objectives include a diverse array of conflict prevention and resolution functions. Job titles include diversity program director or conflicts specialist for a relief organization or government department.

RELATED PROGRAMS

Higher Education and Student Affairs

Political Science and International Affairs

Higher Education and Student Affairs

THE SYLLABUS

What if you could stay in college and get paid to do it? That is basically how Deborah Liverman, Assistant Director in the Massachusetts Institute of Technology Careers Center, describes her job. "I get paid to be on campus and work with highly motivated students every day—it doesn't get any better." Deborah also describes what being a student affairs professional in higher education is all about. "Regardless of the office you work in—for example, Residence Life, Admissions, or, like me, Career Services—you can be sure you'll be doing at least one, if not all of the three main duties of a student affairs professional: advising students, organizing events, and marketing your office." Ultimately, all student affairs professionals work in higher education institutions to enhance and maximize the academic experience for students, including the areas of health and wellness, career counseling, housing, and extracurricular activities. They work in all fields of student life, student development, student services, and other professional areas to generate and modify academic programs, policies, administrative procedures, and other aspects of the institution's academic and student systems.

Graduate programs for higher education and student affairs fall under a variety of degree tracks. Two of the most common programs include the Master of Science in College Student Personnel Administration and Master of Arts in Educational Administration with an emphasis in higher education. The curricula of popular programs follow the standards set by the Council for the Advancement of Standards in Higher Education. Programs incorporate both theory and practice both in the classroom and directly in the university environment. They strive to instill graduates with the knowledge, skills, ethical standards, respect for diversity, and compassion necessary to optimize student experiences. They often involve close interactions with the student affairs professionals on the campus of the graduate program in order to gain practical, hands-on knowledge. Typical courses include history of higher education, college student personnel administration, law in higher education, leadership development, governance and finance in higher education, and student development theory, and almost all require an on-campus internship in a Student Affairs Office.

YOUR CLASSMATES

Graduate students in higher education and student affairs are typically the people who were most involved in on-campus extracurricular activities as undergraduates. They probably worked as residence assistants (RAs), spirit coordinators, and campus tour guides, and held multiple leadership roles on campus. Your cohorts likely will have cheerleader-like enthusiasm for their area of study and be intent on enriching students' college experiences. Overall, they are motivated and demonstrate excellent leadership skills. Many are comfortable in mentoring positions. Most of all, they feel they can relate to students and develop fun and effective programs.

ONLY IN ACADEMIA

Some of the more unusual areas of specific interest include:

- The effects of attending a single-gender high school on college performance
- The effects of drinking on making friends and test performance
- How to stop parents from intervening on behalf of their child in college
- Appropriate boundaries for sex education in residence halls

AFTER COMMENCEMENT

Deborah shares, "I loved being in college, and by my senior year I started trying to figure out how I could stay there. I asked the faculty advisor for the honor society of which I was president how she got into her job, and she explained that professors and faculty were only about half of the people who worked at the university. There I was, in it everyday, and I never really considered all of the people behind the scenes on the 'other' side of my diploma." In due course, graduates of these programs work in colleges and universities in a variety of specialized departments and might be involved in the operations and approaches of Residence Life, Counseling Centers, Academic Advising, Admissions, the Registrar's Office, Student Activities, and many other functional areas of university life. Among other opportunities, graduates hold positions as residential program directors, directors of academic grants, and even deans of university departments.

RELATED PROGRAMS

Public, Urban, and Regional Affairs

Industrial and Organizational Psychology

PSYCHOLOGY PROGRAMS

Clinical Psychology

THE SYLLABUS

Many undergraduate psychology majors, at some point, consider becoming a clinical psychologist, practicing their craft from the comfort of a deep leather lounge in an upscale, private office. Being paid to listen to people share their concerns and ask the occasional insightful question is tremendously appealing to many. Technically, clinical psychology is one of many distinct areas in the field known as applied psychology. This discipline emphasizes the practical application of psychological theory and research, integrating science, philosophy, and practice. Clinical psychologists observe and assess human behavior in various states of mental distress with the purpose of evaluating and developing methods of psychological care. They spend their time doing both research in the field and providing therapy to their clients.

All graduate programs in clinical psychology involve several hundred or even thousands of hours of supervised practice in order for students to develop the competency to maintain a private practice. These hours are usually completed during the second through fourth years of the program. A supervised internship is also a common requirement and is typically completed during the fourth or fifth year of the program.

Graduate programs emphasize critical theory in biological, cognitive, and social behaviors. They also include courses in developmental psychology, personality, and psychotherapy theories. Programs are based around research methodology. The comprehensive nature of the graduate programs' curriculum assures student proficiency in a diverse collection of psychological theories, clinical experiences, and research approaches.

Graduate programs in clinical psychology offer assorted degree options. The PhD (Doctor of Philosophy) degree takes at least five years to complete, stresses research, and requires you to take courses in statistics and experimental design. Also, experimental research is an expected component of the PhD program and generally culminates in a dissertation. The PsyD (Doctor of Psychology) degree program takes four to five years to complete and focuses on the various aspects of clinical work. It is designed for people who are primarily interested in practicing psychology as opposed to doing quantitative research, and it usually consists of more clinical experience than the PhD. PsyD programs also tend to have larger class sizes (40–50 students) than PhD programs (5–10 students). Clinical psychology students can specialize further in health psychology, neuropsychology, developmental psychology, geropsychology, group therapy, or behavioral therapy.

YOUR CLASSMATES

Graduate students in clinical psychology programs have a keen interest in studying and researching human behavior. They usually exhibit critical thinking and analytical skills, and they are dedicated to both practicing and improving clinical psychology methods and standards. Interests in science and math will be common as most will have performed research as undergraduates and have the logical methodology and analytical thought processes necessary for deconstructing psychopathology.

ONLY IN ACADEMIA

Some of the more unusual areas of specific interest include:

- What the "doodles" of high-ranking White House officials (including the president) imply
- Rates of post-traumatic stress disorder (PTSD) in high-risk professions
- Comparing women with and without phobic fear of spiders

AFTER COMMENCEMENT

Following graduate school, clinical psychologists typically pursue careers in clinical work, teaching, or research depending on the degree they have earned. Several go on to develop private practices. Many, however, gravitate toward work as psychologists in managed-care groups affiliated with hospitals. Other practicing clinical psychologists work in family therapy, marriage counseling, psychotherapy, or numerous other specialized fields out of hospitals, rehabilitation clinics, and private offices. Graduates of a PsyD program are the ones most likely to go on to be practicing psychologists. It should be noted that almost every one of these career paths, especially a private practice which has the ability to be reimbursed by a health insurance provider, requires a rigorous certification process beyond graduate-level course work, and the conditions can vary greatly by state.

Developmental Psychology

Addictions and Substance Abuse Counseling

Marriage and Family Therapy

THE SYLLABUS

Just as the program name implies, marriage and family therapy involves providing counseling services to families, couples, and even individuals, in cases where other members of the family are unwilling to attend. Therapists in this field facilitate effective communication and accurate perceptions among group members in order to improve the family dynamic. They work toward understanding and diffusing issues so that individual and family crises are addressed and hopefully prevented in the future. They can be called upon to provide diagnostic services and help clients overcome child and adolescent difficulties, eating disorders, alcohol and drug abuse, couples conflicts, depression, and other mental health issues.

Graduate programs in marriage and family therapy focus on teaching both the practical and the theoretical principles behind healthy relationships. Students graduate with a thorough understanding of the individual, marital, and family dynamic, in addition to assessment skills, and intervention skills. Along with these course sequences, almost every program requires extensive supervised clinical training so that graduates can apply these theories firsthand. A typical curriculum covers child guidance and parenting, intervention and assessment skills, marriage and family therapy models, community psychology, and couples counseling.

Marriage and family therapy graduate programs can result in a Master of Arts (MA) or Master of Science (MS) in Marriage and Family Therapy. Many programs offer the master's degree only en route to a doctorate (PhD). Master's degrees generally take two years to attain while a doctorate program takes four to five years

YOUR CLASSMATES

Your cohorts will include many compassionate people, some of whom were themselves in family therapy at some point and are now firm believers in the counseling process. A passion for helping people overcome trials and tribulations likely fuels their quest to apply effective communication skills and solutions to the countless issues that plague modern-day relationships.

Some of the more unusual areas of specific interest include:

- Sexual addiction and its impact on marriage
- The experience of wives, husbands, and children in polygamous families
- The effects of domestic partnership laws on the health of children
- Why lipstick and push-up bras effectively convey attractiveness to men

After Commencement

After graduation from an accredited program, students must complete two years of post-degree supervised clinical experience before receiving licensure or certification. When the supervision period is completed, students can take a state licensing exam or the national examination for marriage and family therapists conducted by the Association of Marriage and Family Therapists (AAMFT) regulatory boards. This exam is used as a licensure requirement in almost all states. Marriage and family therapists find work in medical settings like hospitals and clinics, in counseling organizations, and in private practices.

Related Programs

Industrial and Organizational Psychology

Addictions and Substance Abuse Counseling

Occupational Therapy

The Syllabus

If there are truly saints among us, then they are the occupational therapists, exceptional individuals who help people develop, preserve, or regain skills that allow them to adapt to life changes, perform daily tasks, and function independently in their home or work environments. In short, they give people their lives back after devastating accidents. Imagine a terrible car accident that leads to a loss of limbs or permanent paralysis. It is unpleasant to consider in passing, but it happens everyday. Surgeons can put you back together, and physical therapists will get you moving again, but what about all the things you used to do with your dominant arm that no longer exists or is paralyzed? All of the things you took for granted such as combing your hair, buttoning your shirts, or pouring a cup of coffee must be learned again. Enter the occupational therapist. Occupational therapists work with clients to improve motor skills and reasoning abilities and teach people how to compensate for permanent loss. Occupational therapists provide assistance to people of all ages, and their clients may include individuals with mental, physical, or developmental disabilities. The populations they work with most frequently include the elderly, car accident victims, and soldiers returning from military combat. As the baby boomer population ages and awareness of therapy programs spreads, the job outlook for this industry is strong.

Graduate programs in occupational therapy emphasize intense clinical training and experience through internships along with courses on the principles and applications of occupational therapy theory. Typical courses include kinesiology, neurology, sensory and perceptual foundations, motor aspects, human functional anatomy, occupational intervention, and research design and dissemination. Graduate programs result in a Master of Arts (MA) in Occupational Therapy degree, the Master of Occupational Therapy (MOT) degree, or the Doctor of Occupational Therapy (OTD) degree. The PhD in Occupational Science is most appropriate for aspiring researchers and professors in the field. These degree options differ mostly in terms of the program length and the type of final project necessary for graduation (e.g., comprehensive exams or a thesis project). Master's degrees require two to three years to complete, and doctorate programs can take an additional one to two years.

YOUR CLASSMATES

Occupational therapists are some of the kindest and most caring people you will ever meet in your life. They are particularly calm and patient people who have to handle ugly and sometimes embarrassing situations with great poise. In their hearts, graduate students in occupational therapy programs are interested in the application of their education to help disabled persons lead independent and productive lives. They feel comfortable working with a diverse range of people and demonstrate patience and understanding when working with others. They are thoroughly trained in the science and methods behind occupational therapy and receive plenty of practical application and clinical experience.

ONLY IN ACADEMIA

Some of the more unusual areas of specific interest include:

- Best practices for handwriting instruction in elementary schools
- Treatment methods for combat casualties in military medical centers
- Inactivity schedules for those living after a stroke
- How to provide reality orientation to the elderly

AFTER COMMENCEMENT

Occupational therapy graduates are employed as clinicians, administrators, researchers, and educators and work in medical and rehabilitation centers, schools, nursing facilities, home care agencies, mental health clinics, and universities. Many will start their own private practice after some years of experience and certification.

Industrial and Organizational Psychology

Clinical Psychology

Experimental Psychology

THE SYLLABUS

Experimental psychologists live to do research. They are intensely curious and intelligent people who are in constant pursuit of knowledge, if for no other reason than for the sake of knowledge itself. A high degree of intrinsic motivation is required for this career path, since the majority of what you do is not prescribed and must be figured out as you go along. On the surface this sounds extremely appealing (and it can be), but in reality, it is very difficult. You are constantly guessing at outcomes and research methods; there are often setbacks and dead ends. In the strictest sense, experimental psychology uses experimental methods to make observations on the thoughts and behaviors of living organisms. Experimental psychologists use a variety of research methods during the course of their work and, due to the several modern divisions of the psychology field, experimental psychologists are often closely aligned with another specific area, such as developmental or cognitive psychology. Just a sample of topics explored by experimental psychologists includes perception, learning, sensation, emotion, and motivation.

Training in experimental psychology involves detailed education in research methods and technology, as well as the applications of these procedures to the psychology discipline. Graduate programs can lead to a Master of Arts (MA), Master of Science (MS), or PhD in Experimental Psychology. Master's programs take about two years to complete and involve course work along with intensive research practice, internship experience, and almost always a thesis project. Other programs may not offer master's degrees individually but rather en route to acquiring the PhD.

Curricula include all the core psychology courses such as learning and cognition, theories of personality, statistics, research design, computer applications, as well as specialized experimental psychology courses including assessments administration, organizational psychology, program evaluation and measurement, and biological bases of behavior. Any decent program places a high emphasis on becoming proficient in at least one computer programming language for statistical analysis.

As most graduate students of experimental psychology will surely engage in a thesis project, most establish an apprenticeship-type relationship with a faculty member. Students perform research under their faculty advisor's direction and generally choose faculty whose research reflects their own interests.

Painfully logical and methodical is good way to describe the students in this area of study. However, the future superstars in this field will be exceptionally creative, almost artistic types, able to ferret out new information and apply old theories and methods for new uses. As the study of experimental psychology endeavors to prepare students for research and teaching positions, students in this domain possess strong math, science, logical, and analytical skills. Oral and written communication skills are also important, as experimental psychologists must interact with people as subjects as well as express ideas and experimental conclusions to other professionals in their fields.

ONLY IN ACADEMIA

Some of the more unusual areas of specific interest include:

- Step length adjustment in running
- How bright lights affect human reaction time
- Developmental differences between urban and rural children
- The motor skills and in-coordination of mice

AFTER COMMENCEMENT

Experimental psychology graduates may end up in other fields of psychology with a strong experimental emphasis, such as social psychology or cognitive psychology, but still allows them to do what they do best: research and experimentation. Those with a master's degree in the field pursue employment at labs, research institutes, government agencies, or educational facilities constructing and carrying out research relevant to the organization. Those with a PhD generally stay in academia as professors or professional researchers.

RELATED PROGRAMS

Developmental Psychology

Industrial and Organizational Psychology

Industrial and Organizational Psychology

THE SYLLABUS

Industrial and organizational psychology (called IO psych by those in the field) is the application of psychology to business and the workplace. Finding ways to make industry more productive and hospitable is at the heart of what industrial psychologists do. Stanton Dennis, a training and development consultant for the auto industry, says: "I get hired to make people work harder and be happy about it. It's very sneaky psychological warfare." He goes on to clarify, "For example, we'll advise adding a well-stocked, comfortable staff room because if none of your employees ever leave the building for lunch and congregate together talking primarily about—what else— work, productivity increases tremendously."

Practitioners in the field spend their time making observations and analyses on individual behaviors, employee-employer relationships, and general staff dynamics. Industrial psychologists conduct research on individuals and entire organizations in literally every industry, and they work with both management and workers to enhance employee satisfaction and company productivity.

Graduate study in industrial and organizational psychology can result in a Master of Arts (MA) or Master of Science (MS) in a variety of areas including human resources, education, and business. A program may also grant a Master of Arts in Counseling and Organizational Psychology (MOA) or a Master's in Organizational Development (MOD). All routes of study involve a combination of psychology course work, research experience, field work and thesis writing. Master's programs take two to three years to complete, unless done as an extension of an undergraduate program, where a total of five years would be required to complete the BA and MA. Students seeking a PhD would need four to five years to complete the doctorate program.

The industrial and organizational psychology graduate program curriculum includes basic courses in statistics, research design, and computer statistical language, as well as focused courses in personnel psychology, organizational psychology, ethics, assessment techniques, and career counseling.

YOUR CLASSMATES

IO grads have a general interest in business and human resources along with a penchant for science and research methods. Industrial and organizational psychologists must be tactful and diplomatic when working in the business arena amid sensitive organizational relationships (employees and bosses) and developments (restructuring and downsizing). Students here find management, team building, executive coaching, organizational development, and employee performance to be exceptionally exciting topics of discussion. All must be able to actively assess and implement remedies for issues in the workplace. Active listening and communication skills are highly prized.

ONLY IN ACADEMIA

Some of the more unusual areas of specific interest include:

- The pros and cons of caffeinated beverages in the workplace
- The under-reporting of sexually harassed males in the workplace
- Managing the pregnant employee
- Nursing in a war zone

IO psych grads often wind up in human resources departments with job titles like human resources manager or diversity program coordinator. But they also hold academic or non-academic research positions delving into a variety of behavioral or organizational topics. Many aspire to work as private consultants on matters including hiring, training and development, diversity, structural change, and performance evaluation.

RELATED PROGRAMS

Experimental Psychology

Marriage and Family Therapy

Addictions and Substance Abuse Counseling

THE SYLLABUS

Substance abuse counseling is one of the rare specialties that you can break into with just a bachelor's degree. So why pursue an advanced degree in the field? It may boost future bids for promotion. Consider this scenario: There is an available middle management position. Two front line counselors have applied and both have worked in the office roughly the same amount of time, and both did well in the interview and have great references. One has a master's degree (perhaps earned part-time, while working) and the other only a bachelor's degree. Who do you think will get the position? More often than not, it is the one with the master's degree (and this rule of thumb is applicable to almost every industry). Setting aside the philosophical rationale for pursuing any advanced degree (to be more knowledgeable about best practices and future developments in your field), the reason for seeking an advanced degree lies in career advancement. Of course, being the boss is not important to everyone and remaining on the front lines delivering group and one-on-one interventions suits many just fine.

Although it is obvious what this field of study is about, what is not so obvious is the tremendous commitment and depth of character that it takes to work in this field. Addictions counseling is not a theoretical pursuit that takes place in the sheltered halls of academia. These counselors work face-to-face with people fighting ugly demons. Do not be fooled: Even the world-class Malibu "spas" where billionaire playboys, models, and actors go to dry out is not as posh as it sounds (the lush accommodations often feature barred windows and padded walls). Plus, they typically only hire MDs. But, as with anything in life, risk is commensurate with reward. As Paul Helson, a psychology graduate who works as a narcotics substance abuse counselor explains, "Right out of college, I got a job at a residential facility were I was basically a babysitter. I'll never forget the second day of training when we learned restraint and submission holds. I'll tell you, I had some serious second thoughts. But I can tell you, over the years, I have had to use all of those holds at one time or another, and it's nothing compared to hearing someone say, 'I've been sober for over a year' or to have a man, with tears in his eyes, thank you personally for reconnecting with a son whom he hasn't spoken to in over 10 years. It's an indescribable sense of pride and success."

Substance abuse counselors are employed in settings as diverse as correctional institutions, hospitals, mental health agencies, drug treatment centers, and community shelters. Substance abuse rehabilitation programs are funded by a wide range of sources including nonprofit local, state, and federal governmental agencies, schools, and churches. Other, more exclusive (and always more expensive), programs are for profit. Some don't even accept health insurance and require direct payments in advance.

Graduate schools generally offer an addictions or substance abuse track within a counseling or mental health master's degree program. Students can attain a Master of Science (MS) or Master of Arts (MA) in Counseling, Mental Health Counseling or Counseling and Educational Psychology with an emphasis in addiction or substance abuse counseling, or even a Master of Public Health (MPH) or Master of Social Work (MSW) in substance abuse.

Typical graduate school courses include group dynamics, substance abuse counseling, assessment and diagnosis, prevention and early intervention strategies, relapse prevention, addictions and treatment, case management, and alcohol and drug abuse. In addition to course work, graduate students must also participate in fieldwork through counseling internships. Master's programs usually take one and a half to two years to complete. Students may also need to meet state licensing requirements before they can practice solo.

YOUR CLASSMATES

Many of the people who decide to go into this field have direct experience with the damage addictions cause, perhaps as the child of an abusive alcoholic father or the friend of the victim of drug-related violence. This can often make for very emotional and powerful classroom sessions. Paul shares, "Even the course work can be draining. I can't tell you how many classes we all walked out of in dead silence because of what had been shared or what we had worked on. It was like, whoa, that was heavy stuff. In my opinion, many of my classmates were there to work out some of their own issues." As a result, graduate programs in addictions and substance abuse counseling attract students who are quite mature and eager to help others in times of crisis. Most of them are very action oriented and focused on identifying real problems and implementing strategic solutions. They are hands-on, not theoretical. Active listening and analytical skills are essential, as well as qualities that demonstrate compassion and sensitivity.

ONLY IN ACADEMIA

Some of the more unusual areas of specific interest include:

- The patch vs. the "cold turkey" method of quitting smoking
- Aggression and substance abuse among bipolar individuals

- Happiness levels in post substance abuse personalities
- The escalation of prescription drug abuse

AFTER COMMENCEMENT

Graduates find positions as substance abuse counselors at a facilities ranging from therapeutic communities to prisons. Addictions and substance abuse counseling students may become addictions counselors in public or private treatment facilities, juvenile or adult probation officers, employee assistance professionals, coordinators of substance abuse prevention services, or eventually counselors in their own private practices.

RELATED PROGRAMS

Clinical Psychology

Marriage and Family Therapy

Developmental Psychology

THE SYLLABUS

Did you know that babies can use sign language to communicate as early as six months old? Did you know that humans can learn up to five languages at the level of a native speaker with ease up to the age of seven and afterward it gets more difficult with age? Have you ever wondered why an elderly person cannot remember what they had for breakfast but they can tell you how many cookies they ate during snack time in kindergarten 70 years ago? These are exactly the types of subjects that developmental psychologists find fascinating.

Students of this discipline concentrate on the development of the human mind throughout the aging process and study the changes in perceptual, social, communication, and cognitive abilities over the life span. They investigate infant brain development, the parental role in child development, and natural instincts among the literally thousands of issues to explore. Studies either span the entire aging process or focus on a specific age range such as infant, toddler, adult, or geriatric. The quest of a developmental psychologist is to determine the reasons behind certain behaviors and human aptitude developments. Several disciplines within applied psychology, such as educational psychology, rely on information gained by developmental psychologists' research.

Graduate students in developmental psychology encounter broad theoretical and empirical training but also have the opportunity to develop an area of expertise within the field. The goal of most programs is to prepare students for roles as researchers and professors. Most programs include seminars that cover basic studies and changes in cognitive, social, emotional, and physiological processes. Typical course titles include statistics, childhood psychopathology, theories of personality, child development, and perception. Developmental psychology programs emphasize that the best way to learn research methods is to practice research so a large portion of a student's time is dedicated to involvement in ongoing research projects.

Most graduate programs expect students to attain a doctoral degree in developmental psychology, and the master's degree (MA) is typically only attained en route to the PhD, which often takes six to seven years to complete although it can be attained sooner. Students have the option of discontinuing their education after receiving the master's degree, which usually takes one to two years, but will find that career options are limited. Some students plan to go into the field of child psychiatry with their developmental psychology background. These students must pursue an MD, which requires four years of medical school and at least three years of residency, followed by a minimum of two years of psychiatric training.

YOUR CLASSMATES

Graduate students in developmental psychology demonstrate an avid interest in research and studying human development. They are curious individuals who are prepared to delve into abstract subjects to determine the reasons and causes for human behavior at all levels of development.

ONLY IN ACADEMIA

Some of the more unusual areas of specific interest include:

- Sexual practices of the elderly (frequency and style)
- Early memory formation and the retention of childhood experiences
- The neurobiology of infant vision
- Why some "adults" seem immature

AFTER COMMENCEMENT

A developmental psychology graduate usually finds research positions with government organizations or private laboratories. He or she may also contribute as both a researcher and a professor at a research university or work as an educator at various institutions. If an MD is attained, a developmental psychology graduate can enter the field of child psychiatry, which focuses on the roots and treatments of mental disorders in children and adolescents as well as provides psychological support.

RELATED PROGRAMS

Clinical Psychology

Occupational Therapy

CHAPTER 8

Q & A with Psychology and Sociology Majors

A FINAL WORD FROM US. . .

By now you should be feeling pretty darn confident about the many opportunities that are available to you as a psychology or sociology major. This book has sought to show you that the skills and knowledge you learned in your studies have market value in the "real world." We've also given you the tools that'll help you get your foot in the door, whether the next step is advanced study, fellowships, or the job market.

But don't take our word for it. We spoke with several former psychology and sociology majors from all walks of life to find out how their degrees have helped and/or hindered their professional career paths. Some of these folks work in business, others in the health sector, and still others in education and/or various nonprofit fields. We asked them about their motivation for choosing a psychology or sociology major, what they learned, how those skills have been useful/not useful in the real world, about internships, their first job search, their current job, the best career advice they received, tips for current psychology or sociology majors, and much more. You'll get to hear straight from them about how being a psychology or sociology major has affected their professional growth.

Remember—this is only the beginning. The next several years will be full of exciting ups and downs, as your future kicks into high gear. So buckle up. And remember to enjoy the journey.

Good luck!

Q & A WITH FORMER PSYCHOLOGY MAJORS

The following professionals dedicated their time to answering our questions:

Danielle McCumber is an enrollment coordinator for a study abroad organization.

Kerry Davis does bilingual psychoeducatonal evaluations for a local school district and also has a private practice in juvenile forensics.

Leslie Quon is an instructor at a community college.

Rebecca Scalera is a neuropsychologist in a private, hospital-affiliated group practice in southern Connecticut.

Yana Myaskovetskaya is an information developer/certified usability analyst for a major technological corporation.

1. Why did you major in psychology?

Danielle: The "theater dream" fell through, and psych seemed interesting.

Kerry: I got my BA in English . . . MA and PhD in psychology. I decided to go for psychology because one of the women my mother most admired was a psychologist in a school. I had always been fascinated by the motivation for behaviors and how our experiences mold us.

Leslie: I found my psychology classes to be the most interesting and practical. The concepts and theories I studied were actually applicable to my daily life. I also knew that I would have a broad choice of careers to pursue with a major in psychology.

Rebecca: I majored in psychology because I had always been interested in learning more about the human condition. It was the only subject that really held my interest because we live it everyday. Psychology and human relationships and dynamics surround us. I thought it would be fascinating to understand people better. I guess I always wanted to know what makes us tick, so to speak.

Yana: When I got to UCLA, I was [an] international sevelopment studies major; I switched to political science major. After one class of political science, I knew that was not for me. I was completely confused. I went to the school book store and started looking at the books; I decided that I would pick a major that I would be interested in reading. After one class of psychology, I knew that I found what I was looking for.

2. What skills or information learned in college do you find yourself making the most use of?

Danielle: Research skills—finding the most and best information in a short amount of time; social skills—how to behave in a professional manner; I greatly improved my ability to write concisely and informatively.

Kerry: The best skill of a psychologist is that of observation. Observing subtle nuances of both behavior and communication can give you insights into a person that they are not even aware of. This also facilitates self-observation.

Leslie: I believe that time-management skills are what I will continue to use for the rest of my life. I learned the importance of balance—getting my work done, but also saving time for rest and pleasure. As far as information, I continue to refer to many theories I learned in social psychology classes.

Rebecca: To be honest, at this point in my career, I'm not readily able to think of skills in college that help me now directly. However, my undergraduate degree absolutely prepared me in an academic sense for graduate school which is where I . . . learn[ed] the nuts and bolts of this field that I use everyday. To become a licensed psychologist, a doctorate degree is required so that is where you really get your training, through that program and your internship and fellowships. In that regard, your undergraduate studies can be quite removed from your clinical training, but it provides the basic foundation . . . and you receive basic training in research methodology that you build on in your PhD program. But it's not like you will come out of a psych undergrad program knowing how to be a therapist; it doesn't work that way. It is a good solid foundation upon which you build further research and clinical skills in graduate school. I also received invaluable advice and guidance from my psych professors in undergrad in terms of career options and what it took to pursue an advanced degree in this field.

Yana: The research skills that I've learned in college have been instrumental. Also the ability to work under pressure has been the skill that [helped] me succeed in the work force. I work in [a] fast-paced environment, and all the work is under pressure and under time constraints.

3. What skills or information learned in college do you find yourself not using at all?

Danielle: Although I benefited greatly from the classes I took, the specific information taught (Contemporary African Witchcraft, for example) is not applicable to daily life.

Kerry: The practice of psychology is so all-encompassing that virtually all information is eventually put to use. History, sociology, biology, math (statistics) all have an important place in understanding the dynamics of behavior.

Leslie: I don't use too many of the very detailed theories that I only really learned for the exam. For instance, the technical process of how exactly our brain processes information, theories on learning, etc. It was interesting at the time, but too much information for me to remember to this day.

Rebecca: Well, I am not currently in an academic or research position; I focus on clinical work. Therefore, I would have to say that, at the moment, all of those research courses and skills are sitting on the sidelines a bit.

Yana: While in college, I had to take three statistics classes for my major; I have yet to use any of that knowledge.

4. Which internships or extracurricular activities that you pursued in college have been most valuable to you personally and professionally? Why?

Danielle: I interned at a drug rehab center for women—after I did that no feat was too small, and I have a much easier time managing and communicating with people (especially angry people).

Kerry: At university (undergrad) I associated the most with foreign students as I also came from Central America, and the United States was a new experience for me in spite of the fact that my parents are from Texas and I was born in Texas also. The experience of being an observer of culture from an outside perspective, both of American culture and the culture of other foreign students, their adaptation strategies, and what they found different, sparked a lifelong interest and profession in cross-cultural psychological evaluation.

Leslie: Doing research with one of my professors was the most valuable to me both personally and professionally. It showed me the realities of what research and graduate school would be like. It also helped establish the connections I needed in the field.

Rebecca: I pursued a clinical internship at a psychiatric hospital when I was a senior in college, and that was really a defining career experience for me. I enjoyed the internship, and I was able to see people in my field working at all different levels and positions firsthand. I really loved seeing the different specialties work together for patient care, and I found the hospital atmosphere to be so stimulating, and I learned so much.

Yana: While in college, I worked in the UCLA Medical Center as an administrative assistant. This enhanced my communication skills. I did an internship for *Forbes* magazine and Symantec. These experiences were most valuable because they helped me decide what I want to pursue as a career. I think internships during college are extremely valuable and important for an individual who is entering the work force.

5. How did you decide which field, either in academia or the real world, to go into?

Danielle: I found a position with an organization that is based out of a city in France where I have a lot of family.

Kerry: I initially became a teacher of English and Spanish at the high school level . . . then a teacher of a migrant tutorial (using my Spanish) at the high school level, then a psychologist after my doctorate. I love assessment, and bilingual assessments are fascinating as they are a puzzle with more and more complex pieces than the usual assessment.

Leslie: I was inspired by one great professor I really admired—this encouraged me to go into teaching. I wanted to positively impact students the way she did.

Rebecca: I decided to pursue a private practice career in neuropsychology with a group that is affiliated with a hospital for several reasons. I wanted to be in private practice to have the autonomy to make my own schedule and be my own boss. I have always been entrepreneurial, so this really worked for me. I also loved the stimulation of a hospital setting, so the affiliation was appealing and gave me the opportunity to continue to work with professionals from different disciplines (medicine, nursing, physical, speech and occupational therapy). I chose to pursue a career in neuropsychology because, while I loved doing traditional psychotherapy and wanted to continue this, I also enjoyed the challenges that come with neuropsychological assessment. This process is like an exploration and there are real opportunities to help people by identifying underlying cognitive problems and making solid recommendations to make their lives or learning experiences easier. (Neuropsychological assessment is conducted to determine if people have learning disabilities or developmental disabilities like autism or attention deficit disorder. This is also used to clarify the extent of injury following a brain injury or a stroke or to clarify the impact of a psychiatric disorder on cognitive functioning.)

Yana: I did a number of internships during college to get a feel for what industry interests me. This helped me to figure out what fields . . . seemed interesting to me [but] did not provide the major career aspects that I was searching for. I think it's very important to get a taste of the industry before just into a career in that field.

6. Did you have a mentor when you entered the workforce/graduate school?

Danielle: No.

Kerry: Yes . . . a supervisor for my practicum and later for my postdoctoral internship. She was a dynamic and forceful psychologist who, to a large extent, reinforced my therapeutic practices.

Leslie: No. That would've been nice though!

Rebecca: Yes. There are many psychologists in my family and one of my cousins in particular helped me during the application process in focusing my interests.

Yana: No, I didn't have a mentor. I think having a mentor would have been beneficial because it would have provided an opportunity for networking.

7. What's the number-one bit of advice you wish you were given before you entered the job market?

Danielle: You don't have to take the first job you're offered—don't feel bad holding out for something if you think you can do better.

Kerry: Find a niche in which there is a real need. Entry-level people are a dime a dozen . . . [so] you have to have some special skill. I was fortunate to have both language and cross-cultural skills and have been able to draw on them.

Leslie: Start early! I waited until I was finished with graduate school before I even began looking. And probably even a few months after that (after a "vacation" of doing nothing, which I felt I deserved)! Not a good idea. There was a lot of waiting around even after I began the search (which I suppose could've served as my vacation instead).

Rebecca: I wish that someone had given me more guidance on networking. When you are in private practice, this is a very important skill—relationship building with other professionals—and I sort of had to figure this out as I went along.

Yana: I wish I would have been told how important experience is. I went to interviews where I was told that I didn't have enough experience right after graduation. I wish I would have been told how important it is to do internships as soon as you get into college. Also, it's better to do an unpaid internship somewhere rather then working in a coffee shop or something; you are missing out on the money at that given time, but you're gaining experiences that will give you an advantage when you start looking for work.

8. What were your job-related expectations when you were still in school, and how did they match up with your experience of the "real world"?

Danielle: I expected to graduate from college and be able to take one of two jobs: a tech in a psych ward, or an entry-level administrative position. I was 100 percent accurate.

Kerry: My expectations in school were largely accurate but I found myself drawn to a field of psychology that was not a field of training (forensics) so I set out to find job experiences that would allow me to gain the necessary supervised experience to practice on my own.

Leslie: I expected to enjoy working much more than being in school. After all, I wouldn't constantly have research and assignments hanging over me. In some sense, it was true. But I also wish I had appreciated being a student at the time.

Rebecca: In my PhD program, there was a very dismal picture of the clinical world painted for budding psychologists. The focus was more on going into academics, and everyone said the changes in insurance reimbursement were going to make it so difficult financially to survive in private practice. While the insurance situation is challenging, and unfortunately, most of us can't survive on the rates that these companies reimburse (hence we go off panels), my experience of the real world has far exceeded my expectations. If you have an important service to provide and you are diligent, passionate, and thoughtful about what you do, you will always be in demand.

Yana: I was expecting for someone to care about the classes I've taken and my GPA. Yet everywhere where I applied for work and the job that I am working at right now, nobody has ever asked me for my GPA.

9. What was your first job out of college? How did you find that job?

Danielle: Enrollment coordinator for a study abroad organization, I applied to a posting on Monster.com.

Kerry: I was a high school teacher for migrant students in south Texas. Being bilingual was so sought after that I just showed up at the district office in November and mentioned that I was bilingual and had an immediate job offer.

Leslie: Working abroad teaching English in Japan. I found it with help from the career center at my school.

Rebecca: I got a job as a bilingual vocational counselor at Easter Seals. I was taking that year to apply for PhD programs and I found this job through a friend of my older sister's who was leaving the job to go back to school herself.

Yana: My first job out of college was as an information developer/usability analyst for Symantec. I did an internship for this department during my last year of college, and after graduation they took me on full-time.

10. If you went straight into the workforce after receiving your bachelor's degree, do you wish you had attended graduate school first? If you went on to grad school, do you wish you had worked first? In either case, why?

Danielle: I went straight to work, and I am glad I did so because I needed more time to figure out what I wanted to do with my professional degree. I also think it's important for people to experience the "working world" before getting back into academics, because people who spend their life in academia have little understanding of how the real world works—both my parents are professors and great examples of this.

Kerry: I worked while going to get my master's. I believe the experience of working gave me a better focus and feeling for exactly what I wanted to do when I finished my master's program. I realized that I could not practice as a psychologist with just a master's degree, so I decided to work as a psychologist in a school (one of the few venues for psychologists with just a master's) while working on my doctorate.

Leslie: I am so glad I worked first before going to graduate school. Although it was a little difficult to get back into the study mode, it was definitely valuable to have some "real-world experience" under my belt. It really gave me perspective when learning new theories—to see which ones were actually practical. Plus, I probably would have absolutely hated school in general had I gone straight from undergrad.

Rebecca: I am happy that I worked for a year before going to graduate school. The real world experience and low pay added to my motivation to continue my education and work very hard in graduate school.

Yana: I went straight into the workforce. I actually did a right thing by working first, because I found out what career I want to pursue. Now with a little experience under my belt, I have better chances of getting into a master's program of my choice and I am sure about what program I want to pursue.

11. What's the best piece of advice you've received from a colleague?

Danielle: Actually the best advice I ever got was from my dad, who told me to do what I loved and the money would follow—don't plan your career path based on potential income.

Kerry: Return your messages every day, and, above all, be ethical.

Leslie: Work should not be something you dread. Weekends should not be the highlight of your life. If so, consider finding a new job.

Rebecca: To have a specialty. Something you become known for.

Yana: I was told by my colleague that in order to succeed an individual needs intelligence, integrity, and motivation. You need to know that you want to accomplish. You need to be able to take responsibility for your work. You need to be able to be diplomatic and work well with others.

12. What's the smartest move you've made since receiving your bachelor's degree?

Danielle: I was realistic about what job my BA could get me and I understood that you have to pay your dues before you can get the job of your dreams. As such, I am never disappointed!

Kerry : Getting a PhD in psychology so I can practice independently without supervision.

Leslie: Traveling. It is so eye-opening to get out there and experience different cultures—and to really immerse yourself in them. It reminds you that life is a lot bigger than just your own little world.

Rebecca: Going on to get my PhD.

Yana: After graduating, I figured out what I want to do and what needs to be done. I've researched my career of choice and found out that taking computer science classes would boost my chances in the workforce. I've started attending a community college to boost my skills.

13. Describe your current job and its major responsibilities.

Danielle: I still work at the study abroad organization. I manage the incoming students. I am the first point of contact for prospective students, students, college advisors, business partners, and alumni. I also oversee all office and administrative duties for the U.S. office.

Kerry: I work full-time for a school district doing their bilingual psychoeducatonal evaluations and have a thriving private practice in juvenile forensics.

Leslie: I am an instructor at a community college. I teach about three courses a semester and also help coach students for speech tournaments.

Rebecca: I am a neuropsychologist in a private, hospital-affiliated group practice in southern Connecticut. I see patients, both children and adults, on an outpatient basis for general psychotherapy and neuropsychological assessment.

Yana: I work as an information developer/certified usability analyst. My job involves working on the user interface content, online help, and user guide manuals for Symantec consumer products. I work on the production of this media as well as testing. As a usability analyst, I conduct research by working with users to see how the products match their needs and what works for our users.

14. What experience was required for it?

Danielle: Prior administrative experience.

Kerry: School practice requires a master's and a state credential. My private practice requires a PhD, extensive supervised experience, and state licensure.

Leslie: A master's degree and teaching experience.

Rebecca: A PhD in psychology as well as relevant externship, internship, and fellowship experiences in the field of clinical neuropsychology. In addition, you must take a national and state licensing exam to become a licensed psychologist in Connecticut.

Yana: I was required to have good research skills, [the] ability to learn quickly, and work well with others. I also went through multiple trainings in order to acquire [the] skills necessary to become a usability analyst as well as training on the content management systems that the company uses.

15. To what extent has your degree helped you in your current role?

Danielle: I deal with people all day long, and psychology is the only reason I can do that well!

Kerry: I could not do my private practice without the PhD. Having been a teacher in schools before being a psychologist gives me tremendous insight and credibility with school staffs that other psychologists don't have.

Leslie: It was a requirement, as you need a master's degree to teach at the college level. It has also given me the knowledge and background I needed to teach the courses.

Rebecca: My degree has helped me enormously in my current role. My PhD program was relevant and important preparation for my current career.

Yana: The knowledge that I've acquired in my major has shown my manager the determination and the willingness to learn that I've brought to our department. I learned valuable research and writing skills while obtaining my degree, and these are two major skills that I use at work on daily bases.

16. What do you like most about it?

Danielle: My job is very flexible because it is a very small operation—I'm one of two employees in the U.S.

Kerry: The school practice has regular hours, good benefits, time off when my children were off, no overhead—and it is not rocket science. Most psychologists in school don't have clinical skills. I love my private practice as I get to use my clinical skills for assessment, diagnosis, and treatment recommendation. I also like interfacing with the courts. Overall, in both settings I really just enjoy assessment . . . it is a big puzzle . . . the bilingual assessments have more pieces to the puzzle.

Leslie: I love being able to interact with and influence students, and I appreciate the fact that each day is different. I also love the fact that I am teaching the very things I studied in college . . . assuring me that all of my studies were not in vain. In addition, it is very rewarding to see how much a student progresses over the semester.

Rebecca: I love working with such a variety of patients from small children to older adults and many adolescents. However, I really enjoy the peer contact, support, and group supervision with my colleagues. This is a huge benefit to being in a group practice. I also love the flexibility of private practice and that I can work part-time now that I have a child.

Yana: I get to work with people from different backgrounds and different countries. We provide the content that gets translated into 23 languages, so I get to meet and discuss issues with people from Japan, Poland, and Ireland. Through my interaction with engineers, managers, and marketing people, I get to learn something new and interesting every day.

17. What aspect(s) of it do you not like?

Danielle: Of course doing admin work is never exciting; the organization is not run in a terribly efficient manner; more colleagues to interact with would be nice.

Kerry: The school practice is circumscribed by the assumption (generally a good one) that the psychologists don't have clinical skills.

Leslie: Grading can be a drag sometimes. But I suppose every job has its price. I do not like dealing with insurance companies and they often do not cover needed services.

Yana: Working in the IT industry is not your typical 9-to-5 kind of job. The hours can be very long, and sometimes you're on call over the weekend, even if you are on vacation or out of town. Working for a big corporate company means that if you make a little mistake, it could end up costing the company a lot of money. So the level of responsibility here is higher than normal.

18. What skills have you had to acquire that your bachelor's degree did not help you cultivate?

Danielle: Looking back on my college experience, the jobs and internships I held have been infinitely more helpful than the courses I took to obtain my degree. I can't say that I have had to learn important new skills because I was so well prepared by my professional experience in college—and my chosen major is the reason I was able to secure all the jobs and internships I had in college.

Kerry: I sought out supervised experience when I wanted to practice juvenile forensics. That involves a skill set that was not available in my university program.

Leslie: Public speaking and interpersonal skills. I believe this comes from . . . well, basically living and interacting with others in this world! Obviously you can't get that from doing research or writing papers.

Rebecca: I have had to acquire networking skills and business skills that were not part of my degree training.

Yana: Working in the IT industry, I had to continue my education into the field of computer science in order to be able to comfortably discuss issues with the engineers and managers.

19. What suggestions would you have for those still in college? Are there any "optional" elements of the undergraduate experience that you would recommend they explore?

Danielle: Make sure you take classes that you find interesting—don't focus solely on getting your requirements out of the way. You'll learn more from the subjects you like. Find out who the best professors are, and take courses from them when you can. Always go to your professors' office hours and speak to them individually— you will learn more that way, and the professor will get to know you, which carries many benefits. I was given great opportunities by being "in" with the faculty. Join as many clubs and teams as your schedule allows because you meet great people that way.

Kerry: If interested in forensic psychology, try to get as much law enforcement/criminal justice exposure as you can. If interested in practice in schools, teach in a school before practicing school psychology as this will give you a huge amount of insight and credibility.

Leslie: I highly recommend studying abroad. Living in a different country really opens your eyes to things about Americans, about others, about yourself, how to cope with challenges . . . and it is so much fun!

Rebecca: Try to get as much hands on experience in your field as possible as an undergraduate. Try to obtain internships in settings that you could see yourself working in, and interview folks in your field who have completed their training; ask what their typical day is like, and try to imagine yourself in that position.

Yana: It is very important to do internships while in college, even if they are nonpaid. Networking with the alumni is also very valuable.

20. Do you have any tips for those entering the workforce/graduate school now?

Danielle: You have the rest of your life to figure out the best career path for yourself. Don't rush into anything.

Kerry: Seek out a mentor. They can be invaluable.

Leslie: Make sure you love what you are going to be studying. Graduate school is very demanding, and if you don't love the subject matter and are just planning to trudge through it to get that degree, it will be extremely difficult.

Rebecca: Be creative about getting the training you need and networking in your field to find opportunities that could lead to career advancement. Don't expect things to fall in your lap. Think of a setting you would like to work in, and seek out professionals in that area to guide and mentor you. There are psychologists in sports, television, law, hospitals—almost every setting.

Yana: If you're entering the workforce, you need to get your resume intact. It shouldn't be long, but it should give the employer a clear picture of what you're bringing to the table. Reading books about resumes and job hunting and having someone give an outsider's opinion of your resume is very important.

21. What's the best way to get a job in your field?

Danielle: Psychology majors should check out job openings at all the nonprofit organizations and psych wards at hospitals in the area. It's great work experience.

Kerry : Schools: Be bilingual or have [a] specialty such as neuropsychology. Forensics: Get supervised experience.

Leslie: Try to make and maintain connections with others in the field. Get as much teaching experience as you can—even in graduate school. Be a TA, lead discussion groups, etc.

Rebecca: Networking—reach out to professionals in your community and check online listings through professional organizations like the APA's website. There are also job listings every month in the back of professional journals.

Yana: Don't assume that just because you're a psychology major you have to do clinical work. I remember in college everyone would tell me, "What can you do with a psychology major? Everyone has that." I realized that I can do anything I want. I'm not limited to any one field, so the best way is to apply—and don't get discouraged if you don't get the job on the first interview. Keep searching for the job that you would really enjoy.

22. What mistake do psychology grads often make?

Danielle: There aren't a lot of jobs specifically in the field of psychology for people with just a BA—a lot of grads stress that their job doesn't relate to their degree. But knowing psychology is always helpful in any job setting!

Kerry: They don't seek out jobs that offer variety. It is true that every assessment has some different elements, and every person who comes to you for therapy has their own story and history, but being able to practice in two settings has been very beneficial for me.

Leslie: Many don't pick a specific area to pursue. Psychology is very broad, offering a bunch of career options. However, that can also be a drawback to those who have no direction.

Rebecca: Some become discouraged and leave the field too soon before playing out all of their options.

Yana: Most psychology grads think that their degree will not get them far if they don't have a master's degree to back it up. In reality, with a psychology degree there are many doors that are open.

23. What's something that you think more psychology grads should do to advance their careers?

Danielle: You absolutely have to get a higher degree—LCSW, MFA, PhD, whatever you choose.

Kerry: Get some experience, even if it's just job shadowing, before applying for jobs.

Leslie: They should try to do research with a professor. The more experience you have doing research, the better. This also helps you establish connections.

Rebecca: Graduate school.

Yana: I can't stress enough the importance of internships. An internship will give you experience, networking, and, if you prove yourself, a job and a career.

24. Who is in the best position to offer a psychology graduate help with his or her resume and cover letter?

Danielle: College psychology advisor—kept in touch with them after you graduate.

Kerry : A mentor who works in the field . . . preferably a supervisor (intern or practicum).

Leslie: One of your professors, or someone who is already working in the field you would like to pursue. The career center at your school will probably be helpful as well.

Rebecca: A supervisor or professor.

Yana: Have someone who has been working for a while look at your resume. This person has probably been to a number of interviews with different types of managers and can give you an inside look into what the interviewing process is like and what employers look for.

25. What pitfalls should psychology graduates avoid when applying to and interviewing for positions?

Danielle: A lot of employers don't realize that psychology degrees require a variety of skills—if you just put "BA in Psychology" they may assume that you know how to run experiments and that's it. Make sure you touch on the fact that psychology also develops analytical, writing, and people skills.

Kerry: Be aware that you are not expected to know everything, but you have to express an enthusiasm and willingness to learn and pay your dues.

Leslie: One pitfall is thinking that their degree alone will be all they need when applying for a position. It's important to remember that many positions also look for experience—so it's critical to get as much of that as possible.

Rebecca: (No response.)

Yana: I remember at the very beginning at every interview I was asked "So why the psychology major?" I felt that when they asked me this question they thought I didn't bring enough to the table. So I thought and realized that I bring more to the table than an average employee because of my major, internships, work experience, education, and background. An employer wants a well-rounded employee, someone who can get the work done and be nice to have around the office. It's the same reason in high school someone who has straight A's and did no volunteer work and no extracurricular activities gets upset that he or she did not get into a top school, and someone with slightly lower grades and extracurricular activities did. You're not just a major; you're a person with knowledge, experience, and skills. When you can prove this to an employer, no field is unattainable.

Q & A WITH FORMER SOCIOLOGY MAJORS

The following professionals dedicated their time to answering our questions:

Antonio Ogas is outreach manager for The Princeton Review—Arizona.

Emily Rosenfeld is legislative assistant for a delegate to the Maryland General Assembly.

Erica Broussard is director of education at The Crocker Museum in Sacramento, California.

Laura Smith counsels low-income, single parents on the employment and short-term training options available to them in order for them to become financially independent.

Marsha Blum is a self-employed interior designer.

1. Why did you major in sociology?

Antonio: I have always been interested in human interaction and the dynamics associated with how people live and play with each other. I've always believed that we are a reflection of who we interact with, and understanding this interaction is what drove my interest. Sociology is the study of societal ambiguity and leaves a lot of room for interpretation. I often refer to it as having a bachelor's degree in *open-mindedness*.

Emily: The main reason I chose sociology as my major had to do with the books assigned for class. I went to the bookstore early in my college career and looked for all the books I wanted to read, just for the sake of reading. When the majority of my pile came from the sociology section, I knew I was hooked.

Erica: At the time I entered college, I was interested in politics and law, not because I liked it, but because my parents thought being a lawyer was respectable. I thought that sociology (political science seemed too dry) would be good preparation for law school. I know now that I was more interested in art or art history but my parents didn't think that was practical enough; how would I make a living?

Laura: I honestly wasn't sure what to major in, but I knew I didn't want to go into my first year undeclared because, at that time, I associated the "undecided" option with someone who didn't have the ability to make a decision or commit to anything.

Marsha: As a teenager in the 1960s, I didn't have a clue as to what I should major in. Since I had no scientific, athletic, or musical talents, I came up with sociology as a major since it seemed serious. I even decided that I could specialize in criminology (which really concerned my parents).

2. What skills or information learned in college do you find yourself making the most use of?

Antonio: Academically speaking, I found courses such as Social Theory and Social Stratification to be the most interesting. Experiencing these classes was like taking a wedge and splitting my brain in half. However, I learned a lot from studying these topics and I've always been able to retain most of the knowledge learned from those two classes. As a sociologist, I was very active on campus, and I craved human interaction. I learned a lot from my practical experiences through my involvement in the various clubs and organizations on campus. You would be surprised how much you learn from taking an active role.

Emily: Analytical reading has proven to be an important learned skill. The ability to identify relevant passages in larger texts is extremely useful in my current position.

Erica: I'm not sure if it's a specific skill, but I feel like I learned to be more organized in college. My job has me supervising several very different departments and I credit being able to keep track of all of them because of the skills I picked up in college juggling multiple courses. I also feel I have a better understanding of people and how to interact with them.

Laura: I believe the basic skills that helped me become a successful student—learning how to "fine tune" my time-management skills, developing better work habits, and becoming more organized so that I was able to complete my work efficiently—are the skills most utilized within my current role.

Marsha: I attended the University of Colorado for two years where I took a number of general sociology classes. The only one that made much of an impact was a course called Juvenile Delinquency. This was a real eye-opener for me. I actually finished up my sociology degree at the University of Wisconsin. What I did realize later on was that I had developed excellent skills in terms of writing papers. When I went on to art school at Pratt Institute, I clearly had superior abilities in doing writing assignments.

3. What skills or information learned in college do you find yourself not using at all?

Antonio: I am always one to admit that the "good" and "bad" are both learning experiences. I found myself learning less from professors that had absolutely no dynamism or charisma whatsoever. So my remedy for that was to learn as much as I could from the situation. If you're planning on studying sociology, I would recommend taking courses that will allow you to explore interesting discussions that challenge every atom of our brain.

Emily: I struggled through a very early Friday-morning Forensic Chemistry course and can honestly say that I have yet to use anything I learned from that course since.

Erica: Test taking. I cannot remember the last time I took a multiple-choice exam or composed a timed essay.

Laura: Information feed during general education requirement courses.

Marsha: During the first semester of my junior year at Madison, I began to realize that I might be majoring in sociology for the wrong reasons. This was made clear to both my counselor and me when we tried to have a discussion at the end of the first semester. Since we were unable to really communicate, she suggested that I speak to her husband who was also a sociology counselor. This second conference only confirmed my belief that I needed to reconsider my direction.

4. Which internships or extracurricular activities that you pursued in college have been most valuable to you personally and professionally? Why?

Antonio: My internship took me to Washington, DC. I worked with the Department of the Interior, Office of Equal Opportunity. I did this for two summers. The reality of a government job, a big city, and living completely on my own facilitated one of the best learning experiences of my life. To put it lightly, I grew up. I had never lived anywhere else except my hometown, and this experience awoke me to an entirely new world. Professionally, it opened up doors and networks that I still carry to this day. Ten years later, I'm still able to send an e-mail or make a phone call to a friend from those summers and know that I have a connection. As far as activities, I took advantage of every opportunity I could . . . [since] participation builds leadership, and leadership builds a future.

Emily: I was a public policy intern at a women's health organization. The political and research experience I gained helped me to be a qualified candidate for my current position as a legislative assistant.

Erica: Working at *CBS Night Watch* during the fall of my junior year was a great experience. It was my first extended stay away from home (it was in DC, and I was in LA) and it exposed me to the "real world" of work, its pressures, expectations, and demands. I learned that I could and should take better advantage of internship possibilities and networking with others because they can both mean jobs.

Laura: Incorporated into my course work were two required practical training projects (volunteer requirements). This allowed me the opportunity to gain exposure into two different work environments within the same occupational area—providing me with insight into two distinct paths.

Marsha: During my three years at Pratt Institute, I had the opportunity to have many part-time jobs (working in a furniture store in Chinatown, working for a solo furniture designer, working for a multidisciplinary firm in Manhattan and working for a firm that both designed and manufactured display items) and although these were not considered internships, they taught me so much about working in firms; a lot of which you could never learn in a classroom. I think these jobs certainly helped me when I went on to full-time work, and I feel that the design schools that integrate internships into their programs are doing the students a great service.

5. How did you decide which field, either in academia or the real world, to go into?

Antonio: This was not an easy process. I would agree that a combination of things took place for me to better anticipate what I wanted to do when I "grew up." First of all, you should always strive for more. Everything I do is another stepping-stone. Bits and pieces of my academic and extracurricular career all had an affect on what I do today. I have done event planning, academic advising, crisis counseling, public speaking, public health education, activism, curriculum development, and leadership development. These are all bits and pieces from my course work and extracurricular involvement.

Emily: I felt I would be happy entering a job in either health care or education. I think mostly I've always wanted a job where I can help other people and foster positive growth for myself and the world. When I had a position doing direct service work in a community health center, I realized that I actually like the policy end better.

Erica: I finally decided to pursue what I thought about my freshman year—the arts— but my parents did not support that, and so it took a lot of other jobs and pursuits to finally come full circle and help me determine what I did not want to do.

Laura: I was fortunate enough to select a work-study position within the Career Services Office—the staff within the department drilled into me the importance of networking as part of the internship/job development process. It was through their help that I was able to connect with representatives from local agencies in order to learn more about their profession and role within the agency. It was through this process that I gained a better understanding of which field would be the best fit for me.

Marsha: Back at CU during my sophomore year I had taken one interior design class since it had the reputation of being an 'easy A' class. Since I had enjoyed the class, I took another interior design class that first semester at Wisconsin. I had always felt that interior design was not relevant, that it was just something for people of wealth to do, but the fact that I couldn't stay awake past midnight studying for a sociology test, but could do an all-nighter for my design project was a giant clue for me. It became clear that I should follow something that interested me rather than something I thought I should do.

6. Did you have a mentor when you entered the workforce/graduate school?

Antonio: I did when I entered graduate school. I had close connections with my advisors and professors. These were individuals who I looked up to and often sought out when I was in need of a good "slap in the face." Many of these professors are now my friends, and I still keep in touch with some of them almost 10 years later. To be honest, it has been harder to find that mentor in the real world. I dare say that it's a bit more cutthroat out here in the dense world, and a lot of people are looking out for number one. To me, a good role model is someone who is training the next person in line to take their job.

Emily: No.

Erica: Yes, her name was Kikanza and I owe her a great deal. She came into the café where I was working and we started to chat; before she left I had an interview to be her personal assistant. Obviously, she hired me and became my first mentor. She taught me if you're a man and tough at work, you're a performer. If you're a woman and tough at work, you're a "b-tch." She taught [that] being a "b-tch" isn't all bad.

Laura: No.

Marsha: I really, really wish I had had a real mentor in the early stages of my design career not only because I made so many mistakes, but to give me a better perspective on the real meaning, the importance of design to the human soul.

7. What's the number-one bit of advice you wish you were given before you entered the job market?

Antonio: Never have more than one credit card with a balance of more than $500. You'll have more money in your pocket if you have fewer bills to pay.

Emily: I was given the advice that people often have several different career paths throughout the course of their lives. The idea that it's okay to explore diverse interests and opportunities—and that I'm not locked into anything—was a very comforting thought.

Erica: Do your very best because you never know what this job may lead to next.

Laura: Fortunately, I had a lot of advice through my on-campus employment experience; however, some of it didn't become real to me until after graduation.

Marsha: I had the training in how to approach a project as far as design solutions, but needed more knowledge in so many other areas, both technical and more ephemeral aspects. If a mentor had taken an interest in me, that would have been much better for my career.

8. What were your job-related expectations when you were still in school, and how did they match up with your experience of the "real world"?

Antonio: Although my internships attempted to prepare me for the real world, the mentality is different. As an intern, you're still a student. You still have homework and may live in the dorm or with your parents. The real world is just that—the real thing. It's a tough place, and you should expect it to be. Expect the bar level to be risen on you. Expect that you should work hard, work late, and feel underpaid. Expect that you'll have to pay your dues and that you may not have all the resources you need to do your job. Expect to have the challenge of your life.

Emily: I expected it would be easier to adjust to a 9-to-5 lifestyle. Getting up, ready, and sharp for early mornings five days a week was a big adjustment from my very flexible college schedule.

Erica: My expectations were too high, and they did not match the real world. I thought it would be simple to one day land a high-paying job, but it is much harder than you think, especially if you do not pursue a career that requires you to learn a trade or specific skill (e.g., accounting, dentistry, etc).

Laura: Aside from working in the Career Services Office, I also completed an internship with the judicial branch in juvenile probation. I knew that I wasn't going to start out making as much money as my fellow accounting and graphic design classmates; however, I also knew that the experience would provide me with the practical training I needed to become a probation officer or a related position.

Marsha: You need other people skills, and you need information about best business practices. It would have been better for me to have learned this in school rather than by trial and error.

9. What was your first job out of college? How did you find that job?

Antonio: My first "official" job out of college (at least the job that was tied to my purpose in being in college) was as an event coordinator at a university. I got this job because the director of the department knew me and offered me the opportunity to get out of my hometown. It is most certainly true when they say, "It's who you know." How did I know her? From student government. And they say getting involved doesn't make a difference?

Emily: I worked for several months at a local restaurant (where I'd worked during school vacations) while I searched for something more permanent. My first job was as an access-to-care coordinator at a community health center. I found the job posting on Craigslist.com.

Erica: My first job out of college was in retail sales at a department store called I. Magnin in the Gifts/Home Wares Department. A woman I was babysitting for was a manager there and got me the interview.

Laura: I accepted a position as a social worker within a substance abuse treatment center. The center was on my list of agency referrals while working as a probation intern. It was through maintaining my relationships with those I knew would be in the position to help me advance that my internship became even more worthwhile.

Marsha: I left New York for Denver after grad school and applied to a large number of architectural and design firms. My first job was with a small interior design group.

10. If you went straight into the workforce after receiving your bachelor's degree, do you wish you had attended graduate school first? If you went on to grad school, do you wish you had worked first? In either case, why?

Antonio: I'm very glad that I went straight into graduate school. It's nice to be able to say that I finished it when I was 24. I think my appreciation level was lower than it would have been had I waited, but nonetheless it has helped me climb the latter a bit more successfully. My graduate degree has not been a certainty. I don't always earn wages for my degree but I am often given a certain level of respect for having it.

Emily: I am happy to have taken the time to work. I want to go back for grad school, but I want to be sure that I will be using my degree for many years to come. The opportunity to work and learn more about my professional likes and dislikes has been very helpful.

Erica: Without question, I'm glad I took time off for two reasons: first, I was simply burned out on school; second, the time allowed me to really consider all the different options available. It was almost six years before I enrolled in grad school and I'm certain that time gave me the focus necessary to not only get through, but ensure I would do something that I truly wanted to do for a career.

Laura: No. My hope is that my employer will pay for any of my advanced degree plans.

Marsha: I think my portfolio and the reputation of my grad school were helpful in landing the job.

11. What's the best piece of advice you've received from a colleague?

Antonio: "Take the job!" A former colleague of mine advised that I leave a previous job where I had become pretty stagnant and unhappy. The job I took didn't come with a big pay raise, but it was certainly a better opportunity for professional and personal growth. It's risky sometimes, and when you become comfortable in a situation, it's hard to give that up. I feel 10 times stronger as a result of taking that risk.

Emily: Try your best to leave work at work and home at home, and don't beat yourself up when you can't.

Erica: Finish what you start. Then go on to something new.

Laura: It never hurts to ask for what you want—the worst anyone can do is tell you "no."

Marsha: The profession is a little like being a hairdresser; you need to listen to your client and interpret what they are saying.

12. What's the smartest move you've made since receiving your bachelor's degree?

Antonio: Moving away from home. I'm the quintessential, homegrown "mama's boy," and for me, getting out and seeing the world is what changed me. That diploma will only take you as far as you're willing to go.

Emily: Leaving a job where I was somewhat unhappy, and couldn't see advancement potential.

Erica: Getting my master's degree.

Laura: I try and sign up for as many additional training workshops and seminars that come through my department to become more marketable.

Marsha: Going to art school.

13. Describe your current job and its major responsibilities.

Antonio: I'm the current outreach manager for The Princeton Review—Arizona. I am in charge of all marketing and outreach for the entire state. I work closely with high school counselors, university advisors, student groups, and partnering organizations to promote the company. I provide resources for assisting students to get into the college or university of their dreams. I do public speaking engagements where I talk about the essentials of standardized tests and work to promote stronger methods in which to score better. I plan all major and minor events for our office. I also serve as customer service personnel on a day-to-day basis.

Emily: I am a legislative assistant for a delegate to the Maryland General Assembly. I field and respond to constituent concerns, and aid my delegate in legislative research.

Erica: Currently, I am director of education at The Crocker Museum in Sacramento, California. The Crocker is a midsize museum with approximately 50 full-time staff. I lead the entire education department, which means I supervise 90 docents [and] 5 full-time and 2 part-time employees. My staff provides all of the programming offered by the museum. This includes but is not limited to: museum tours, art classes, lectures by artists, and the occasional concert. The audiences we specifically target are: adults, children, families, and school groups.

Laura: I basically counsel and advise low-income, single parents on the employment and short-term training options available to them in order for them to become financially independent.

Marsha: As an interior designer, I really enjoy the fact that I have great diversity in the tasks that are required of me. A large part is creative work, which is gratifying, but there is also a lot of organizational work as well as paperwork that wasn't taught when I went to school.

14. What experience was required for it?

Antonio: Some of the skills that were required for this job included the ability to interact with other people on a professional level. Sound familiar? Good organizational skills, a higher educational background, experience working with youth, knowledge of college life and beyond, and having a college degree didn't exactly hurt my chances. Overall, my company was looking for someone who was energetic, outgoing, and willing to learn quickly in a fast paced environment.

Emily: My public policy experience helped. The nice thing about politics is that people come from a variety of backgrounds, so employment can be flexible.

Erica: A bachelor's and master's degree, knowledge of art history, and art education and museum work experience.

Laura: A bachelor's degree in psychology, sociology, or related area, as well as at least one practical training opportunity. I am fluent in Spanish, so that was an advantage given my client population.

Marsha: Many people think that being a designer is just about having good taste, but there are many aspects that are quite technical, involving lighting, acoustics, etc.

15. To what extent has your degree helped you in your current role?

Antonio: I work with people every day of my life. Understanding someone's personality can really help to assess a situation, and since I work in customer service occasionally, our customers are looking for empathy. Empathy is such an important element in your daily job, no matter what you do. Empathy is not always easy to learn, but studying human interaction is a good start. Apply what you learn to your own life and use yourself as an example (i.e., put yourself in their shoes).

Emily: When attempting to represent a region of people, understanding social behavior is key. I also think the research skills I honed in college are being well used.

Erica: Credentials are just as important as work experience in the museum field; a master's is a standard requirement at this point.

Laura: My degree not only gave me the necessary classroom training I needed, but it also offered room for practical training and volunteer opportunities to complement my classroom learning.

Marsha: I think that between understanding the design process and having good drafting skills (now done mostly on computers) it is essential to have received specialized training in school.

16. What do you like most about it?

Antonio: Creative freedom. I am encouraged, on a daily basis, to use my skills and experience to help our company succeed. I am recognized for those efforts and also given open, constructive feedback to help reach my goals. Also, I work for a company where almost everyone I work with is open-minded. There is very little that cannot be said because so many of my colleagues have acquired the wonderful skill of empathy.

Emily: I like the flexible schedule, and the opportunity to meet and work with many people.

Erica: Being around art and artists is definitely the best. Teaching others about art and helping them appreciate it is another big plus.

Laura: I enjoy helping others see the options available to them—providing them with the resources and tools they need to be informed decision makers and better providers for their families.

Marsha: I have really enjoyed having the opportunity to meet many different types of people and being able to interpret their design challenges. I love the variety of not always doing the same thing over and over. I love working with colors, materials, and finishes.

17. What aspect(s) of it do you not like?

Antonio: There are times when the workload seems a bit too much, and it becomes easy for details to become lost. When you work in an environment where change is constant and information flies by like a bat out of—well, you know—then sometimes it can be a bit stressful. However, that is the challenge you have to accept and use it as a learning experience.

Emily: Because politics is so competitive, it is difficult to find a trustworthy mentor or trainer.

Erica: Administration and managing different personalities.

Laura: Sometimes options have limitations. The options I can present to some of my clients—the realistic options—may not necessarily be the options they would like to consider, but I try and help them make connections and see relationships so that they realize sometimes starting small can lead to something big.

Marsha: The aspect of my profession that is the most distressing is the need to depend on other people to do various parts of the work necessary to complete the projects. I must rely on furniture, wallpaper, or fabric manufacturers plus painters, installers, delivery people, and so on. When these people don't follow through, the client always looks to the designer, and the situations can be very stressful.

18. What skills have you had to acquire that your bachelor's degree did not help you cultivate?

Antonio: A college degree will almost never teach you how to network. That is something you will almost certainly have to learn on your own. Getting involved will help with that, but you will have to learn how to adjust your own personality and learning style to how you "schmooze." It's good to know people. Have dinner parties, volunteer, join a group, and get out of the house. I can't begin to tell you how much this has helped me in the real world.

Emily: I'm working on learning how to let negative comments roll off my back. I'm also learning more about the individual state's legislative process.

Erica: Pretty much everything around the business aspect of my job. Accounting, creating budgets, administration, and management skills.

Laura: That's a hard question because I am a satisfied customer and believe I have had a good return on my investment.

Marsha: This profession has grown to the point where there are distinct specialties, similar to the medical profession. Designers often work solely in retail, health care, or hospitality since those fields have many specialized aspects. Also, it is always helpful to have a broad knowledge about the general trends such as designing for disabled/ADA, "green" design, "aging in place" design, etc.

19. What suggestions would you have for those still in college? Are there any "optional" elements of the undergraduate experience that you would recommend they explore?

Antonio: Pay your bills on time, and try not to get too many student loans. Just get the essentials. Volunteer as much as you can. Spend one Saturday a month to one dedicated program. If you're going to have a job, try and get a job on campus; it helps you stay focused. Finally, listen to classical music when you study. Later on in life when you take your first date out to a symphony concert, you can talk about how this piece of music influenced you.

Emily: I would encourage students to explore all of their interests. I think sometimes people gravitate toward "resume boosters." I was a manager for my university's men's basketball team in college. Every job interviewer I met with asked about the position because it was unique, particularly because I am a woman. This was a great conversation starter, particularly since I felt so comfortable with the subject.

Erica: Do as many internships as possible, and join clubs. Meet people—you never know when they may able to help you out in the future.

Laura: I didn't participate in study abroad. I believed that my language skills and practical training opportunities gave me the exposure I needed in learning more about cultural diversity and global awareness. I believe a study abroad opportunity may have taken it one step farther into reality.

Marsha: I feel that once residential designers get large commissions, they will be working with architects and should have some knowledge and background in architectural basics.

20. Do you have any tips for those entering the workforce/graduate school now?

Antonio: Always keep your resume updated. Keep a portfolio of everything that you do, particularly with your first job. If someone praises you in a letter or e-mail, put it in your portfolio. If you are particularly proud of something then throw that in there as well. One last thing, save important e-mails; you never know when you'll need them.

Emily: Whenever you can afford to, be patient. And don't be discouraged because your econ major friends have entry-level jobs that pay two or three times your annual salary. If you enjoy what you do, and can do it without incurring major debt, I say go for it.

Erica: Learn as much as you can about all the aspects of your job or program so that you can explore options within your field and always have choices.

Laura: Be patient and realistic. Networking is wonderful way to learn about the world of work and the people and professions in it. The job-search process is a full-time job; what you get out of it is a result of what you put in to it.

Marsha: The whole profession is affected by the economy, so a designer looking for a job during an economic slowdown has to realize that the cycles always reverse eventually.

21. What's the best way to get a job in your field?

Antonio: Have a bachelor's degree and open-mindedness.

Emily: Politics is often about who you know. I recommend networking as much as possible and not being afraid to use your contacts.

Erica: Network, join national organizations, and do informational interviews at the places you want to work. Keep in mind: You'll most likely have to start at the bottom for horrible pay; it weeds out those who are serious and those who aren't.

Laura: Networking—and practical training.

Marsha: For students trying to obtain their first job, a strong portfolio is a must. Having good references from internships would be a great bonus as well.

22. What mistake do sociology grads often make?

Antonio: I think I walked away from campus with my degree in hand and said, "Okay. Now hire me." Well, it doesn't work that way. You have to learn how to sell yourself and learn how to apply what you have learned in college to what it is you are reaching for. The job market is more competitive than ever, and if you don't stand out you will most certainly get lost in the crowd.

Emily: They listen to all those people who say, "Sociology? What the heck can you do with that?" If nothing else, studying social science will certainly make you a more thoughtful human being.

Erica: Assuming your major is so general that you are qualified to do anything. Find a specific area to specialize in; if possible, create a niche for yourself.

Laura: Some, unfortunately, only see direct relationships as opposed to indirect relationships. I decided on one of the "typical" paths; however, I know other sociology majors who are now working in the field of finance.

Marsha: I can't really speak to that since most of the people in my profession are art school graduates. I'm not an expert on resumes, but I think a well-organized page that is both informative and graphically pleasing will make a good first impression. After all, the people reading these resumes are usually designers themselves.

23. What's something that you think more sociology grads should do to advance their careers?

Antonio: Get your head out of the book. Do something practical, and apply what you are learning to real scenarios. As a sociologist, the field is wide open for interpretation. Your skills have to be adaptable to your environment and you have to be flexible. You may not get what you want right out of college so use each experience as another step. More specifically, do something that makes you uncomfortable.

Emily: Because the major is so broad, I'd recommend people eventually attend grad school if they've chosen a very specialized field.

Erica: Develop an expertise, and network.

Laura: Gain exposure into the field, but select two different environments or populations.

Marsha: Looking presentable, having strong communication skills, and basically being able to persevere are all important.

24. Who is in the best position to offer a sociology graduate help with his or her resume and cover letter?

Antonio: Anyone who tells you to keep it short and sweet. It's not an epistle. One of my first mistakes out of college is that I thought employers like to read—that is so not the case. Keep to the basics and give the facts. Let the interview be the moment to shine in your glory!

Emily: I do recommend using the college Career Center. That's their job! I also recommend having a peer editor. They may be able to point out some interesting facts/skills about yourself that you never even thought of.

Erica: I'd say there are two options: Anybody who works specifically in the field that you want to enter or a general career counselor.

Laura: An assistant or adjunct professor of sociology, a professional within the field, or someone from Career Services; it depends on your comfort level—who are you most comfortable talking to?

Marsha: (No response.)

25. What pitfalls should sociology graduates avoid when applying to and interviewing for positions?

Antonio: Stay away from sounding too academic, and use some of your practical experiences when you're applying for a job. Employers like to hear specific examples that are relevant to the job you're applying for. Stay away from sounding to "theoretical" or "observational." Anticipate that you will be asked questions that will want you to cite your own experiences. One last bit of advice: When you are asked for your strengths and weaknesses, be honest. Employers can see through this. Don't overindulge with your strengths, and construct your weaknesses so that you utilize them to your advantage. Remember, you are always learning from them. It's okay to make mistakes.

Emily: Don't assume your material arrived in one piece—follow up, and reiterate your interest. Also don't take it personally if you don't get the job, even if you had your heart set on it. Not getting one position just means you'll be more available when another one comes along.

Erica: Not knowing what you want to do and, worse yet, not being able to explain it.

Laura: The same pitfalls any graduate faces—one, putting all of your eggs in one basket—or relying on the internet to find you a job.

Marsha: (See response to question 23.)

APPENDIX A
Fellowships

FOREIGN SERVICE

THE INSTITUTE FOR INTERNATIONAL PUBLIC POLICY FELLOWSHIP PROGRAM

www.uncfsp.org/iipp/content/program.cfm

The IIPP Fellowship aims to prepare students for entry into a career in international affairs. Students from across the country apply during their sophomore year and participate in multi-year policy institutes, language training, study abroad, and graduate studies.

THE PAMELA HARRIMAN FOREIGN SERVICE FELLOWSHIP

www.wm.edu/harriman/harrimanfellowship.html

This competitive fellowship, awarded annually to three undergraduate students from across the nation, funds a summer in a professional position with the United States Department of State. The fellowship offers a $5,000 stipend to cover travel and living expenses. Service is typically completed over the course of 11 weeks.

TRUMAN SCHOLARSHIP

www.truman.gov/candidates

Students planning on pursuing graduate degrees within a public service field should think about applying for a Truman Scholarship. Those selected are offered up to $30,000 in funding. Only current college juniors will be considered. The Truman Foundation also provides career counseling, internship placement, and professional development.

THE WOODROW WILSON NATIONAL FELLOWSHIP FOUNDATION

The Thomas R. Pickering Graduate Foreign Affairs Fellowship

www.woodrow.org/public-policy/graduate.php

The Pickering Fellowship is intended for those interested in pursuing a career within the Foreign Service, an organization dedicated to representing American concerns abroad. Applicants should be enrolled in a two-year master's program in international affairs, public policy, or public administration or studying within academic fields like economics, foreign languages or political science. Funding covers room, board, tuition, and mandatory fees, as well as reimbursement for books and travel.

GERONTOLOGY

THE GERONTOLOGICAL SOCIETY OF AMERICA

www.geron.org/fellows.htm

The Gerontological Society of America offers a fellowship for their members who have made outstanding contributions to the field. To meet the requirements, you must retain society membership for five years and be nominated by a current fellow.

HEALTH SERVICES

HOWARD HUGHES PRE-DOCTORAL FELLOWSHIPS IN BIOLOGICAL SCIENCES

www.nationalacademies.org/fellowships.hhmiprogram.html

This fellowship promotes excellence in bio-medical research, helping future scientific scholars obtain quality graduate education. Applicants must have completed at least one year of postbaccalaureate study in the biological sciences, whether within a master's or doctoral program or outside of a degree program. This fellowship does offer a stipend.

THE WELLSTONE FELLOWSHIP

www.familiesusa.org/about/wellstone-fellowship-about.html

Working in conjunction with Families U.S.A.'s Minority Health Initiatives Department, Wellstone Fellows help draft fact sheets, policy briefs, and other copy for a variety of publications. Fellows gain a thorough understanding of Medicaid, Medicare, and of efforts to achieve universal health coverage. Fellows receive an annual stipend along with health benefits.

HUMAN RIGHTS

THE AMERICAN CIVIL LIBERTIES UNION FOUNDATION AND HUMAN RIGHTS WATCH

The Aryeh Neier Fellowship

www.hrw.org/about/info/hrw-aclu-fellowship.html

This two-year fellowship is open to recent law school graduates. Fellows spend one year at each organization, working on joint initiatives to foster concern for human rights within the United States. The job typically entails preparing reports, advocacy, and development of litigation strategies.

THE CARR CENTER FOR HUMAN RIGHTS POLICY—JFK SCHOOL OF GOVERNMENT, HARVARD UNIVERSITY

National Security and Human Rights Program Fellowship

www.ksg.harvard.edu/cchrp/nshr_fellowship.shtml

The NSHR Program examines national security issues from a humanitarian and human rights perspective. Fellows spend one year at the Carr Center though no stipend is available. Start and end dates are negotiable. It is mandatory that applicants have a military and/or national security background.

THIRD MILLENNIUM FOUNDATION (TMF)

Third Millennium International Fellowship in Human Rights

www.seedsoftolerance.org/initiative_intl_fellowship.html

A practical training fellowship, TMF offers fellows the opportunity to either start or advance their career in the field of human rights. Work is conducted in the home country as well as in a developing nation. The fellowship is open to both students (undergraduates and graduates) as well as practitioners. Applicants will need two sponsoring organizations that are engaged in human rights work.

INTERNATIONAL POLITICS

COUNCIL ON FOREIGN RELATIONS

International Affairs Fellowship

www.cfr.org/about/fellowships/iaf.html

This fellowship, open to young professionals (between the ages of 27 and 35), grants exposure to both policy studies and policymaking. This unique blend of research and formation allows each fellow to gain a well-rounded perspective. Both academics and those working in the private sector are encouraged to apply, as are government officials.

THE NATIONAL ENDOWMENT FOR DEMOCRACY

Reagan-Fascell Democracy Fellows Program

www.ned.org/forum/reagan-fascell.html

This program enables activists, scholars, and journalists to learn more about the facets of democracy and strengthen their ability to promote democratic change throughout the world. Twelve to fifteen follows are hosted each year for periods ranging from 3 to 10 months. There are two separate tracks fellows can pursue—practitioner or scholar.

RAND CORPORATION

Transatlantic Postdoctoral Fellowship for International Relations and Security (TAPIR)

www.rand.org/about/edu_op/fellowships/transatlantic

TAPIR seeks candidates who have recently completed their doctorate in the social or political science or economics. Applicants' academic focus and research should pertain to international relations and security. Fellowships are for 24 months and prepare fellows for a career in policy-oriented research.

LAW ENFORCEMENT

THE NATIONAL ORGANIZATION OF BLACK LAW ENFORCEMENT EXECUTIVES (NOBLE)

Law Enforcement Fellowship Program

www.noblenational.org/displaycommon.cfm?an=1&subarticlenbr=41

Established in 1987, this fellowship program is open to active law enforcement employees. Fellows can serve for anywhere from six months to one year at NOBLE headquarters. The work entails conducting or assisting with research on various technical assistance projects.

W.E.B. DuBOIS FELLOWSHIP PROGRAM

www.ncjrs.gov/pdffiles1/nij/sl000753.pdf

Sponsored by the National Institute of Justice (NIJ), an agency of the U.S. Department of Justice and an arm of the Office of Justice Programs, this fellowship aims to further the understanding of crime, violence and the administration of justice. Fellowship grants typically last for 12 months, and researchers are encouraged to apply no matter what their academic discipline.

PSYCHOLOGY

AMERICAN PSYCHOLOGICAL ASSOCIATION MINORITY FELLOWSHIP PROGRAM (MFP): MENTAL HEALTH AND SUBSTANCE ABUSE SERVICES FELLOWSHIP

www.apa.org/mfp/cprogram.html

This federally funded program is aimed at psychology doctoral students who are preparing for careers in counseling, clinical, school, or other programs that allocate mental health services. Applicants must be American citizens or permanent resident aliens with a strong commitment and interest in serving ethnic minority communities.

YALE CHILD STUDY CENTER PREDOCTORAL INTERNSHIP AND POSTDOCTORAL FELLOWSHIP

www.med.yale.edu/chldstdy/training/psychfellowship

This program is primarily designed for trainees from clinical programs, though candidates from other programs may apply if their prior experience and future plans are in line with the center. Applicants must have completed all course work toward the doctorate and all practicum experiences required prior to internship. Fellows receive an annual stipend as well as health insurance and vacation time.

SOCIAL SERVICES

ECHOING GREEN FELLOWSHIP PROGRAM

www.echoinggreen.org/index.cfm?fuseaction=Page.viewPage&pageID=41

Echoing Green bestows two-year fellowships to emerging social innovators. Fellows are chosen based on their creative models aimed at tackling seemingly insurmountable social challenges. Fellowships are given to either individuals or partnerships of two.

SEEDCORPS FELLOWSHIP

www.socialservice.com/jobdetails.cfm?jid=19566&RequestTimeout=500

Fellows work in conjunction with SeedCorps for a period of 5 months (with an option of extending up to 10 months). Workers provide free tax preparation assistance to low-wage workers throughout New York City.

SOCIOLOGY

AMERICAN SOCIOLOGICAL ASSOCIATION

www.asanet.org/page.ww?section=Funding&name=Funding+Opportunities

This professional organization provides a number of funding and fellowship opportunities for graduate students and those with a doctorate degree in sociology. These include the Minority Fellowship Program, the Community Action Research Initiative, and the ASA Congressional Fellowship.

THE CHARLOTTE W. NEWCOMBE DOCTORAL DISSERTATION FELLOWSHIP

www.woodrow.org/newcombe/index.php

This fellowship is designed for PhD candidates who have chosen to explore ethical or religious values within some realm of the humanities and social sciences. Fellows might also decide to research values influencing political decisions as well as the moral codes of foreign cultures.

INSTITUTE FOR HUMANE STUDIES

Humane Studies Fellowships

www.theihs.org/scholarships/id.775/default.asp

The HSF awards scholarships of up to $12,000 for both undergraduate and graduate students. Scholarships are generally awarded to those studying the practices, principles, and institutions necessary to sustain a free society.

WRITING AND JOURNALISM

AMERICAN PROSPECT WRITING FELLOWS PROGRAM

www.prospect.org/web/page.ww?section=root&name=Writing+Fellowships

This program offers young journalists two full years of employment at the American Prospect, during which time they are expected to produce three to four full-length articles as well as some short pieces. They are also expected to provide general editorial support. Fellows also receive a stipend for living expenses.

INTER-AMERICAN PRESS ASSOCIATION SCHOLARSHIP

www.sipiapa.com/otheractivities/scholarships.cfm

This scholarship supports young journalists or journalism school graduates (ages 21–35) who are interested in studying and reporting abroad in Latin America or the Caribbean. Applicants must have an excellent grasp of the language in which they plan to report.

INTERNATIONAL RADIO AND TELEVISION SOCIETY FOUNDATION SUMMER FELLOWSHIP PROGRAM

www.irts.org/programs/sfp/sfp.html

Fellows participate in a nine-week all-expenses-paid program during which they are exposed to various forms of media, take related field trips, and attend industry events. Career-planning advice is also included.

NATIONAL ENDOWMENT FOR THE ARTS LITERATURE FELLOWSHIPS: CREATIVE WRITING

www.nea.gov/grants/APPLY/Lit06/index.html

These fellowships are for published authors of prose (fiction or creative non-fiction) or poetry who show exceptional talent. The sum of the fellowship ($20,000) allows the author time to research, write, and travel.

Jobs and Internships

BUSINESS/FINANCE

EFINANCIALCAREERS

www.efinancialcareers.com

eFinancialCareers is a highly detailed website covering a number of financial realms including accounting, risk management, investment banking, hedge funds, operations, and commodities. Industry neophytes can take advantage of employer profiles, salary surveys, market news, and articles about the top MBA programs.

FINANCIAL JOB NETWORK

www.fjn.com

Financial Job Network has emerged a top recruiting site for companies located domestically and abroad. Registration is free, and job seekers will find a multitude of financial openings within a number of industries.

FINANCIAL JOBS

www.financial-jobs.com

Financial Jobs has listings for those searching for jobs within corporate finance, accounting, banking, and investment. The website is simple to navigate and users can search for positions based upon job function and geography.

SUSTAINABLEBUSINESS.COM

www.sustainablebusiness.com/jobs

This website provides internship and job listings for those interested in working for businesses with an environmental bent. Positions can be found throughout the country.

www.vault.com

Vault is one of the leading job sites for those within the financial community. Users are privy not only to job listings but also career advice, networking opportunities, and industry information pertaining to everything from salary research to top graduate programs.

CHILD CARE

GREATAUPAIR

www.greataupair.com

GreatAuPair is a fairly comprehensive site featuring nanny and au pair openings within the United States and abroad. Job seekers can investigate family profiles, gaining insight into prospective employers.

NANNYJOBS.COM

www.nannyjobs.com

NannyJobs.com is a resource that caters to nannies, agencies, and families alike. Those contemplating a foray into the world of child care can peruse numerous openings along with finding links to professional organizations and educational and training prospects.

NATIONAL WOMEN'S LAW CENTER

Internship with Child Care Group

www.nwlc.org/details.cfm?id=2168&section=Jobs

The National Women's Law Center is a legal advocacy group that works to enhance and protect the rights of women. Interns with the Child Care Group assist with outreach activities, help organize child care conferences, and conduct research for articles. Undergraduates who are majoring in education, political science, women's studies, English, and pre-law are especially encouraged to apply.

EVENT PLANNING

HOSPITALITY CAREER NETWORK (HCN)

www.hospitalitycareernetwork.com

Hospitality Career Network provides users with the opportunity to search for coveted openings within the hotel, gaming, cruise, spa, and restaurant industries. Registration is free, and once your resume is uploaded, you can look forward to hearing from an HCN consultant.

MEETING PROFESSIONALS INTERNATIONAL

www.mpiweb.org/cms/mpiweb/default.aspx

This high-profile site retains job listings for event planners and meeting industry professionals. Those using the job bank can qualify their search by region, position, salary, and key words among other things. Users must register before gaining access to the listings.

FOREIGN SERVICE

FOREIGN POLICY ASSOCIATION

www.fpa.org/jobs_contact2423/jobs_contact.htm

The Foreign Policy Association has the inside scoop on a number of phenomenal foreign policy opportunities. While they do have postings for positions around the globe, the majority of jobs are located within the greater Washington, DC area. Their vast listings run the gamut—from entry-level jobs to management positions.

THE U.S. DEPARTMENT OF STATE

http://careers.state.gov

Those serious about pursuing a career within the Foreign Service should explore any and all opportunities within the State Department. They staff a variety of positions, from Foreign Service Officer to civil service jobs. They even offer several student programs.

Gerontology

AgeWork.com

www.agework.com/agework

AgeWork features a number of positions within the growing field of gerontology. Job seekers can upload their resume, making subsequent visits highly convenient. The site posts openings from around the country.

ElderJobs.com

www.elderjobs.com

Texas residents with a passion for gerontology should investigate this site. Users are able to upload their resume and research company profiles.

MedicalWorkers.com

www.medicalworkers.com/employment/gerontology-jobs.aspx

The demand for gerontology professionals is rapidly increasing and MedicalWorkers.com is constantly deluged with the latest openings. Those in search of a job can request free email notification whenever a new listing has been posted.

Health Services

Absolutely Healthy Care

www.healthjobsusa.com

This comprehensive website is a highly beneficial resource for anyone interested in pursuing a career within medicine or healthcare. The listings cover a broad spectrum of positions—nurse, pharmacist, medical technician, physician assistant, respiratory therapist, physical therapist, occupational therapist, and speech language pathologist.

Access Nurses

www.accessnurses.com

Access Nurses is one of the country's leading staffing agencies within the nursing industry. Job seekers can find travel, per diem, and full-time positions.

ALLIED HEALTH SERVICES

http://alliedhealthservices.com/registration

Allied Health Services is a great site for anyone looking for physician, nursing, or pharmacy jobs. Additionally, users have access to health care news items and salary surveys.

ALLTHERAPYJOBS.COM

www.alltherapyjobs.com

A visit to AllTherapyJobs.com is a must for anyone pursuing a career within any realm of therapy. This comprehensive site posts positions within a number of sub-fields including massage therapy, occupational therapy, physical therapy, radiation therapy, and art therapy.

HEALTHSERVICESJOBS.COM

www.healthservicesjobs.com

This site provides access to a multitude of jobs within the health services and medical industry. Positions advertised include emergency medical technician, orderly, registered nurse, and pharmacist. Recent graduates will appreciate the site's additional resources, including links to resume guides and career consultations.

HUMAN RIGHTS

HUMAN RIGHTS FIRST

www.humanrightsfirst.org/about_us/jobs/interns.htm

Human Rights First, an advocacy organization that protects refugees and victims of discrimination and human rights violations, offers several internships throughout the year. Those who intern during the academic year typically work around 10–12 hours a week. Summer interns often work full-time. Human Rights First welcomes both undergraduate, graduate, and law students as well as recent graduates.

HUMAN RIGHTS JOBS

www.humanrightsjobs.com

Grads passionate about reversing injustice will definitely want to surf on into Human Rights Jobs. Listings primarily fall into one of three categories: legal, campaigning, or administrative. Viewers can choose to browse by location and openings from around the world are advertised.

IDEALIST.ORG

www.idealist.org

A project of Action without Borders, Idealist offers a global clearinghouse of non-profit resources, including jobs, internships, mailing lists, and nonprofit resources by state and country.

INTERACTION

www.interaction.org

InteAction is a coalition of U.S.-based international development and humanitarian nongovernmental organizations. Working to defeat poverty and promote social justice, InterAction offers incredible opportunities both home and abroad. Their listings are primarily for international relief and development agencies. Openings vary from paid to volunteer.

RIGHTS INTERNATIONAL

The Frank C. Newman Internship Program

www.rightsinternational.org/intern.html

Rights International provides students with an extraordinary opportunity to become involved in human rights litigation. An active litigation docket affords interns the chance to work on actual human rights cases, drafting pleadings, writing legal briefs and interviewing clients. Applicants must have a background in civil rights/liberties law and proficiency in a second language is highly recommended.

INTERNATIONAL POLITICS

THE AMERICAN FOREIGN POLICY COUNCIL

www.afpc.org/op.shtml

The AFPC is a nonprofit organization designed to supply information to those who both influence and create the United States' foreign policy. Unpaid internships are offered year round, with interns expected to commit at least 20 hours per week. Though responsibilities often vary, interns work provide editorial assistance with publications, foreign policy research, special-event planning, logistical support for foreign delegations in Washington, and a multitude of administrative tasks.

THE HENRY L. STIMSON CENTER

www.stimson.org/about/?SN=AB2001110511

The Stimson Center is a nonpartisan, nonprofit institution dedicated fostering international peace and security via both outreach and analysis. Interns are assigned to specific project areas such as Southwest Asia, Cooperative Nonproliferation, and Domestic Preparedness and Homeland Security.

INTERNATIONAL JOB CENTER

www.internationaljobs.org/index.html

Job-seekers searching for employment with an international bent might want to investigate the International Job Center. Though paid membership is required (pricing is reduced for students, recent graduates, and volunteers), benefits give members access to a weekly paper with over 500 current international job vacancies. Listings include internships and positions within foreign affairs, development, health care and education.

JOBS ABROAD

www.jobsabroad.com/listings.cfm/interntypeID/85

Jobs Abroad is yet another useful resource for those contemplating working overseas. The site provides job and internship listings along with information regarding language schools, air fare, hostels, and vital tidbits every ex-pat should know.

JOBSTER

www.jobster.com/find/US/jobs/for/international+relations

Though devoted to a number of industries, Jobster offers a plethora of international relations listings. Users can refine their search criteria, choosing to view openings by date posted. This beneficial tool allows people to gain quick access to the most recent openings. Notably, Jobster features a "People are Talking..." section which displays interviews with employees from a variety of companies. These interviews are a fantastic way to gain insight into potential employers.

THE POLITIX GROUP

www.politixgroup.com/dcjobs.htm

For a nominal, one-time $10 donation fee, employment seekers and politics alike can become a member of The Politix Group. Membership will entitle you to job and internship bulletins, policy and think tanks, campaigns, openings in Congress, newsletters, and a variety of international opportunities.

THE RILEY GUIDE

www.rileyguide.com/internat.html

Students and recent graduates interested in all things international should spend some time on this website. The Riley Guide features job opportunities across the globe. While users cannot post their resume, they will be able to find a multitude of job links that are sure to lead to the ultimate position.

LAW ENFORCEMENT

AMERICAN POLICE BEAT

www.apbweb.com

Chock-full of news and humorous anecdotes, this website also provides employment listings ranging from border patrol jobs to positions as college campus officers and public safety dispatchers.

FEDERAL JOBS NET

www.federaljobs.net/law.htm

Students contemplating a career in law enforcement will do themselves a favor by exploring this comprehensive site to get information on a variety of positions such as U.S. Marshals, prison guards, investigators, Secret Service, etc. The website also offers information on interviews and various civil service entrance exams

FEDERAL LAW ENFORCEMENT TRAINING CENTER

www.fletc.gov/student-information/college-intern-program

The FLETC's College Intern Program allows students to participate in federal law enforcement training. Three 12-week sessions are held throughout the year. Interns are expected to live on premises and receive a stipend to cover the cost of food, travel, and incidentals. Applicants must either be a senior in college or enrolled in graduate school.

INTERNATIONAL ASSOCIATION OF POLICE CHIEFS

www.theiacp.org

The IACP site provides listings for positions throughout the U.S., with a strong focus on police work. A variety of information is also available on topics ranging from training programs, industry publications, and legislative activities. There is a "members only" section which offers numerous benefits including networking opportunities.

INTERPOL

www.interpol.int/Public/Icpo/Recruitment/stages.asp

Those interested in international law enforcement should explore internship opportunities at Interpol's headquarters in Lyon, France. Applicants must have a thorough command of English. Knowledge of French, Spanish, or Arabic is also quite useful (though proficiency is not a requirement). Interns are responsible for finding their own housing accommodations and obtaining their own visa. However, Interpol does offer a monthly allowance.

OFFICER.COM

www.officer.com

This comprehensive website features law enforcement employment opportunities available across the country as well links to industry news, products, and discussion forums.

PSYCHOLOGY

ASSOCIATION FOR BEHAVIOR ANALYSIS INTERNATIONAL (ABA INTERNATIONAL)

http://apps.abainternational.org/start/jobs.aspx

ABA International's job page allows visitors to search for employment opportunities via specialized categories—autism, brain injury, clinical, developmental disabilities, education, faculty, and research. Users can find both jobs and internships, though listings for the former far outnumber the latter. The site allows seekers to upload their resume.

HAZELDEN FOUNDATION

Pre-doctoral Psychology Internships

www.hazelden.org/web/public/predoctoral.page

One of the foremost drug and alcohol rehabilitation centers, Hazelden offers a unique APA accredited internship. Taking a clinical approach, interns focus on treatment for drug and alcohol dependency and related mental health conditions and complications.

PSYCCAREERS—THE AMERICAN PSYCHOLOGICAL ASSOCIATION'S (APA) ONLINE CAREER CENTER

http://psyccareers.apa.org

The APA's career center is an extremely valuable resource. Job-seekers can post their resume, search for potential employment, peruse interview tips, get advice on professional development, and gain deeper insight in the field of psychology.

THE READING HOSPITAL AND MEDICAL CENTER

Internship in Clinical Psychology

www.readinghospital.org/content/psych_intern.htm

Reading Hospital sponsors a one year, APA-accredited pre-doctoral internship. It provides clinical training within a community mental health setting. Interns experience three clinical rotations, working with outpatient clients and conducting inpatient psychological assessments.

SCHOOL PSYCHOLOGY JOB CENTER

www.schoolpsychology.net/p_jobs.html

The School Psychology Job Center includes job and internship openings within both secondary school and university settings. Importantly, the website also provides a plethora of links to a variety of professional organizations and websites focusing on specific disorders and advertising additional job openings.

RECREATION AND LEISURE

THE MARYLAND-NATIONAL CAPITAL PARK AND PLANNING COMMISSION

Department of Parks and Recreation

www.pgparks.com/info/intern.html

The Department of Parks and Recreation features internships in a number of areas including community recreation, planning, design, therapeutic recreation, sports, and horticulture. Students may intern during the fall, winter/spring, or summer.

FITNESSJOBS.COM

www.fitnessjobs.com

FitnessJobs.com obtains listings for a variety of positions within the health, fitness, and recreation industry. Importantly, the "Trade Talk" section provides links to a number of articles pertaining to health and fitness issues.

THE NATIONAL INTRAMURAL-RECREATIONAL SPORTS ASSOCIATION

www.nirsa.org

The NIRSA supports the development, education, and research of collegiate recreational sports. The organization's website has a wealth of information pertaining not only to jobs but also tips on networking opportunities, upcoming conferences, and publications.

National Recreation and Park Association

www.nrpa.org/careerCenter

The NRPA has long promoted recreational opportunities involving the creation and maintenance of parks. Their career center features openings for like-minded individuals, with listings ranging from aquatics director to park naturalist and wilderness trip leader. Visitors to the site will also learn about the latest industry publications and conferences.

The Oaks at Ojai

www.internsearch.com/directory_recres.htm

A residential health resort located in Southern California, the Oaks at Ojai provides full-time internships to college students. Applicants must have, at minimum, sophomore standing, and those with health, fitness, and management majors are especially encouraged to apply.

Social Services

HSPeople.com

www.hspeople.com

Those curious about social services and the nonprofit world will find a stop at HSPeople.com beneficial. Visitors can search for jobs and internships while finding interview tips and career planning suggestions.

Human Services Career Network

www.hscareers.com

The Human Services Career Network covers a number of social service vocations. Those searching for work will find exciting opportunities in areas such as mental health, corrections, education, case management, and social work. Amongst the gems on this site is the "Good Works" section, which offers inspiring stories from the social service trenches.

Nonprofit Career Network

www.nonprofitcareer.com

This organization's primary members include nonprofits operating within the business and economic world. Visitors to the site can upload their resume for free. It will be kept online for a period of 90 days.

NonProfit-Jobs.org

www.nonprofit-jobs.org

NonProfit-Jobs.org is a fairly straightforward site with postings from a variety of nonprofits. Openings can be found all over the country but a majority of the listings feature more senior positions.

SocialService.com

www.socialservice.com

Job seekers can upload their resume onto SocialService.com free of charge, allowing employers to find you and simplifying the application process. Users can also generate a "job agent" which notifies them of new job postings. Listings include domestic positions as well jobs in Canada and the United Kingdom.

Social Service Network

www.socialservicenetwork.com

The Social Service Network displays both a national job board along with a job board dedicated solely to positions open throughout Minnesota. Job-seekers can find a number of openings within industries that fall under the generic umbrella of social services—everything from working with at-risk youth and crisis management to foster care and shelter work. First-time resume writers can take advantage of the sample resumes posted on the site.

SocialWorkJobBank

www.socialworkjobbank.com

SocialWorkJobBank is a user-friendly site featuring positions across the country. Job-seekers can generate job alerts, which notify applicants of newly posted openings that match their criteria. Additionally, users can set up an account allowing them to upload a resume and keep track of applications and cover letters.

Sociology

The American Sociological Association

www.asanet.org

This professional organization devotes a portion of its website to employment opportunities. Members have full access to the job bank while nonmembers can pay $19.95 for 30 days of access. College students and recent graduates will appreciate that the site offers career preparation advice for those who are majoring in sociology.

SocialService.com

www.socialservice.com

Job seekers can upload their resume onto SocialService.com free of charge, allowing employers to find you and simplifying the application process. Users can also generate a "job agent" which notifies them of new job postings. Listings include domestic positions as well jobs in Canada and the United Kingdom.

WRITING AND JOURNALISM

JournalismJobs.com

www.journalismjobs.com

JournalismJobs.com is a comprehensive career site, serving both the rookie reporter and the seasoned news veteran. Interested parties can upload their resume free of charge. Resumes remain listed for six months at which time users must re-register. A variety of journalistic powerhouses have posted openings on the site including CNN, Time Inc., *The Wall Street Journal*, NPR, and PBS.

THE JOURNALIST'S TOOLBOX

www.journaliststoolbox.com/newswriting/jobs.html

This extensive site covers every imaginable niche to be found within journalism: newspapers, broadcast/media, magazines, sports, photojournalism, etc. Importantly, there's a plethora of information to comb through, from reporting tips to editing tools—all rather useful for a journalist-to-be.

MEDIABISTRO

www.mediabistro.com

Mediabistro is currently one of the leading jobs sites for those desiring a career within journalism, writing, and/or publishing. Registration is mandatory, albeit free, and users can find openings in cities across the United States. The site also keeps abreast of the latest media news and trends and advertises media courses and events.

THE NATION INSTITUTE JOURNALISM INTERNSHIP PROGRAM

www.nationinstitute.org/internships

The Nation Institute, working in conjunction *The Nation* magazine, offers an inclusive internship for those desiring a career in journalism and magazine publishing.

Interns gain invaluable editorial and publishing experience, working on everything from fact-checking and evaluating manuscripts to assisting with advertising and circulation. A total of nine interns are selected for each session, eight for the New York office and one for the Washington, DC office.

NEWSLINK

http://newslink.org/joblink.html

Those looking to burst onto the journalism scene might want to investigate Newslink, an inclusive website providing the most up-to-date job listings. In addition to employment openings, the site also offers links to numerous periodicals and media sources.

THE WRITE JOBS

www.writejobs.com

Much like the name implies, The Write Jobs is a niche career site with a focus on jobs within journalism, publishing, and media. The comprehensive site also offers links to both career advice and career resources.

NOTES

NOTES

NOTES

NOTES

NOTES

NOTES

FINDING THE FUNDS
What you should know about paying for your graduate school education

Furthering your education is an investment in your future. Laying down $120,000 — probably more — in exchange for a top-notch graduate school education requires just as much research and planning as deciding which school you'll hand that money over to.

The good news is that you still have a little time before you have to really worry about signing on the dotted line for any type of financial assistance. That gives you some time to research options, to properly calculate the actual costs of going to graduate school beyond just the sticker price, and to create a plan so that your potential future earnings cover your costs of living when you're out of school and using that degree you will have worked so hard for.

You're going to be responsible for the choices you make. Cutting your ancillary expenses for the next few years and building up an out-of-pocket school fund before you ever register for that first class might save you thousands of dollars in interest payments down the road. But how will you know if you don't come up with a plan?

No doubt you've accumulated some sort of credit history, most likely through undergrad student loans and/or some high-interest credit card debt, so you might think you have it all figured out when it comes to paying for graduate school. While you might understand the basics about how federal loans work and how scholarships, grants, and fellowships can help to cut down the final bill, there are lesser-known and fairly new options out there that can make your postgraduate life a little easier to enjoy.

OTHER PEOPLE'S MONEY

Scholarships and Grants
These are the best form of financial aid because they don't have to be paid back. Remember, though, that most scholarships require a minimum GPA and that some grants are good for only one year. When evaluating your payment options, make sure there is a reasonable expectation that the financial aid package being offered will be available for the full term of the degree requirement or that you have a way of managing funds if they are not enough.

Fellowships and Stipends
Fellowships come in many different forms. Sometimes partial tuition scholarships are called fellowships. These university-sponsored fellowships consist of a cash award that is promptly subtracted from your tuition bill. You can earn the amount of the award by teaching for a department or by completing research for a faculty member. The percentage of students who receive this type of fellowship and the amount paid to each will vary depending on the intended degree and field, enrollment status (full- or part-time), and years of enrollment.

It is important to note that survival on a fellowship alone is unlikely. Fellowships are taxable income—federal, state, county, and city—and you may be expected to pay for school fees, supplies, and books out of your fellowship, as well as tuition. If the fellowship doesn't cover the full cost of your attendance, you'll have to explore other financing options.

Employer-financed Opportunities
Some employers will offer a tuition reimbursement or a limited financial sum for employees to attend graduate school part time. Employers expect the advanced degree to enhance your performance on the job or to make you eligible for a different job within the company. Be sure you understand all aspects of your employer's tuition reimbursement program before you sign on and be prepared to meet any commitments expected of you.

LOANS

When scholarships, grants, and fellowships don't cover the full cost of attendance, many students take out loans to help out with the rest.

The government only lends money directly to you under the Federal Direct Loan Program. Lenders provide loans guaranteed by the federal government the Federal Family Education Loan Program.

Avoid loans if you can. A loan can best be described as renting money. There's a cost and it may not be an easy cost to bear.

Here's an interesting anecdote. Many students graduate without knowing what types of loans they received, who the lender was and how much they owe. The first time many students become aware of the scope of their obligation is when they receive their first bill—six months after graduation.

This is often because students are passive participants in the financial aid process and do not educate themselves or ask questions. Most students receive a list of "preferred lenders" from their financial aid office and simply go with the lender recommended to them. Over the course of the previous year, relationships between financial aid offices and lenders have been called into question by State Attorneys General, the Department of Education, and regulators. Financial aid offices in certain cases received revenue from lenders in exchange for being placed on the "preferred lender list." Some schools have even rented out their name and logo for use on loan applications. These practices occur without disclosure to parents and students.

It is important to know that the "preferred lenders" may not offer the best deals on your loan options. While your financial aid office may be very helpful with scholarships and grants, and is legally required to perform certain duties with regard to federal loans, many do not have staff researching the lowest cost options at the time you are borrowing.

Remember that your tuition payment equals revenue for the school. When borrowing to pay tuition, you can choose to borrow from any lender. That means you can shop for the lowest rate. Keep reading. This will tell you how.

TYPES OF LOANS

The federal government and private commercial lenders offer educational loans to students. Federal loans are usually the "first resort" for borrowers because many are subsidized by the federal government and offer lower interest rates. Private loans have the advantage of fewer restrictions on borrowing limits, but may have higher interest rates and more stringent qualification criteria.

Federal Loans

There are three federal loan programs. The Federal Perkins Loan Program where your school lends you money made available by government funds, the Federal Direct Loan Program (FDLP) where the government lends its money directly to students, and the Federal Family Education Loan Program (FFELP) where financial institutions such as MyRichUncle lend their own money but the government guarantees them. While most schools participate in the Federal Perkins Program, institutions choose whether they will participate in either the FFELP or FDLP. You will borrow from FFELP or FDLP depending on which program your school has elected to participate in.

The Federal Perkins Loan is a low-interest (5%) loan for students with exceptional need. Many students who do not qualify or who may need more funds can borrow FFELP or FDLP student loans. Under both programs, the Stafford loan is the typical place to start. The Stafford loan program features a fixed interest rate and yearly caps on the maximum amount a student can borrow. Stafford loans can either be subsidized (the government pays the interest while the student is in school) or unsubsidized (the student is responsible for the interest that accrues while in school). Starting July 1, 2007, the maximum amount a student can borrow for graduate school is $20,5

It is often assumed that the government sets the rate on student loans. The government does not set the rate of interest. It merely indicates the maximum rate lenders can charge. These lenders are free to charge less than the specified maximum rate of 6.8% for Stafford loans. There is also a maximum origination fee of up to 2% dropping to 1.5% on July 1, 2007. In some cases you may also be charged up to a 1% guaran fee. Any fees will be taken out of your disbursement.

Historically lenders have hovered a the maximum rate because most loans were distributed via the financial aid o whereby a few lenders received most of the loans. The end result was limited competition. At 1,239 institutions, one lender received more than 90% of the number of Stafford loans in 2006.

The GradPLUS loan is a federal loan that is another option for graduate and professional students. GradPLUS loans can be used to cover the full cost of attendance and have a fixed interest rate. The maximum rate a lender can charge for a GradPLUS loan is 8.5%. GradPLUS loans also have an origination fee of up to 3%, and a guarantee fee of up to 1%. Any fees will be taken out of your disbursement. Getting approved for one might be easier than getting approved for a private loan, so long as you don't have an adverse credit history.

For either program, the borrower submits a federal application known as the Free Application for Federal Student Aid (FAFSA). The application is available online at www.fafsa.ed.gov.

Certain lenders offer rate reductions, also known as borrower benefits, conditioned on the borrower making a certain number of on-time payments. Unfortunately, it is estimated that 90% of borrowers never qualify for these reductions.

Last year, MyRichUncle challenged this process by launching a price war. The company cut interest rates on Stafford loans and Graduate PLUS loans and introduced widespread price competition. These interest rate cuts are effective when students enter repayment and do not have any further qualification requirements. In addition, students only lose the rate reduction if they default.

Your financial aid office is legally required to certify for lenders that you are enrolled and based on your financial aid package, the amount in Federal loans you are eligible to borrow. You are free to choose any lender even if the lender is not on your financial aid office's preferred lender list.

To shop for low cost Federal loans, call a number of lenders before applying to determine their rates and fees. This is an effective approach because your application will not impact the price. Once you are comfortable that you have the lowest cost option, apply and submit

the Master Promissory Note to your lender of choice.

Private Loans

Private student loans can make it possible to cover the costs of higher education when other sources of funding have been exhausted. Additionally, when you apply for federal loans, you can borrow up to what your institution has pre-defined as the annual cost of attendance. If your anticipated expenses are above and beyond this predefined cost because of your unique needs, it will take a series of appeals before your institution will allow you to borrow more federal loans. Private loans help you meet your true expectation of what you will need financially. Private loans can pay expenses that federal loans can't, such as application and testing fees and the cost of transportation.

When you apply for a private loan, the lending institution will check your credit history including your credit score and determine your capacity to pay back the money you borrow. For individuals whose credit history is less than positive, lenders may require a co-borrower: a credit-worthy individual who also agrees to be accountable to the terms of the loan. While private loans do not have annual borrowing limits, they often have higher interest rates, and interest rate caps are higher than those set by Federal loans. Generally, the loans are variable rate loans, so the interest rate may go up or down, changing the cost.

To shop for a private loan, after you've researched several options, apply to as many of them as you feel comfortable. Once you are approved, compare rates. Pick the lowest cost option.

EXTRA LESSONS

Borrow the minimum

Just because someone is offering to lend you thousands upon thousands of dollars doesn't mean you should necessarily take them up on that offer. At some point, you'll have to repay the debt and you'll have to do it responsibly. Wouldn't it be better to use your money for something more worthwhile to you?

Know your rights

Currently, student lending is an industry that is under heavy scrutiny. It is important, now more than ever, for . parents and students to have an active voice and to make educational and financial choices that are right for them.

Some schools work with "preferred lenders" when offering federal and private loans. You are not required to choose a loan from one of these lenders if you can find a better offer. With respect to federal loans, the financial aid office has a legislated role which is to certify for the lending institution that you the borrower are indeed enrolled and the amount you are eligible for. They are not legally empowered to dictate your choice of lender and must certify your loan from the lender of your choice. You have the right to shop for and to secure the best rates possible for your loans. Don't get bullied into choosing a different lender simply because it is preferred by an institution. Instead, do your homework and make sure you understand all of your options.

Know what you want

When it's all said and done, you will have to take a variety of factors into account in order to choose the best school for you and for your future. You shouldn't have to mortgage your future to follow a dream, but you also shouldn't downgrade this opportunity just to save a few bucks.

MYRICHUNCLE
STUDENT LOANS

Call us:
1-800-926-5320

or learn more online:
MYRICHUNCLE.COM/PSYCHOLOGY

MYRICHUNCLE

Who we are:
MyRichUncle is a national student loan company offering federal (Stafford, PLUS and GradPLUS) and private loans to undergraduate, graduate, and professional students. MyRichUncle knows that getting a student loan can be a complicated and intimidating process, so we changed it. We believe students are credit-worthy borrowers, and that student loan debt should be taken seriously by borrowers and lenders alike. We propose changes in the student loan industry that will better serve parents, schools, and most importantly, students.

Why it matters:
Your student loan will be your responsibility. When you enter into a loan agreement, you're entering into a long-term relationship with your lender—15 years, on average. The right student loan with the right lender can help you avoid years of unnecessary fees and payments.

What we do:
MyRichUncle pays close attention to the obstacles students face. Removing these obstacles drives everything we do. MyRichUncle discounts federal loan rates at repayment rather than requiring years of continuous payments to earn the discount, which saves you money right from the start. We help you plan ahead, you can choose the best loans and save.

Our credentials:
MyRichUncle is a NASDAQ listed company. Our symbol is UNCL. In 2006, MyRichUncle was featured in FastCompany Magazine's Fast 50 and in Businessweek's Top Tech Entrepreneurs. MyRichUncle and its parent company, MRU Holdings, are financed by a number of leading investment banks and venture capitalists, including subsidiaries of Merrill Lynch, Lehman Brothers, Battery Ventures and Nomura Holdings.